PASSOVER AND EASTER

TWO LITURGICAL TRADITIONS

Volume 6

Passover and Easter

The Symbolic Structuring of Sacred Seasons

Edited by

PAUL F. BRADSHAW

and

LAWRENCE A. HOFFMAN

University of Notre Dame Press
Notre Dame, Indiana

Library of Congress Cataloging-in-Publication Data

Passover and Easter : the symbolic structuring of sacred seasons /
edited by Paul F. Bradshaw and Lawrence A. Hoffman.
     p.   cm. — (Two liturgical traditions ; v. 6)
Includes bibliographical references and index.
ISBN 0–268–03858–9 (cloth : alk paper). — ISBN 0–268–03860–0
(pbk. : alk. paper)
1. Easter. 2. Passover. 3. Judaism—Relations—Christianity.
4. Christianity and other religions—Judaism. I. Bradshaw, Paul F.
     II. Hoffman, Lawrence A., 1942- . III. Series.
BV55.P2753   1999
263′.93—dc21   98-41341

The author and publisher thank the following for permission:

The Pastoral Press, for the use of Lawrence A. Hoffman's
essay "The Great Sabbath and Lent: Jewish Origins?" which
appeared originally in somewhat different form as "The Jewish
Lectionary, the Great Sabbath, and the Lenten Calendar:
Liturgical Links between Christians and Jews in the First Three
Christian Centuries," in *Time and Community: In Honor of
Thomas Julian Talley,* ed. J. Neil Alexander (1990).

Worship, for the use of Lawrence A. Hoffman's essay
"A Symbol of Salvation in the Passover Seder," which
appeared originally as "A Symbol of Salvation in the
Passover Haggadah," *Worship* 53, no. 6 (1979).

Contents

Abbreviations   vii

Introduction
Passover and Easter: The Symbolic Shaping of Time and
Meaning   1
* *Paul F. Bradshaw and Lawrence A. Hoffman*

PART 1
PREPARING FOR SACRED TIME: HISTORY AND TYPOLOGY IN GREAT SABBATH AND LENT

The Great Sabbath and Lent: Jewish Origins?   15
* *Lawrence A. Hoffman*

Preparation for Pascha? Lent in Christian Antiquity   36
* *Maxwell E. Johnson*

Lent in Perspective: A Summary Dialogue   55
* *Lawrence A. Hoffman and Maxwell E. Johnson*

PART 2
THE AFTERMATH OF SACRED TIME: FROM PASSOVER/EASTER TO SHAVUOT/PENTECOST

From Passover to Shavuot   71
* *Efrat Zarren-Zohar*

From Easter to Pentecost   94
* *Martin F. Connell*

PART 3
SYMBOLS AND THE ARTS IN
SACRED CELEBRATION

A Symbol of Salvation in the Passover Seder   109
• *Lawrence A. Hoffman*

Haggadah Art   132
• *Joseph Gutmann*

Passiontide Music   146
• *Robin A. Leaver*

PART 4
A SYMBOLIC MODERN DILEMMA

Should Christians Celebrate the Passover?   183
• *Frank C. Senn*

Contributors   207

Index   209

Abbreviations

HUCA	Hebrew Union College Annual
JBL	Journal of Biblical Literature
JJS	Journal of Jewish Studies
JQR	Jewish Quarterly Review
PAAJR	Proceedings of the American Academy of Jewish Research
PL	Patrologiae Cursus Completus, Series Latina, ed. J. P. Migne
REJ	Revue des Études Juives

Introduction

Passover and Easter:
The Symbolic Shaping of
Time and Meaning

PAUL F. BRADSHAW AND LAWRENCE A. HOFFMAN

Just prior to each January, millions of modern men and women buy appointment books for their pockets, pocketbooks, and desks. The empty pages of these date books, as they are sometimes known, reveal the modern concept of time as an empty vessel that wise executives learn to fill. Failure in business is betrayed by having "time on your hands," while success entails filling up each page with commitments, even to the point of complaining constantly that we have no time left. Time is valuable; it is a rare commodity. "Time is money," we say. On occasion, we can "buy some time," though more often than not, we run out of it. We take consolation only if we know we have spent it wisely, for time wasted cannot be made up again.

By extension, we think of our lives as governed by time, ticking down like clocks. As middle-aged adults, we may stop at birthdays to take stock of how much time we are likely to have left, or what we have accomplished with it, and what will happen if we reach the end of our time prematurely. Such is the modern—one might even say, the business or corporate—sense of time.

Most religions share something of this perspective, but differ in other regards. The religious outlook too knows that life is finite and the duration of a lifetime uncertain. But it rarely imagines that time is an empty container waiting only to be filled by enterprising human actors. The goal is usually not human productivity but goodness. Failure is moral, not economic.

1

Time may therefore satisfactorily be spent in nonproductive enterprises like meditation, prayer, acts of loving kindness, and sacred community. Tasks are prescribed by tradition, not invented by corporate managers who measure their worth by the ability to set and then to meet arbitrary deadlines.

The religious calendar therefore comes prepackaged; it is hardly the empty date book for anxious executives to fill productively. It is, rather, the patterned unfolding of sacred moments around which religious men and women plot their lives, in accord with an inheritance of memories that matter and a cycle of rituals that revisit them.

Volume 5 was devoted to the history of Easter and Passover; volume 6 considers the way in which liturgical celebration combines text, art, and symbol to shape the faithful's conceptualization of time.

Before saying more about the contents of volume 6, a caveat is in order: It should be recognized that the division into two distinct volumes, one dealing with the evolution of our liturgical texts, and the other with the symbolic structuring of sacred time, is somewhat arbitrary. The arts, for instance, can appear in either category. In addition, as Paul Bradshaw illustrated in his introduction to volume 5, much of Christian liturgical scholarship has dealt precisely with the shaping of time. By contrast, Jewish research has centered on the development of a specific text for a single ritual event: the Haggadah for use at the Passover eve seder. But the fact that Jewish scholars have usually studied the growth of a text rather than the flow of sacred time may say more about the scholars than about the tradition they study. When Joanne Pierce, for instance, looks at medieval accretions in Christian liturgy (in volume 5), she focuses her attention on the stretching of the Easter "season" into an entire holy week, rather than the simple triduum of antiquity; Israel Yuval's parallel essay in volume 5 demonstrates the same sort of concern among medieval Jews. The Jewish community has cared deeply about the way Jewish time is structured. Traditional Jewish scholarship has just overlooked that facet of the Passover experience.

We have not, however, asked this volume's contributors to apply theories of sacred time to their research on ritual. They were asked to concentrate on what we know about their topics from within Jewish and Christian tradition, not to survey the developing field of ritual studies in order to derive models that then could be applied to their Jewish or Christian evidence. Their data should be seen as a dual case study of how two religious traditions structured the way their adherents came to see the flow of their respective sacred seasons.

Behind our organizational scheme are some basic postulates regarding the way liturgy functions for communities who engage in it.

1. *Stories that matter attract a ritual way of being told. These sacred stories become reference points for the way people conceptualize their lives. As the ritual changes, so too does the story, and also the way people think about who they are.*

Bedtime stories, memorable family moments, and master narratives of sacred origins all matter enough that they are graced with rites of reiterative retelling. Children practically memorize their favorite story books, which are recited at tell-tale times along with predictable ritualized pauses, hugs, and giggles. Likewise, at wedding anniversaries we repeat the tale of how Mom met Dad, or how Grandpa lost his way when picking up Grandma; here too, the story is told in conjunction with ritualized moments like the cutting of a cake, with the family in worshipful attendance.

The child's favorite story may be recalled also in exegetical passing at occasions other than bedtimes—as when parents remind a crying child that the hero in the bedtime book felt the same way the child now does but survived; and a family moment may get honorable mention at other times too ("Poor Grandpa, he always was somewhat absent-minded; remember when he forgot to pick up Grandma?"). Similarly, the story of Israel's Exodus and the recollection of Jesus' passion, death, and resurrection are specially reserved for the right moment of their telling; but they are not reserved exclusively to the Passover-Easter season. In one way or another, they are liturgical staples every day, and they play exegetical roles that explain and reinforce each religion's ideal types, ethical principles, and brands of spirituality.

We need to know more about how sacred tales become ritual events; and we should wonder also how they function exegetically in the daily life of a worshiping community. In the essays that follow, the latter concern does not arise explicitly, but the former one does, under the assumption that how we allot the ritual retelling to specific parts of a specific season influences what tale gets told and what exegeses are available. Volume 6, then, is especially interested in the way a story gets spread out over time, how people prepare for it, and how they live in the aftermath of its getting told.

2. *Stories can get told all at once, or can be seen as chapters in a larger master narrative that is spread over time. To the extent that the latter is the case, a particular season becomes an opportunity for us to live out the larger narrative. A tradition's calendar is thus an extension of its story, and like the story, it too evolves continually.*

In volume 5, Paul Bradshaw's introduction and the essays by Joanne Pierce and John Melloh refer to Kenneth Stevenson's unitive model of the Easter celebration, which emphasizes the basic sense by which communities see moments of sacred time as different chapters in the same story. But as Bradshaw also notes, the liturgical celebration to which the word "Easter" refers "changes its form and function quite radically in the course of history." It is easy to imagine that Lent was always just as it is, or that Holy Week was always in place, when in fact, just the opposite is the case. Even the Easter vigil changed from the focus of celebration in antiquity to a relatively minor liturgical event in our own time. From the perspective of volume 6, such changes in emphasis are not merely textual phenomena (the growth or decay of specific liturgical texts and practices). They are different ways of telling the sacred narrative, and they change the way the flow of Easter time is conceived by those who keep it. To the extent that Easter is paradigmatic for Christians, the changes in emphasis alter their own self-perception as well.

One proper approach to liturgical phenomena, therefore, is chronicling liturgical change as exemplifying (1) readjustments in a community's master narrative and (2) parallel readjustments in the way time is seen to cohere. What matters more, Good Friday or Easter Day, for instance? And why? If Easter Day is the focus for the entire period of time, such that Good Friday begins it and sunrise Sunday marks its culmination, Saturday's all-night vigil becomes tensely anticipatory—as indeed, it originally was. If, by contrast, popular imagination sees Easter Day as cut off theologically from Good Friday, and also if economic marketing forces have conspired to make Easter Day into a day of fashion on New York's Fifth Avenue,[1] then the vigil loses its point.

The same can be said of the Jewish view of the Passover season, although we know much less about it than we do about the Christian view of Easter. As we said above, Jewish scholarship has largely ignored issues of sacred time, preferring instead to study liturgy as if it were purely a text, and to analyze it only by asking such questions as how, when, and why particular prayers in the Haggadah came into being. Jewish sources are very clear, however, on the centrality of calendrical concerns. Already in the second century, Jews were preparing for Passover by a specially designed lectionary cycle. With historicist intent, scholars have studied that cycle to ascertain the pericopes that were read, but have insufficiently linked the lectionary choices to the way the Rabbis perceived the flow of time. They have therefore missed paying proper attention to how the lectionary prepared its rabbinic devisers for Passover, no less than a preparatory lectionary and fast prepared Christians for Easter.

Ideally, we would be able to chart the subjective view of time's passage in both traditions. We would be able to explain when and why views have changed. We would also know how those changing views reflect parallel changes in the master narrative and how they got to be accompanied by changes in liturgical celebration.

3. *Ritualized time requires preparation and afterthought.* Only if liturgical celebration is entirely "non-unitive," that

is, if there is no particular story to be told, can celebration emerge full-blown with nothing before and nothing after. But even rituals that are relatively devoid of an accompanying story tend to attract a period of building up to the moment that matters and a similar period of denouement. Birthday parties, for instance, may occasion the advance ordering of a chocolate ice-cream cake, and freezing part of it for later distribution to relatives who cannot make the big day: both events may be more than practical matters, since the particular kind of cake may be related to Grandpa's tastes and family traditions, and the practice of family dropping over for an aftertaste may come replete with tales about Grandpa's idiosyncratic cousins who never show up on time. These may not be *religiously* "sacred" tales, in that they do not refer to ultimates in the same way that the stories of Passover and Easter do, but they rank as sacred within the family context. All the more sacred are the ultimate narratives of our traditions that demand large blocks of time in which to live out the various chapters that comprise them. It is not enough to show up at the seder. Already in antiquity, Jews were expected to attend synagogue some three weeks prior and listen to the Torah's instructions to prepare for the day by wiping away impurity in home and heart. By the Middle Ages, if not earlier, Jews had a preparatory Great Sabbath as well. On the Christian side of things, attending church only on Easter Day was insufficient, since the first two days of the triduum prepared for the third one. And by the fourth century, if not earlier, when the triduum was taken for granted as a single event demanding its own preparation, some form of universal Lent was becoming normative. Volume 6 explores the growth of liturgical traditions that provide moments that build and moments that follow from the "main chapter" of the Jewish and Christian story. It emphasizes more than the single moment or set of moments that we call Passover eve or Easter Day. It is about how, in the course of their evolution, those moments were enlarged both backward and forward, like sacred elastic bands being stretched through time; and how the communities that call them sacred live through the entire elasticized period.

4. *Ritual as story-telling is an artistic thing.* All ritual involves artistry. Traditions like Zen, where ritual is everything, and where there may be no coherent story to recapitulate, have their own ways of training the adept to do the right ritual acts with proper care and finesse. The artistry of a story-telling tradition follows suit, with the additional caveat that its artistry reflects the story. As the story changes, the artistry will too; and as the chapters of the story are spaced out over time, the arts will be called on for the new blocks of time that were hitherto unimportant, but which begin to take on meaning as preparation or denouement for the main chapters that had been emphasized all along.

By ritual artistry, however, we have more in mind than the obvious recourse to painting or music.[2] Consider food, for instance, the ritual presentation of which is an art in itself (witness the Japanese tea ceremony, or the care with which the eucharist is choreographed). Both Christians and Jews use foods for ritual purposes, bread and wine being the best examples here. These are ordinary foods, but they take on liturgical roles when they are eaten symbolically, that is, not for how they fill or satisfy but for what they mean. As in *maror,* Passover's bitter herbs that "mean" slavery, taste may matter; so too may color (red wine means blood better than white wine does). In such cases, symbols function iconically—they point beyond themselves the way smoke points to fire. Sometimes the iconic connections are not so evident, as when Edmund Leach considers the possibility that both red traffic lights and red ink mean "Stop, danger is near." Is that because red "means" blood which means "danger"?[3] Real-life examples are Victor Turner's instances of red and white (from the sap of a "milk tree") as icons among the Ndembu of Africa for blood and breast feeding, respectively.[4] On the other hand, Claude Levi-Strauss knows that symbols are largely arbitrary; they mean what we want them to. Colors like red and white can mean exactly opposite things, even in neighboring cultures.[5]

The point is not to arrive at a theory of how symbols work, but to recognize that ritual is symbolic, and that we never know for sure what a symbol means until we do the necessary ethnographic observation of a ritual in practice, or the necessary literary analysis of the texts that reveal the way our forebears practiced this or that ritual once upon a time. Volume 5 was not unconcerned with symbols. How could it be? But volume 6 turns specifically to studies in how the sacred stories of Passover and Easter are illustrated artistically, and how ordinary foods take on symbolic meanings in our ritualized narratives.

Volume 6, therefore, begins with sacred time, exploring the ways in which Easter and Passover attracted preparatory periods and sacred residues or aftermaths. The most celebrated case may be the lengthy preparation in Lent.

Lent has received considerable attention, especially since 1986, when Thomas Talley published his influential *Origins of the Liturgical Year.* Talley demonstrated the abundant early Lenten traditions, many of which contradict each other.[6] In 1990, Lawrence Hoffman published an account that traced the Christian Lent to Jewish practice, holding that Jews prepared for Passover by means of a lectionary cycle of readings going back some three weeks prior to the onset of Passover.[7] The three-week period coincided with a three-week preparation for catechumens that Talley had located in Rome and elsewhere. Maxwell Johnson now questions some of Hoffman's conclusions, drawing on Bradshaw and others who have indicated that the common three-week period is irrelevant, since the three-week catechumenate did not coincide everywhere with Easter and could not, therefore, have anything to do with Lent. Only later did baptism of converts universally coincide with the Christian Pascha.

The issue is complex, so our example of sacred time is best served, in part 1 of this volume, by reprinting Hoffman's article and Johnson's alternative reconstruction, followed by a dialogue between the two parties laying out the issues in question and the different ways of understanding them.

A similar instance of extended preparation is the Great Sabbath, a term taken from John 19:31 but commonplace in medieval Jewish texts as the name given to the Sabbath prior to Passover. Zeitlin did the pioneer work here, which

Hoffman summarizes as part of his essay on Lent. Zeitlin, thinking that Jews would never consciously emulate Christian practice, imagined an early Jewish custom that had gone underground until being resurrected as part of a medieval world where authorities no longer recalled just how the Great Sabbath had even begun. Yuval's bold reconstruction of Jewish-Christian relations is especially relevant here. In volume 5 ("Easter and Passover As Early Jewish-Christian Dialogue"), Yuval questions Zeitlin's assumptions. In his view, medieval Jews did indeed borrow from their Christian environment; the Great Sabbath was entirely a Christian matter, until Jews adopted it as part and parcel of their Jewish celebration.

Hoffman raises the question of the symbolic meaning of the Great Sabbath. The term is taken purely historically by traditional scholarship, which wants to know what day it was and whether the same day was kept by Jews as well as by Christians. The martyrologies of Polycarp and Pionius have therefore attracted substantial literature as to the precise day on which the two saints were killed, since they are both said to have died on a Great Sabbath. Hoffman replaces historicity with symbolism, suggesting that the Great Sabbath was a typological consideration having nothing to do with a specific day of the year on which the two men perished.

If sacred moments attract times of preparation, they also develop follow-up periods whereby the sacred is allowed to extend into the ordinary, rather than come to a sudden halt with the official end of the day in question. Much more work has to be done on this phenomenon, which is less well recognized than the preparatory prologue to the holy day's onset. Jewish tradition knows of such things as fast days following the three pilgrim festivals, and the extension of the period of atonement beyond Yom Kippur to the end of Sukkot, or even farther in some traditions. The aftermath of sacred time is especially evident, however, in the seven-week period from the onset of Passover to Shavuot, a period known to the Bible as the Omer.

The name is drawn from the sheaves of grain that are harvested each spring and are designated by the Bible as an "Omer" offering in the Temple. Later Jewish tradition builds upon the Bible by adding to the period's sanctity through a mélange of practices and beliefs that emphasize its penitential quality. It develops another name—not just Omer but *S'firah,* the days of "counting." Efrat Zarren-Zohar's essay in part 2 of this volume is a look at the customs associated with the period, as residue from Passover and preparation for Shavuot. The parallel piece by Martin Connell establishes the way in which Easter is part of a larger scheme that culminates in Pentecost.

Part 3 of this volume turns explicitly to the arts. In volume 5, Carole Balin explored the use of illustrations along with novel textual variants in the way that new Haggadah texts adapt the traditional Jewish narrative to modern Jewish life. In this volume, Joseph Gutmann explores what we know about the beginning of the Haggadah artistic tradition, and Robin Leaver turns to the role of music in explicating the Easter narrative in the sixteenth century and beyond. The other contribution to part 3 is Lawrence Hoffman's essay on bread as "A Symbol of Salvation in the Passover Seder." Some of the essays in volume 5 refer to this article, first published in *Worship* Magazine[8] and included here as a consideration of how shared symbols permeated Christian and Jewish ritual in the era when Christianity and rabbinic Judaism were jointly coming into being.

If we assume that liturgy is essentially symbolic, and that worshipers are therefore inevitably thrust into symbolic universes that structure time, provide root narratives, and govern self-perception, we can understand, finally, the way those same worshipers may find themselves in conflict over a particular liturgical act that is an essential constituent not only in their own story, as they see it, but in someone else's symbolic universe as well. In our time, that dilemma is particularly evident for Christians who want to adopt the Passover seder as a Christian event reminiscent of Jesus' lifetime as a Jew. We conclude this volume with Frank Senn's consideration of the dilemma in which such Christians find themselves, a dilemma that is entirely symbolic. What would keeping a seder as a Christian properly entail? Can it be kept at all?

We adopted Passover and Easter as our topic for volumes 5 and 6 of this series on the liturgical traditions of Jews and Christians because these sacred periods so prototypically intertwine in Jewish/Christian consciousness. The essays that we have collected explore the two traditions not only as they developed in isolation from each other, but also as they influenced each other, and thus exemplify the double helix that binds Jews and Christians in their common path as they swirl about each other through time.

What is true of Passover and Easter is probably true of other periods as well. Sacred time has its own way of behaving: stretching its bounds to include build-ups and residues; and stretching the boundaries of the medium in which the sacred is presented, drawing on both text and art to constitute a sacred theater of ritual display, in which each participant is a sacred actor, provided with lines and gestures designed to evoke the sense that God is present.

Passover seders culminate in a door flung open to receive the messiah, that "Next year we might be in Jerusalem." Easter vigils end with the glorious shout that "Christ has risen." Nothing bespeaks the spirit of hope that is common to Jews and to Christians better than the sacred springtime seasons that we explore in these pages. We dedicate these pages to the realization of this fervent hope that we share.

NOTES

1. See Leigh Eric Schmidt, *Consumer Rites* (Princeton, 1995), pp. 193–243.

2. See Lawrence A. Hoffman on liturgy as art form, in volume 2 of this series, Paul F. Bradshaw and Lawrence A. Hoffman, eds., *The Changing Face of Jewish and Christian Worship* (Notre Dame, 1991), pp. 15–21.

3. Edmund Leach, *Claude Levi-Strauss* (Middlesex and New York, 1970), pp. 17–21.

4. Victor Turner, *Forest of Symbols* (Ithaca, N.Y., 1966), pp. 20–25.

5. Claude Levi-Strauss, *The Savage Mind* (Chicago, 1962), pp. 64–65.

6. Thomas J. Talley, *The Origins of the Liturgical Year* (New York, 1986), pp. 163–230.

7. Lawrence A. Hoffman, "The Jewish Lectionary, the Great Sabbath, and the Lenten Calendar," in J. Neil Alexander, ed., *Time and Community* (Washington, D.C., 1990).

8. Lawrence A. Hoffman, "A Symbol of Salvation in the Passover Haggadah," *Worship* 53, no. 6 (1979): 519–37.

PART 1

Preparing for Sacred Time:
History and Typology in
Great Sabbath and Lent

The Great Sabbath and Lent:
Jewish Origins?

Lawrence A. Hoffman

The Great Sabbath

My primary topic, Lent and its Jewish origins, depends on a passing familiarity with the Jewish lectionary, so it is convenient to begin with some background on the Great Sabbath, as an illustration of the way the lectionary works; then to move on to a consideration of Lent; and finally, to return to the Great Sabbath and its typological usage in early Christianity.

The Jewish lectionary for Sabbaths and holy days contains a Pentateuchal (Torah) and a prophetic (*Haftarah*) reading. Scholars are undecided as to when either of them came full-blown into being.[1] We know, however, that some sort of Torah cycle was in effect by the first century, possibly in two systems. One is associated with Palestinian synagogues and is called (somewhat misleadingly) "triennial"—it was really variable, taking three to four years to complete; the other (the one we use today) became normative in Babylonia and was annual, beginning and ending at the same time every year. Both followed the system known as *lectio continua,* that is, they began at the beginning of the Torah and continued *seriatim* until the end, whether one year or some three to four years later. Special calendrical occasions commanded their own readings, however, and these took priority over the normal lection of a Sabbath on which they fell, with the result that the normal reading would be postponed.

A fixed *Haftarah* cycle developed later, possibly out of the eventual piecing together of several independent smaller lectionary lists. Unlike the Pentateuchal reading, the Prophets were never read *seriatim*, and to this day there are different traditions as to which *Haftarah* accompanies some of the Torah readings. The question of whether by the first century prophetic readings were already assigned to particular Sabbaths depends largely on one's reading of Luke 4:17.[2] In any event, the identity and order of the prophetic reading for the triennial cycle has generally eluded investigators. Of late, however, a list of *Haftarah* readings has been reconstructed by Joseph Offer, and it is now widely regarded as an authentic set, if not necessarily the only set available in the immediate post-talmudic period.[3] Our purposes require the recognition that both Torah and *Haftarah* readings were in effect by the second century, with the result that particular Sabbaths could be named after either of the readings found therein.

Rabbinic literature normally names individual Sabbaths according to their Torah portion: "The Sabbath of [the name of the Pentateuchal reading]." However, some Sabbaths are known by their prophetic readings. An example of a Pentateuch-derived name is "Sabbath Noah," that is, the Sabbath in which the story of Noah is read. Examples of a prophet-derived name are Sabbath "Comfort," the Sabbath following the 9th of Av (the anniversary of the Temple's destruction) when the *Haftarah* begins with Isaiah 40:1 ("Comfort [my people]"); and "The Sabbath of 'Return,'" the Sabbath between Rosh Hashanah and Yom Kippur, which features Hosea's call (Hosea 14: 2–10), "Return O Israel to the Eternal your God."

Sabbath names are thus derived formulaically, by citing the appropriate Pentateuchal or prophetic reading. We can further distinguish names as being derived either (a) primarily from the lectionary readings (Sabbath Noah, for example), or (b) primarily from the calendar and only secondarily from the reading (which was chosen to begin with only because of its calendrical relevance). The Sabbath of "Return," for example, may in the narrowest sense draw its name from the Hosea lection, but that reading was selected in the first place because the calendrical occasion (the Sabbath between Rosh

Hashanah and Yom Kippur) demands repentance. Calendrical determination is often the norm with *Haftarah* readings, which, following no continuous cycle, were easily selected with calendrical concerns in mind. It is also true of some Pentateuch-derived names, namely, where special Torah readings replace or augment the continuous lectionary.

The two calendrically driven and Pentateuchally derived names that will concern us later are the Sabbath of the [red] Heifer (*Parah*) and the Sabbath of "This Month" (*Hachodesh*), which feature Numbers 19:1–22 and Exodus 12:1–20, respectively. These Sabbath names are not applied when the cycle arrives at Numbers 19 or Exodus 12 as part of the continuous lectionary, but only on the two occasions when they are read out of order. Exodus 12 is reread for calendrical purposes to announce the new month of Nisan, and Numbers 19 is selected the week before (for reasons that we will see). Since they are read out of order, they are calendrically driven; but since they are Torah, not *Haftarah* readings, they are Pentateuchally derived.

Another specially named Sabbath is *Shabbat Hagadol,* "the Great Sabbath." But what kind of name is that? In some places, in thirteenth-century Italy, for instance, the term referred to the Sabbath preceding several holy days,[4] but more generally it meant (as it does today) only the Sabbath preceding Passover; it seems, therefore, to belong to the calendar-derived category. Following the formulaic pattern of naming, we would expect to find the word "Great" in the prophetic or Pentateuchal lections for the day, and in fact, we do, for the prophetic portion is Malachi 3:4–24, which promises "the great . . . day of the Lord." However, the Mishnah and the Talmuds, which recognize other specially named Sabbaths, are absolutely and mysteriously silent about this one. Not until the Middle Ages do rabbis discuss the Great Sabbath, by which time, preferring homiletics to history, they offer a host of other explanations for the name.[5] The Tosafot, for example—a generic term encompassing Franco-German rabbis of the twelfth and thirteenth centuries—imagine it goes back to biblical

times, because on that day, the Israelites took the lamb they
were to slaughter, and forever after recalled it as the time of
the "great" miracle [of Passover].[6] Easily the most amusing
etiology comes from *Shibbolei Haleket*, a thirteenth-century
Italian source: "On this Sabbath, people stay late at synagogue
to hear the sermon of the rabbi who preaches until the middle
of the day, practically into the afternoon . . . so that [the day]
appears to them as drawn-out and long [*gadol*, here translated
as 'great' in time, not stature]."[7] Others opine that it may be
a mistake, *Hagadol* being erroneously derived from the word
Haggadah, since on this Sabbath it is customary to read the
Passover Haggadah in anticipation of the seder; or it may be
a transfer of terminology from *Hallel Hagadol* (The "Great
Hallel"). Clearly, what we have are guesses that do not help us
determine the actual origin of this important Sabbath in the
Jewish year.

The problem of the Great Sabbath's origin attracted the attention of the earliest generation of scientific scholars, who
noted the oddity that even though Jews keep the Great Sabbath, early Jewish texts do not mention it; whereas Christianity, which did not continue the Great Sabbath, bequeathed us
early texts (beginning with the Gospel of John) which do contain it.[8] Jellinek, for example, assumed that the Christian literature in question was referring to extant Jewish practice at
the time; he therefore dated the Great Sabbath in Judaism not
later than the first or second century.[9] In 1859, on the other
hand, the great Leopold Zunz concluded that it must have
originated among Christians, whence it was borrowed by the
Jews.[10] Most scholars prefer Jellinek's reconstruction, but if so,
how can we explain the Great Sabbath's Jewish origin?

Solomon Zeitlin turned to this task in 1948,[11] drawing on
an explanation that he found in *Sefer Mateh Moshe*, a halakhic
treatise largely on the holidays, which was originally published
in Cracow in 1591. Noting that a "Great Sabbath" occurs in
both John (19:31) and the *Apostolic Constitutions* (5:18) as the
Saturday before the resurrection, Zeitlin concluded that Jews
must already have celebrated the Sabbath in question by the

second century. He explained its name by looking at the calendrical event and its associated *Haftarah* reading:

> It was the prevalent opinion among a group of Jews, particularly the Apocalyptists, that God would redeem the Jews on the first day of Passover, and on the eve, God would send Elijah to herald the coming of the Messiah. Thus we may understand why the chapter on Malachi dealing with Elijah was assigned. . . . [Since the reading in question promises, "Behold, I will send you Elijah the prophet before the coming of the *great* and glorious day of the Lord," the Sabbath when Malachi was read] was therefore called the Great Sabbath.[12]

That Elijah's coming was also crucial to early Christians, Zeitlin learns from Matthew 27:47–49 (and Mark 15:35–36), where Jesus is misunderstood by those around him as calling on Elijah to save him; and from Justin Martyr, who avers, "For we all expect that Christ will be a man [born] of men, and that Elijah, when he comes, will anoint him. . . . Does not Scripture say that Elijah shall come before the great and terrible day of the Lord?"[13] Hence Zeitlin concludes that the church took over the idea of a Great Sabbath, but transferred it to the Saturday before the resurrection rather than the Sabbath before Passover. The Rabbis polemicized against the church's successful transformation of the Great Sabbath by omitting all discussion of the term from the Talmud. "However, the sages did not succeed in entirely eradicating the observance of the Sabbath before the Passover as the Great Sabbath. Hence the rabbis of the Middle Ages, not finding any reference to it in the Talmud, advanced different reasons for its name."[14]

Zeitlin's reconstruction is far from foolproof, but it has its attractions, not the least of which is its solution to two grammatical problems inherent in the troublesome term *shabbat hagadol*. (1) *Shabbat* is feminine and requires a feminine modifying adjective, and (2) *hagadol* contains the definite article, and requires that the noun it modifies does so too. Thus *shabbat hagadol* should read *hashabbat hagedolah*. Alternatively, we might follow the model of *shabbat kodesh*, a normal rabbinic expression, usually rendered "the holy Sabbath," but literally being "the Sabbath of holiness"; we might then accept *shabbat gedulah* ("the Sabbath of greatness") as well. In either case, *shabbat hagadol* will not do—unless, of course, *gadol* never did modify *shabbat,* but was borrowed from another context where the noun it modified was masculine—such as "the great day," *hayom hagadol,* in Malachi. Moreover, Zeitlin's scheme makes this Sabbath name fit the model of the others. It is calendrically determined but prophet derived, named by virtue of the *Haftarah* lection chosen to express an annual calendrical theme. On the other hand, Sabbaths are named elsewhere after the first word or two of a lection, not after a lectionary verse near the end, and we have no independent evidence that Malachi was even read on the Saturday in question as early as the first or second century.

The other possibility is that until the Middle Ages, Jews kept no Great Sabbath at all. It is lacking in rabbinic literature because it was a Christian invention to begin with. Only in the Middle Ages did Jews borrow it from the church, at which time they naturally looked for Jewish precedent, and finding none, derived the various exegetical interpretations that I have summarized above. That is Israel Yuval's conclusion, presented in his essay "Passover in the Middle Ages," in volume 5. I find it compelling.

Either way, however, a Great Sabbath was certainly known to John, and (as we shall see) it figured prominently in the thinking of Polycarp and Pionius. Whether a Jewish term to start with or a Christian invention that Jews eventually borrowed, it demonstrates the way Sabbaths are sometimes named: according to lections (secondarily), but determined in the first instance by calendrical considerations. Later, I will return to *Shabbat Hagadol,* but for now, let us turn to two other special Sabbaths named after their lections but actually calendrically determined: *Shabbat Parah* and *Shabbat Hachodesh,* which I cited earlier. They are related to preparation for Passover, and in that regard, serve as models for what eventually became Lent.

Shabbat Parah *and* Shabbat Hachodesh: *Their Impact on Lent*

Thomas Talley has summarized Lenten traditions known from antiquity.[15] Egeria's fourth-century account from Jerusalem describes eight weeks of five days per week for the stipulated number of forty days. But the forty-day requirement is probably a late imposition on earlier systems that numbered something other than forty originally. Even in Jerusalem, Egeria's system could not have been universal, or else it was short-lived, since her account is not in agreement with that city's Armenian lectionaries from less than half a century later. It is therefore hard to know what Egeria's experience reflects; at the very least, it is not necessarily a measure of what people in the fourth century were doing all over Jerusalem, let alone in other centers and other times.

Earlier than Egeria, we have Hippolytus's *Apostolic Tradition* from Rome (c. 200), where the number of days of the catechumenate was not fixed at all; one's status as a catechumen might last as long as three years. True, an unspecified period at the end was kept more severely, but what weeks or even months were they? Did it occur any time in the year, or was it planned to coincide with the period preceding Pascha? Though the text does not stipulate the latter, I have assumed it here as the hypothesis most in keeping with the facts. On that hypothesis, it follows that Hippolytus knew of a lengthy catechumenate culminating in an intensive Lent-like period for an unspecified time before Easter. Still, precisely because it is unspecified, this helps us as little as Egeria for our purposes of narrowing down specific pre-Easter time periods in which the nascent church practiced its Lent. Likewise, from that early period—in fact, about a hundred years before Hippolytus—the *Didache*'s early chapters, which may be a catechesis, tell us nothing about the length of time allotted to the process.

Talley also cites Socrates' fifth-century *Ecclesiastical History,* which confirms the existence of several time periods. In Greece and Alexandria, people fasted for six weeks, while unspecified "others" fasted seven. Both groups called their fast "the forty days." We are back where we started with Egeria: a time when various customs (six, seven, or in Egeria's case, eight weeks) have been theologically harmonized to arrive at the number forty. Similarly, Athanasius writes from Rome (where he was in exile) in 340 back to his friend Serapion, saying that forty days (of some sort) are common everywhere except in Egypt. The process of theoretical standardization around the number forty seems to have been concluded, therefore, somewhere between the fourth and the fifth centuries.

There is one glaring exception to the rule: a Roman custom of fasting for only three successive weeks and not calling it forty days at all. Chavasse concludes that this custom must have existed prior to the end of the third century but disappeared between 354 and 384,[16] for a letter by Jerome written in 384 confirms the fact that the six-week fast that replaced it was then already in effect.[17] But even in the later system, we have the otherwise inexplicable application of the term *Dominica mediana* to the fifth Sunday of Lent, and *hebdomada mediana* to the week preceding it, thus signaling again an original core of three weeks to which other days were added later on in order to round out their number to forty. All of this merely accords with the assumption that as time went on, every effort was made by all parties to call their fasts—whatever their original length—"Forty Days," and that still in the middle of the fourth century, earlier customs prevailed to which the arbitrary designation "forty-day" had not yet been applied.

Thus, a three-week Lent was an early custom known before the middle of the fourth century, at least in Rome, and possibly elsewhere as well. It eventually got swallowed up by other customs in an effort to arrive at the total of forty, patently impossible if there are only three weeks with which to work.

The question arises: why three weeks? The explanation favored by Chavasse, and repeated thereafter elsewhere,[18] is the inherent ambiguity in the Roman calendar. On the one hand, it retained the pre-Christian empire's date of March 1 as its new year; but on the other hand, Easter Sunday could not occur until the spring, that is, March 22 at the earliest, so that the new year from a Christian perspective would not occur until then. People must have dedicated to the preparation for Easter the minimum amount of time separating the beginning of the chronological Roman year (March 1) from the earliest date that Easter could fall.[19] This certainly seems reasonable enough for Rome, but others may have celebrated a three-week Lent as well. The Armenian Lectionary, composed some time between 417 and 439, indicates the possibility that there had once been a three-week fast in Jerusalem.[20] One can surely grant that the three-week structure posed a solution to the Roman calendrical anomaly, without assuming that the idea of three weeks was created *ex nihilo,* as it were, solely with that end in mind. The question remains: why three weeks to start with?

Given its possible existence in Jerusalem, I want to ask whether a three-week preparation for Easter may be traced to Jewish precedent. Not that it must be, or even that it logically should be, especially if the three-week Lent was Roman in origin and then spread elsewhere, to Jerusalem, for example. On the other hand, a good deal of give-and-take characterized the late empire, so that a custom known in Rome need not have originated there; and in any case, the Jewish population of Rome, even in the first century, was considerable. Jewish influence was hardly limited to Palestine. It was, for example, a regular concern of Chrysostom in Antioch as late as the fourth century, which Robert Wilken calls "Not Yet the Christian Era."[21] At the very least, we shall see that the specially designated Sabbaths prior to Passover provide us with an interesting three-week parallel to the three-week Lent.

We saw above that Sabbaths are often known by designations borrowed from the lections they carry. Even the Great Sabbath, *Shabbat Hagadol,* follows that rule, if it is related to the lectionary's *Haftarah* still read on that day, Malachi's prophecy of the "great . . . day [*hayom hagadol*] of the Lord." Whether Zeitlin is right in antedating the day and its reading to antiquity, or whether Yuval is correct in seeing both as medieval innovations, the linkage of name and lection remains. But even if there were no linkage, even if, that is, the Great

Sabbath is somehow different from the others, the fact remains that the Mishnah (c. 200) lists other named Sabbaths which are definitely known to Jews of the first two centuries, and which unquestionably take their name from their Pentateuchal readings. The two which interest us have already been mentioned here: *Shabbat Parah* (The Sabbath of the [red] heifer) and *Shabbat Hachodesh* (The Sabbath of "This month . . . ").

The Mishnah's text is unambiguous:

> If the first day of the month Adar falls on the Sabbath, they read the Pentateuchal portion "Shekels" (Exod. 30:11–16); if it falls in the middle of the week, they read it ["Shekels"] on the prior Sabbath; and on the next Sabbath they take a break [reading no special portion at all then, but instead, reading the regularly scheduled lesson and waiting until the week after for the next special reading]. On the second [special Sabbath, which invariably falls also on the second Sabbath of the month of Adar] they read the Pentateuchal section, "Remember what Amalek did . . . " (Deut. 25:17–19). On the third [Sabbath of the month] they read "The [red] heifer" (Num. 19: 1–22). On the fourth, they read, "This month shall be for you . . . " (Exod. 12:1–20).[22]

The Mishnah is phrased as if it counts the Sabbaths from the beginning of Adar, the last month of the year. But suppose we count backward from the month that follows Adar, Nisan. It would then become evident that the fourth of the special lections, "This month . . . ," is reserved precisely for the Sabbath that introduces Nisan. Appropriately, it warns, "This month shall be for you the beginning of months . . . the first of the months of the year. . . . On the tenth of this month . . . each [household] shall take a lamb" (Exod. 12:2–3). Since Passover falls on the night of the 14th, there can be a maximum of two sabbaths in Nisan before it. If, that is, Passover Day (the 15th) falls on a Sunday, then Nisan 14 and Nisan 7 would be Sabbaths, and Nisan 1 would fall the Sunday before that. In that case, the Exodus reading "This month . . . " would occur on Adar 29, the last day of the old year, the very day before the month being heralded, and *three Sabbaths* (!) prior to Passover.

The same scheme would hold if Passover fell on Monday

through Friday. There would always be (1) two Sabbaths of Nisan before it, then (2) still counting back, Nisan 1, falling sometime during the prior week, and (3) the announcement of the new month via the lection from Exodus on the Saturday before that. That Saturday would also be three Saturdays—though not exactly three weeks—before Passover itself. The only way a difference might occur would be if Nisan 15 fell on Saturday. In such a case, Nisan 1 would also fall on Saturday, and the reading announcing it could occur that very day, rather than being moved up one week so as to anticipate the new month falling some time within the week following. In such an instance, the Jewish calendar would feature *Shabbat Hachodesh* only two rather than the usual three weeks prior to Passover, and *Shabbat Parah* would be read three weeks before.

Let us look also, then, at *Shabbat Parah,* the Sabbath of the [red] Heifer, normally found four weeks before Passover, but sometimes (when Passover falls on Saturday) three weeks before. On the face of it, the Mishnah seems to be counting its special lections from the viewpoint of Adar. But in actuality, the text conflates two traditions, the first being the initial two readings which are Adar-based, and the second being our two readings here, which happen to be read next, but are actually dependent not on Adar but on Passover, just as Lent is dependent on Easter. Numbers 19:1–22 describes the biblical practice of slaughtering and burning a red heifer, the ashes of which are then reserved for the purpose of washing away the ritual impurity of those who have come in contact with a corpse. Corpse-uncleanness is directly related to Passover, since Numbers 9:9 explicitly prohibits the offering of the Passover sacrifice to "any of you who are defiled by a corpse." Continuing biblical precedent, the Mishnah aptly worries about people who "mourn their near kindred [and who would normally be presumed to have contacted impurity while guarding and preparing the corpse], or who relocated the bones of their dead [from their temporary burial place to the permanent ossuary]."[23] The Mishnah returns to the theme of uncleanness at the time of the Passover offering in 9:4, without, however, stipulating that corpse-uncleanness is intended; but the Tosefta glosses the Mishnah to correct the record: "When the Passover offering is eaten in a state of uncleanness: [that is] one who has contracted corpse-uncleanness."[24] To be sure, the actual practice of the red heifer as a means of alleviating corpse-uncleanness may have long fallen into desuetude,[25] but taking its place were the rabbinic enactments of ritual bathing, which appropriately are given as the proper remedy for people suspected of being impure.[26] Obviously, the purifying regulations read on *Shabbat Parah,* and *Shabbat Hachodesh*'s summons *the very next week* to prepare for the Passover, are intimately connected, as the Palestinian Talmud itself maintains:

> Rabbi Levi said in the name of Rabbi Chama bar Chanina: you may not interrupt the lectionary between *Parah* and *Hachodesh.* [If, that is, the first of the four special readings had been read early[27]—thus necessitating an extra, fifth Sabbath, on which one would have to return to the regular lectionary—the interruption must occur between two of the other special readings, but on no account between these two.] Rabbi Levi said: The cups of Passover wine provide an analogy to help us remember this, for the Mishnah teaches us that people may drink all they like between one cup and another, but not between the third and the fourth cup. There, no extra drinking may occur. Rabbi Levi said in the name of Rabbi Chama bar Chanina: Logic might lead you to argue that we should first read *Hachodesh* and only then [on the Sabbath thereafter, where there is no special reading] read *Parah,* since the Tabernacle was completed on the first of Nisan, and the red heifer was burned on the second. Why then is the account of the heifer read first? Because it details the cleansing of Israel.[28]

Rashi, looking back on the Mishnah's order from his vantage point at the end of the eleventh century, corroborates the connection assumed here by the Palestinian Talmud: "[We read the account of the heifer first] to admonish all of Israel to purify themselves, so that they may offer their Passover sacrifices in a state of purity."[29]

Even from the plain meaning of the biblical texts, we see that these two Pentateuchal readings, each a possible option for the Sabbath three weeks before Passover, are ideal proto-types for Lenten themes: preparation for the sacrifice (Exodus 12) and cleansing from impurity (Numbers 19). Let us return briefly to the calendar, to see where Easter Sunday would fall relative to the Sabbaths in question.

Martimort, Dalmais, and Jounel summarize the matter well:

> It was not until the early years of the second century that there was any thought of celebrating a specifically Christian feast of Easter, and even then, the Church of Rome waited until the second half of the century before accepting it.
>
> Until Pope Victor intervened (189–198), two ways of calculating the date for Easter were in use. The Churches of Asia Minor were bent on Christianizing the day of the Jewish Passover, the 14th of Nisan, so they stopped their fast on that day. The other Churches celebrated their paschal feast on the following Sunday, the "first day of the week." The Roman Church, in particular, followed this second way, and it became the rule for all from the beginning of the third century.[30]

In other words, the Jewish calendar was critical to the pre-Nicean Church, especially in Asia Minor, where for a while there was no Easter Sunday at all, but instead, a Christianized Passover held on the date of the Jewish celebration itself. Alternatively, Christians outside Asia Minor, and especially at Rome, kept Easter on the Sunday after Passover. In no case, however, was there a third possibility. Easter always corresponded with Passover or took place at most one week after it.

What matters even more than the actual calendrical overlap between Passover and Easter, however, is the theory behind it. For the churches in Palestine and Asia Minor, Passover *was* Easter. But even for churches outside Asia Minor, those which moved Easter to the Sunday after Passover, Easter was still seen as the Pascha, with Jesus the newly sacrificed lamb whose blood saved the new Israel, just as the blood of the lamb in Exodus saved the old. "For the Pascha was Christ afterward sacrificed," says Justin Martyr. "As the blood of the Passover saved us who were in Egypt, so also the blood of Christ will deliver those who have believed from death."[31] As the new

month of Nisan dawned, then, Exodus 12's announcement to
prepare for Passover was as relevant to Christians as to Jews;
and so too was Numbers 20's demand for pre-paschal purity,
without which participation in the sacrifice was impossible.

Of course, the best evidence for Jewish influence on the
Lenten calendar would be a direct connection between the lectionaries of the Rabbis and the early church, and in fact, it is
there. Chavasse lists Exodus 12:1–14 as an early reading for
Good Friday, albeit balanced by the prophetic text of Hosea
6:1–6, "which illustrates exceptionally well the idea of a new
sacrifice."[32] The case with Numbers 19 is a bit more complex.
I am not aware of its existence as a Lenten reading, but let us
look at the prophetic accompaniment to it in the early synagogue. The Mishnah records only the Pentateuchal readings
for the special Sabbaths in question, but the Tosefta supple-
ments the Mishnah's data by giving the prophetic reading also.

> For the prophetic lection [that accompanies "the red Heifer"]
> they read [the passage beginning], "I will sprinkle clean water
> upon you, and you shall be clean from all your uncleanness, and
> from all your idols I will cleanse you" (Ezek. 36:25).[33]

The early church readings from the Hebrew Bible would have
preferred prophetic readings in any case, and one need not look
very far before discovering this one as part of the Lenten lectionary. In his comparison of the Georgian and the Armenian
lectionaries, Lages lists Ezekiel 36:25–36 as the reading for the
Wednesday of the fifth week of Lent.[34] The *Wurzburg Epistolary* prescribes Ezekiel 36:23–28 for the Wednesday of the
fourth week, which would put it roughly about two and one-
half weeks prior to Easter, not very far from its placement in
Jewish tradition.[35] The common usage of Ezekiel 36 dovetails
with what we know of its centrality in the Jewish-Christian
debate.[36] For Jews there was but one covenant, the saving blood
of which was visible in two commandments: the Passover offering and circumcision. Within its homily on *Hachodesh*(!),
the earliest midrash to Exodus even polemicizes against Christian claims that a new and spiritualized covenant is intended
here.[37] Apparently, the Ezekiel reading may already have been

common in the second century in both Jewish and Christian preparation for their respective feasts, so that Jewish exegetes took pains to explain the Jewish understanding of its message.

Of course, there can be no certainty here. But we do have the common themes, the probability of common lections, and above all, a three-week Lent which here takes on specific meaning as a Christian application of Judaism's insistence that one count back three weeks from Passover in order to cleanse oneself and prepare for the sacrifice of the paschal lamb.

Great Sabbath: From Chronology to Typology

We can now return to the Great Sabbath and in particular, the way Christian sources use the term. As we saw, John 19:31 understands the Sabbath *prior to the resurrection* to be a Great Sabbath. If the term was indeed Jewish, then John is using the Jewish term but transforming it for Christians from the Sabbath prior to the Passover to the Sabbath afterward—since for John, the Passover sacrifice had taken place on Friday, the day before. If, on the other hand (following Yuval), he was inventing it himself, he was still using it in a non-calendrical but typological way. In either case, John's Great Sabbath is not a calendrical designation; it is a concept, by which he means the Saturday connected with the day of salvation. He may be borrowing the term already used by Jews for the equivalent Saturday prior to their own day of salvation (the Passover), and announcing that the resurrection now takes the place of that Passover. Alternatively, following Yuval's claim that Jews borrowed the Great Sabbath later on from Christians rather than Christians borrowing it early from Jews, he is inventing a new term for the Saturday in question. But either way, he is speaking not in calendrical but in theological terms.

Seeing John's use of the term "Great Sabbath" as theological, not chronological, goes a long way toward solving the puzzle of its use in the *Acts of the Martyrs*. We find it twice, once in the Martyrdom of Polycarp, and then again in the Martyrdom of Pionius. Both are said to have been martyred in Smyrna on a Great Sabbath, the former in 155[38] and the latter in 250. Can both men really have died in Smyrna on exactly the same day? And if so, what day was it, given the fact that the martyrdoms occurred in February, while the Great Sabbath of which John speaks is tied to Passover and cannot possibly have occurred that early in the year?

A recent attempt to solve the problem has been made by Robin Lane Fox, who bases his reconstruction on the prior study of Willy Rordorf,[39] which in turn goes back all the way to Lightfoot's claim in 1889.[40] Recognizing the impossibility of the Great Sabbath of Passover falling in February, Lightfoot posited the theory that the same term can be used generically for any Sabbath on which "a festival or other marked day in the Jewish calendar" falls. Thus, says Rordorf, the *Sabbaton mega* of the martyrs "does not designate the first day of Passover but simply a special Sabbath." But which one? Rordorf draws our attention to the account of Pionius, where we discover that the pagan population was celebrating a feast, and suggests that the author, himself a Christian, used the term *Sabbaton* not in its Jewish sense of the Sabbath but merely as a weekday name, Saturday. Hence no particular Jewish holy day is intended. Rather we have February 23, which is the end of the civil calendar in the Roman empire. Jews, Rordorf says, were not working because it was a Sabbath for them, and pagans too were mischievously idle because they were celebrating a holiday. In a festive mood, the two groups conspired twice within a century to kill the two Christians. Fox accepts most of this, with embellishments and alterations. The pagan festival was the ancient Dionysia, but it must have been a Jewish holiday too, he thinks. He dismisses the special Sabbaths of Adar on the mistaken notion that they were probably not around yet in the third century.[41] Actually, as we saw, they existed, but the term Great Sabbath was never used of any of them. Fox is right in rejecting them as a possible solution, albeit for the wrong reason. So Fox isolates Purim as the culprit. The Pagans were celebrating Dionysia, and the Jews, Purim— the very day of bloody and vengeful deliverance from the biblical Haman. What better day than that for Christian-bashing?

But Fox still has the incontrovertible problem that except for some isolated exceptions late in the Middle Ages,[42] the term Great Sabbath is never used for any Sabbath but the one known to John, the Sabbath prior to Passover.

I suggest a different type of solution, one that does not depend on fitting a term to an actual calendar day. We have seen that John was speaking theologically, not calendrically. A direct line reaches from John through both Polycarp to Pionius. Eusebius quotes Irenaeus, himself a disciple of Polycarp, as testifying that the latter knew "those who had seen the Lord," but especially John, who is singled out by name. Tertullian also says he was a disciple of John, who even appointed him to his bishopric.[43] As for Pionius, none other than he is credited with preparing the final copy of the account of Polycarp's martyrdom.[44] Musurillo notes that the accounts of the two martyrdoms are composed in similar style, highly dependent on gospel paradigms, full of rhetorical devices, and dedicated to the moral of "stress[ing] above all the poignant lack of sympathy which the Christians experienced as aliens in a hostile world . . . attributed to the malevolence of the Demon, whose aim is to conspire with Pagans and Jews to destroy the saints."[45] He doubts much of the historical veracity of the Pionius narrative, finds "undisguised anti-Semitism" in both accounts, and finds an overall theme according to which the martyrs are portrayed *as imitating Jesus's own death.*[46]

This theme is the key. The martyrs imitated Jesus' own death, according to their master, John. How much of the accounts we should therefore credit as history and how much as typology is indeed questionable. Arguing strenuously for the historicity of Pionius, Fox is left with the need to believe that both martyrs died on the same "Great Sabbath" ninety-five years apart. He must then explain that remarkable circumstance by locating something unique about the date; and thus, he is led to identify the "Great Sabbath" as a Jewish feast in February. It is far more likely, following Musurillo, that both accounts are highly skewed pictures. From (1) Polycarp's arrest by the police chief conveniently named Herod (to whom "destiny had given the same name, that Polycarp might fulfill the lot that was appointed to him, becoming a sharer with Christ, and those who betrayed him might receive the punishment of Judas" [para. 6]), to (2) the "mob of pagans and Jews" who "shouted aloud in uncontrollable rage" (para. 12), to (3) they "swiftly collected logs and brushwood [to burn him alive], with the Jews—as is their custom—zealously helping," we have no historical narrative, but a literary masterpiece in which theological characterizations replace historical fact.

The Great Sabbath could not possibly have occurred in February. But if the designation of the date is a typological desideratum, it need not have. It cannot be mere coincidence that (1) John is the only gospel to make the typological breakthrough of seeing the Great Sabbath as the day preceding God's deliverance; (2) John is also mentor par excellence of Polycarp, who himself is the model for Pionius; and (3) the deaths of these and only these two martyrs are associated with the Great Sabbath. I suggest that the Great Sabbath for the authors of these martyrologies is not an objective date in February but simply an extension of John's typology. It is the Sabbath associated with the deaths of martyrs who want in every way to come as close as they can to Jesus' death, and who therefore are killed, by definition, on a Great Sabbath—the authors having decided that any Sabbath in which they died should be so named.

NOTES

Originally published in somewhat different form as "The Jewish Lectionary, the Great Sabbath, and the Lenten Calendar: Liturgical Links between Christians and Jews in the First Three Christian Centuries," in J. Neil Alexander, ed., *Time and Community: In Honor of Thomas Julian Talley* (Washington, D.C., 1990), pp. 3–20.

1. Cf. classic studies by Adolph Büchler, "The Reading of the Law and Prophets in a Triennial Cycle," *JQR*, o.s., 5 (1893) and 6 (1894), reprinted in Jakob J. Petuchowski, *Contributions to the Scientific Study of Jewish Liturgy* (New York, 1970), pp. 181–302; and *The Bible as Read and Preached in the Old Synagogue*, vol. 1, by Jacob Mann (1940), and vol. 2, by Jacob Mann and Isaiah Sonne (1966),

reprinted with "Prolegomenon" by Ben Zion Wacholder (New York, 1971). In addition, see modern studies by Wacholder (abovementioned "Prolegomenon"), Joseph Heinemann, "The Triennial Lectionary Cycle," *JJS* 19 (1968): 41–48, and M. D. Goulder, *The Evangelists' Calendar: A Lectionary Explanation of the Development of Scripture* (London, 1978).

2. See Büchler, "Reading of the Law and Prophets," p. 240.

3. Joseph Offer, "Seder Nevi'im Ukh'tuvim," *Tarbiz* 58 (1988): 155–89.

4. See Solomon ben Hayatom's testimony, "The Great Sabbath before Passover, Shavuot, Rosh Hashanah and Sukkot," in Ismar Elbogen, *Der Jüdische Gottesdienst in seiner geschichtlichen Entwicklung* (1913; reprint, Hildesheim, 1962), pp. 550–51, note d.

5. See Issachar Jacobson, *Chazon Hamikra* (Tel Aviv, n.d.), p. 232, for synopsis.

6. Tos. Shab. 87b, d.h. *v'oto yom.*

7. *Shibbolei Haleket,* section 205.

8. Translations of the Greek *mega* vary, but it is "literally: 'great.'" Raymond E. Brown, *The Gospel according to John: Introduction, Translation and Notes* (Garden City, N.Y., 1970), p. 934.

9. A. Jellinek, "Literarische Analekten: Sabbat Ha-gadol," *Der Orient* 18 (1851): 287–88.

10. Leopold Zunz, *Der Ritus des synagogalen Gottesdienstes,* (Berlin, 1919), p.10.

11. Solomon Zeitlin, "The Liturgy of the First Night of Passover," *JQR,* n.s., 38 (1948): 431–60; see esp. pp. 457–60. Reprinted in *Solomon Zeitlin's Studies in the Early History of Judaism,* vol. 1 (New York, 1973), pp. 62–91.

12. Ibid., pp. 458–59 (=89–90).

13. *Dialogue with Trypho,* 49; cited by Zeitlin, in his *Studies,* p. 90, n. 320.

14. Zeitlin, "Liturgy of the First Night," p. 459.

15. Thomas J. Talley, *The Origins of the Liturgical Year* (New York, 1986).

16. Antoine Chavasse, "La structure du Carême et les lectures des messes quadragesimales dans la liturgie romaine," *La Maison-Dieu* 31 (1952): 84.

17. Cf. Chavasse, ibid., p. 84, and M. Ferreira Lages, "Étapes de l'evolution du Carême à Jérusalem avant le Ve siècle," *Revue des Études Arméniennes,* n.s., 6 (1969): 69.

18. See, e.g., Cyrille Vogel, *Medieval Liturgy: An Introduction to*

the Sources, revised and translated by William G. Storey and Niels Krogh Rasmussen (Washington, D.C., 1986), pp. 309-10.

19. Chavasse, "Structure du Carême," p. 84.
20. Lages, "L'evolution du Carême à Jérusalem," p. 98.
21. Robert L. Wilken, *John Chrysostom and the Jews: Rhetoric and Reality in the Late Fourth Century* (Berkeley, 1983), pp. 29-33: quotation from Bickerman, p. 33.
22. M. Meg. 3:4.
23. Pes. 8:8.
24. T. Pes. 8:9.
25. As had the biblical practice of providing a second Passover one month later for those who were unclean on Nisan 14 (Num. 9:11).
26. M. Pes. 8:8.
27. See M. Meg. 3:4, cited above.
28. P. T. Meg. 3:5.
29. Rashi to M. Meg. 3:4.
30. A. G. Martimort, I. H. Dalmais, and P. Jounel, *The Church at Prayer,* vol. 4 (Collegeville, 1983), pp. 33-34.
31. *Apology* I, 66:3. Cf. Israel Yuval, "Passover in the Middle Ages," in volume 5 of this series; Lawrence A. Hoffman, "A Symbol of Salvation in the Passover Seder" in this volume; and I. H. Danielou, *Sacramentum Futuri* (Paris, 1950).
32. Chavasse, "Structure du Carême," p. 95.
33. T. Meg. 3:3.
34. Lages, "L'evolution du Carême à Jérusalem," p. 99.
35. See Adrian Nocent, *The Liturgical Year,* vol. 2, *Lent* (Collegeville, 1977), p. 248. On the *Wurzburg Epistolary,* see Vogel, *Medieval Liturgy.*
36. Cf., for example, Bernhard Blumenkrantz, *Die Judenpredigt Augustins* (Paris, 1973), and Marcel Simon, *Verus Israel: Études sur les relations entre Chrétiens et Juifs dans l'Empire romaine* (Paris, 1948), pp. 135-425.
37. Mekhilta *Pascha,* chap. 5.
38. The exact date is debated. See Boudewijn Dehandschutter, *Martyrium Polycarpi: Een literair-kritische studie* (Louvain, 1979), p. 281; Herbert Musurillo, comp., *The Acts of the Christian Martyrs* (Oxford, 1972), introduction, p. xiii; and Robin Lane Fox, *Pagans and Christians* (New York, 1987). Fox dispenses also with Eusebius's version of the year for Pionius's death; see p. 468.
39. Cf. Fox, *Pagans and Christians,* pp. 468-73, 485-87; and Willy

Rordorf, "Zum Problem des 'Grossen Sabbats' im Polykarp- und Pioniusmartyrium," in *Pietas: Festschrift für Bernhard Kötting* (Munich, 1980), pp. 245–49.

40. J. B. Lightfoot, *Apostolic Fathers* 2:1, pp. 709ff; cited in Rordorf, "Zum Problem," p. 246, n. 11.

41. This mistaken notion is attributed (Fox, *Pagans and Christians*, p. 758, n. 71) to Elbogen, *Der Jüdische Gottesdienst*, pp. 155–59. In fact, Elbogen says no such thing, but cites instead the Mishnah noted above. I mention it here not because I think the Great Sabbath was one of these special Sabbaths, but because I want to retain the historicity of the special Sabbaths for the Tannaitic period, for the purposes of my thesis regarding their relationship to the origin of Lent.

42. See above, n. 5.

43. Cf. Eusebius, *History* 5:20, Tertullian's testimony in *De Praescr.* 32:2, and other similar accounts, all cited in E. C. E. Owen, *Some Authentic Acts of the Early Martyrs* (Oxford, 1927), p. 31, and in Musurillo, *Acts of the Christian Martyrs* p. xiii.

44. Musurillo, *Acts of the Christian Martyrs*, pp. 19–20.

45. Ibid., pp. xiv–xv, xxviii–xxix.

46. Ibid., pp. xii, xiv, xxviii.

Preparation for Pascha?
Lent in Christian Antiquity

Maxwell E. Johnson

It was once commonly assumed that the forty-day period of pre-paschal preparation for baptismal candidates, penitents, and the Christian community in general known as "Lent" (*Quadragesima* or *Tessarakoste*) had its origin as a gradual backwards development of the short preparatory and purificatory fast held before the annual celebration of Pascha.[1] According to this standard theory, the one- or two-day fast before Pascha (as witnessed to by Tertullian in *De ieiunio* 13–14) became extended to include:

1. the entire week, later called "Great" or "Holy Week," beginning on the preceding Monday,
2. a three-week period (at least in Rome) including this "Holy Week," and finally,
3. a six-week, forty-day preparation period assimilating those preparing for Easter baptism to the forty-day temptation of Jesus in the desert.

That this pre-paschal period finally became forty days in length in the fourth century has been traditionally explained by an appeal to a shift in world view on the part of the post-Constantinian Christian community. That is, instead of a church with an eschatological orientation to the imminent *parousia* of Christ little concerned with historical events, sites, and time, the fourth century reveals a church whose liturgy has become principally a historical remembrance and commemoration of the *past:* a liturgy increasingly splintered into separate commemorations of historical events in the life of Christ. As

36

the primary and most influential proponent of this theory of fourth-century "historicism," Gregory Dix, explained it:

> The step of identifying the six weeks' fast with the 40 days' fast of our Lord in the wilderness was obviously in keeping with the new historical interest of the liturgy. The actual number of '40 days' of fasting was made up by extending Lent behind the sixth Sunday before Easter in various ways. But the association with our Lord's fast in the wilderness was an idea attached to the season of Lent only *after* it had come into existence in connection with the preparation of candidates for baptism.[2]

Recent scholarship, however, most notably that of Thomas Talley,[3] has necessitated revising previous theories. We can no longer speak of a *single* origin for Lent. Rather, there are multiple origins for this period which, in the fourth-century post-Nicene context, become universally standardized and fixed as the "forty days" that have characterized pre-paschal preparation ever since.

The Primitive Pre-Paschal Fast

Third-century sources indicate that the two-day fast on the Friday and Saturday before the celebration of Pascha was becoming a six-day pre-paschal fast in Alexandria and Syria.[4] Although this extension has often been interpreted as the initial stage in the development of the forty-day Lent (since this week is included in the overall calculation of Lent in later liturgical sources), this six-day preparatory fast is better interpreted as the origin of what would come to be called "Holy" or "Great Week" throughout the churches of the ancient world. Thomas Talley observes that within the later Byzantine tradition, Lazarus Saturday and Palm Sunday divide Lent, which precedes them, from the six-day pre-paschal fast of Great Week which follows, and these days were known already in fourth-century Jerusalem.[5] Rather than being related specifically to the origins of *Lent*, therefore, the two-day (or one-week) fast in these third-century sources (with the possible exception of *Apostolic Tradition* 20)[6] seems to have been an

independent preparation of the faithful for the imminent celebration of the Pascha itself. Already in the third-century
Didascalia Apostolorum, this fast is related chronologically to
events in the last week of Jesus' life. In other words, the *Holy
Week* fast, properly speaking, is not *Lent* but a pre-paschal fast
alone, which overlaps with, but should not be confused with,
an earlier preparatory period that comes to be known as Lent.

Thanks to the "historicism theory" of Gregory Dix in particular, the development of Holy Week has often been explained as the result of post-Nicene preoccupation with Jerusalem, whose "liturgically minded bishop," Cyril, was fixated
on the liturgical commemoration of historical holy events at
the very holy places where they once occurred.[7] From Jerusalem as a pilgrimage center, then, these commemorations spread
to the rest of the church and tended to shape the way this week
was celebrated elsewhere.

In fact, however, as early as the pre-Nicene *Didascalia Apostolorum,* this week had already been assimilated to events in
Jesus' last week. As Robert Taft and John Baldovin have demonstrated for Jerusalem,[8] the situation cannot be explained
adequately as a simple interpretive shift from a pre-Nicene eschatological orientation to a fourth-century historical one.
"Eschatology" and "history" are not mutually exclusive. As we
shall see, even prior to Nicea, the date of Easter, the assimilation of the six-day pre-paschal fast to a chronology of Jesus'
final week, and an assimilation of a forty-day fast to the forty-
day post-baptismal temptation of Jesus in the desert—although
not to a pre-paschal "Lent"—were already accomplished. Post-
Nicene Lenten trends were liturgically evolutionary, not revo-
lutionary, trends, and were not suddenly instituted by individual influential figures (like Cyril) in response to the changed
situation of the Church in the post-Constantinian world.[9]

A Three Week Pre-Paschal Preparation

The fifth-century Byzantine historian, Socrates, describes
his understanding of the variety of Lenten observances throughout the Christian churches of his day:

The fasts before Easter will be found to be differently observed among different people. Those at Rome fast three successive weeks before Easter, excepting Saturdays and Sundays. Those in Illyrica and all over Greece and Alexandria observe a fast of six weeks, which they term "the forty days' fast." Others commencing their fast from the seventh week before Easter, and fasting three to five days only, and that at intervals, yet call that time "the forty days' fast." It is indeed surprising to me that thus differing in the number of days, they should both give it one common appellation; but some assign one reason for it, and others another, according to their several fancies.[10]

What is most intriguing about Socrates' statement is his reference to a three-week Lenten fast at Rome. Since he corrects himself about Saturdays as non-fasting days in Rome later in this work, and since Athanasius (in his Festal Letter of 340),[11] Jerome (in a letter to Marcella in 384),[12] and Pope Siricius (in a letter to Himerius of Tarragona in 385)[13] refer to an established pattern of a forty-day Lent there too, his statement is inaccurate as a fifth-century description. Nevertheless, his reference to "three successive weeks" of fasting appears to be corroborated by later sources of the Roman liturgy. Such evidence includes:

1. the provision of three *missae pro scrutiniis* (masses for the scrutinies of baptismal candidates) assigned to the third, fourth, and fifth Sundays of Lent in the Gelasian Sacramentary (seventh century);
2. the course reading of the Gospel of John during the last three weeks of Lent (beginning in the *Würzburg Capitulary,* the earliest Roman lectionary [c. 700], on the Friday before the third Sunday in Lent and reaching its conclusion on Good Friday); and
3. the titles *Hebdomada in mediana* (week in the middle) and *Dominica in mediana* (Sunday in the middle), applied, respectively, to the fourth week and fifth Sunday of Lent in various *ordines Romani* and Roman lectionaries.

In light of all this, Socrates' inaccurate fifth-century description may well indicate the remnant of a well-ingrained three-week Lenten period in Rome some time earlier. Such, at least, was the conclusion of Antoine Chavasse[14] from his analysis of the Johannine readings of the last three weeks on Lent, which he was able to reconstruct as an independent set of lections that must once have constituted an original three-week Lenten period, including Holy Week.[15] Along similar lines, Thomas Talley has also concluded that Socrates' reference may reflect an earlier, if not fifth-century, Roman practice.[16]

The possibility of an original three-week Lent, however, is not limited to Rome. On the basis of a detailed structural analysis of the contents of the fifth-century Armenian Lectionary, a lectionary generally understood to reflect fourth-century Jerusalem practice, Mario F. Lages has argued that early Jerusalem practice knew an original three-week Lenten preparation period of catechumens for paschal baptism.[17] Along with these contents—including a canon of Lenten readings with concluding psalmody assigned to Wednesday and Friday gatherings at Zion and a list of nineteen catechetical biblical readings assigned to Lenten catechesis (which parallel the pre-baptismal catecheses of Cyril of Jerusalem)—Lages also pointed to the introductory rubric in the ninth- or tenth-century Armenian rite of baptism and to a pertinent rubric in the fifth-century Georgian Lectionary. The Armenian baptismal rubric reads in part:

> The Canon of Baptism when they make a Christian. Before which it is not right to admit him into the church. But he shall have hands laid on beforehand, *three weeks or more* before the baptism, in time sufficient for him to learn from the Wardapet [Instructor] both the faith and the baptism of the church.[18]

The Georgian Lectionary, while listing the same nineteen catechetical readings as Cyril and the Armenian Lectionary, specifically directs that catechesis is to begin with these readings on the Monday of the fifth week in Lent, that is, exactly *nineteen* days (or approximately three weeks) before paschal baptism.[19]

The early three-week Lenten period in Rome and Jerusalem was customary in other liturgical traditions as well. I have suggested elsewhere[20] that a similar three-week period of final preparation for baptismal candidates is discernible from an analysis of the last three weeks of the forty-day Lent in North Africa, Naples, Constantinople, and Spain. For Spain, in particular, this three-week period appears to be confirmed by the first canon of the Second Council of Braga (572), which directs that bishops

> shall teach that catechumens (as the ancient canons command) shall come for the cleansing of exorcism twenty days before baptism, in which twenty days they shall especially be taught the Creed, which is: I believe in God the Father Almighty. . . . [21]

What Socrates says about the "three successive weeks" of pre-paschal fasting at Rome, therefore, should be seen as the memory of an early Christian practice which was much more universal than Roman in its scope.

On the basis of this discernable pattern in Christian liturgical sources, Lawrence Hoffman has suggested that this practice has its ultimate roots in Judaism.[22] Hoffman notes that, according to rabbinic sources, the feast of Passover itself is preceded by lectionary readings (Exodus 12 or Numbers 19) on the third Sabbath prior to its arrival that stress either preparation for the passover sacrifice or the necessity of being cleansed from impurity. The Exodus 12 reading, he notes further, was cited by Chavasse as an early reading for Good Friday at Rome, and the prophetic reading of Ezekiel 36:25–36 (accompanying Numbers 19, according to the Tosefta) appears on the Wednesday of Lent IV (the fourth week of Lent) in early Roman lectionaries, that is, two and one-half weeks before Easter. According to Hoffman, therefore, the early three-week Lent—at least in Jerusalem and Rome—was "a Christian application of Judaism's insistence that one count back three weeks from Passover in order to cleanse oneself and prepare for the sacrifice of the paschal lamb."[23] If Hoffman is correct, then, as Talley writes, "this could well suggest that the three-week preparation for Pascha antedates its employment as the framework for baptismal preparation."[24]

The strength and appeal of Hoffman's theory are that it appears to provide a firm rationale for the Christian choice of a *three-week* period of preparation. The problem, however, is that when we first see whatever evidence there is for this three-week "Lent" (with the exception of Socrates' general reference to fasting), it is

1. already closely associated with the final preparation of catechumens for baptism, and
2. not always clearly associated with *Easter* baptism.

The Armenian baptismal rubric, for example, stresses three weeks of preparation for baptism without specifying when that baptism is to take place. But the early Syrian and Armenian traditions favored baptism on Epiphany, not Easter, since they understood Christian initiation as the *mimesis* of the Jordan event interpreted in light of the rebirth imagery of John 3 rather than the paschal imagery of Romans 6. The three-week period of preparation was therefore more probably associated with catechumenal preparation for baptism without having anything to do with Easter.[25] Similarly, thanks again to the work of Talley, it is now common knowledge that prior to the post-Nicene context of the fourth century, the Alexandrian tradition knew neither Easter baptism nor a pre-paschal "Lent" longer than the *one* week of the paschal fast. And, it must be noted, the reference to "three weeks" in the Constantinopolitan liturgy is actually a reference in the *typica* to the enrollment of baptismal candidates exactly *three weeks* before the celebration of baptism on Lazarus Saturday (the day before Palm Sunday and a full week before Easter), a day which in current Byzantine usage still contains the vestige of a baptismal liturgy in its entrance antiphon.[26]

Because of the primary association of this three-week period with baptismal preparation, the real question, therefore, is whether or not this period must necessarily be connected to Easter and consequently to a pre-paschal Lent. Talley has stated that "Pascha was becoming the preferred time for baptism in many parts of the Church" in the third century,[27] but Paul Bradshaw has recently surveyed the evidence for this assertion and comes to a much different conclusion.[28] According to Bradshaw, the most that can be said about Easter baptism before the fourth century is that there is a *preference* expressed for this practice, a preference limited to third-century North Africa (Tertullian) and Rome (Hippolytus), with its possible celebration on other days by no means excluded. Only in the post-Nicene context of the fourth century does paschal baptism, along with a Romans 6 reinterpretation of baptism as incorporation into the death and resurrection of Christ, become a nearly universal Christian *ideal*. Even then, however, it does not appear to become the only or dominant custom outside of Rome or north Italy. The letter of Pope Siricius to Himerius of Tarragona (385), one of the earliest Roman references to a forty-day Lent, reveals a variety of baptismal occasions in Spain (i.e., Christmas, Epiphany, and the feasts of apostles and martyrs). Evidence from Leo I demonstrates that Epiphany was also a baptismal day in Sicily and that the feasts of martyrs were baptismal occasions elsewhere in Italy. A sermon of Gregory Nazianzus shows, similarly, that Epiphany baptism was a common practice in Cappadocia. These examples, along with those of Alexandria and Constantinople referred to above, lead Bradshaw to say that "baptism at Easter was never the normative *practice* in Christian antiquity that many have assumed. The most that can be said is that it was an experiment that survived for less than fifty years."

What, then, may be concluded about Socrates' three weeks and the origins of Lent? As we have seen, references to this three-week period are discerned primarily within the context of final baptismal preparation. But what is most striking is that not all of these sources refer to *Easter* baptism. We seem therefore to have a three-week period of (final) catechetical preparation for baptism that only later gets associated with Easter. It becomes "Lent" simply because Easter gradually becomes the preferred day for Christian initiation. Whenever baptism occurred, it was preceded, as the Armenian baptismal rubric says, by "three weeks or more" of preparation. For those

churches (North Africa and Rome) which "preferred" to celebrate initiation at Pascha, we may speak of this three-week period as a kind of primitive "Lent." For those which did not
have such an early preference, this three-week period was not
"Lent" but merely a final catechetical baptismal preparation.
Only when paschal baptism becomes the normative *ideal*—as
Bradshaw says, in the second half of the fourth century—
do these variations become blurred, harmonized, and thus
brought into universal conformity as part of the newly-
developed pre-paschal *Quadragesima* or *Tessarakoste*.

The Forty Days as a Pre-Paschal Season

As already noted, the pre-paschal Lent of forty days, like
the universal ideal of paschal baptism, appears to be a fourth-
century post-Nicene development. Talley writes:

> the Council of Nicea is something of a watershed for the fast of
> forty days. Prior to Nicea, no record exists of such a forty-day fast
> before Easter. Only a few years after the council, however, we en-
> counter it in most of the church as either a well-established cus-
> tom or one that has become so nearly universal as to impinge on
> those churches that have not yet adopted it.[29]

From where, then, does this forty-day fast as a pre-paschal
preparation period emerge? Following the initial work of
Anton Baumstark and R.-G. Coquin,[30] Talley has provided
what is rapidly becoming the standard answer to this question
by directing scholarly attention to Alexandria. I have already
noted that within this tradition, neither Easter baptism nor
a pre-paschal fast of more than one week was customarily
known. Nevertheless, there are references in the sources of this
tradition to a *forty-day fast* separate from this one-week pre-
paschal fast. Such references appear in Origen's *Homilies on
Leviticus*, in the context of remarks concerning the reconciliation of penitent apostastes in Peter of Alexandria's *Canonical
Epistle* (c. 305), and in the *Canons of Hippolytus* (c. 336–340),
the earliest document derived from the *Apostolic Tradition:*

(Origen, *Hom. in Lev.*, X.2): They fast, therefore, who have lost the bridegroom; we having him with us cannot fast. Nor do we say that we relax the restraints of Christian abstinence; for we have the *forty days consecrated to fasting,* we have the fourth and sixth days of the week, on which we fast solemnly.[31]

(Peter of Alexandria, *Canon* 1): for they did not come to this of their own will, but were betrayed by the frailty of the flesh; for they show in their bodies the marks of Jesus, and some are now, for the third year, bewailing their fault: it is sufficient, I say, that from the time of their submissive approach, *other forty days* should be enjoined upon them, to keep them in remembrance of these things; *those forty days* during which, though our Lord and Saviour Jesus Christ had fasted, He was yet, after He had been baptized, tempted by the devil. And when they shall have, during these days, exercised themselves much, and constantly fasted, then let them watch in prayer, meditating upon what was spoken by the Lord to him who tempted Him to fall down and worship him: 'Get behind me, Satan; for it is written, Thou shalt worship the Lord thy God, and Him only shalt thou serve.'[32]

(*Canons of Hippolytus* 20): The fast days which have been fixed are Wednesday, Friday, *and the Forty.* He who adds to this list will receive a reward, and whoever diverges from it, except for illness, constraint, or necessity, transgresses the rule and disobeys God *who fasted on our behalf.*[33]

While in two of these sources the forty days of fasting are explicitly related to Jesus' own post-baptismal temptation in the desert, none of them speak of this period in relationship to either Pascha or to baptism. It would be very difficult, therefore, to interpret these "forty days" as clearly referring to a period connected to a pre-paschal forty-day Lent in Egypt. Might they, however, be references to a unique and early Alexandrian custom and season? Talley certainly believes so, and after a detailed analysis of admittedly later Egyptian liturgical sources, concludes that this unique and early Alexandrian forty-day fast soon became a forty-day *pre-baptismal* fast for catechumens begun on the day after Epiphany (January 6), a feast which celebrated the baptism of Jesus. Following the chronology of the Gospel of Mark—the Gospel traditionally associated with the Church of Alexandria—this fasting period concluded forty days later with the solemn celebration of baptism and, in light of Canon 1 of Peter of Alexandria, perhaps with the reconciliation of penitents.

In conjunction with baptism a passage was read from a now lost secret Gospel of Mark (the *Mar Saba Clementine Fragment*),[34] which describes an initiation rite administered by Jesus himself to an unnamed Lazarus-like figure whom Jesus had raised from the dead six days earlier in Bethany. And, it is important to note, the next chapter in Markan sequence (Mark 11) describes Jesus' "Palm Sunday" entrance into Jerusalem. If Talley is correct, the "forty days" of Lent ultimately have an Alexandrian origin. At the same time, this post-Epiphany practice at Alexandria would also explain the Constantinopolitan custom of baptism on Lazarus Saturday as well as the use of Lazarus Saturday and Palm Sunday to distinguish and separate Lent from Great Week.[35]

The question remains, however: *How* does this Alexandrian forty-day post-Epiphany baptismal-preparation fast become the pre-paschal Lent? For this there is no clear or easy answer. Coquin thinks that Lent became a universal forty-day pre-paschal period as the result of the Council of Nicea's determination of the calculation to be employed for the annual celebration of Easter throughout the church.[36] The sudden post-Nicene universal emergence of the forty days of pre-paschal preparation for Easter and for baptism at Easter does suggest that the Nicene settlement included this preference for Easter baptism. This preference was now seemingly followed everywhere except at Alexandria, which, although shifting its traditional forty-day period to a pre-paschal location in order to conform generally to the rest of the church, continued to celebrate baptism itself at the very end of this forty-day period, first on Good Friday, and second, because of the addition of another week of fasting later attached to the beginning of Lent, on the Friday before Holy Week. A vestige of this tradition continues in the Coptic Church today, where baptisms are not allowed between Palm Sunday and Pentecost.[37]

When, after Nicea, the forty days of Lent became attached to pre-paschal preparation throughout the churches of the ancient world, different manners of calculating the actual duration of this season were employed. This resulted in both the differing lengths of Lent and the different fasting practices during Lent within the various churches, which caused Socrates to express his surprise that all of them, nonetheless, used the terminology of "forty days" to refer to this period. In Rome, for example, the forty days began on the sixth Sunday before Easter (called *Quadragesima*) and thus, including the traditional pre-paschal two-day fast on Good Friday and Holy Saturday, lasted for a total of forty-two days. Since Roman practice did not know fasting on Sundays, the total number of fast days was actually thirty-six. Only much later, with the addition of four fast days beginning on the Wednesday before *Quadragesima* (later called *Ash Wednesday* because of the penitential practices which came to be associated with it), does Roman practice come to know an actual forty-day Lenten *fast* before Easter.[38]

Like Rome, Alexandria (as witnessed to by Athanasius's Festal Letters of 330 and 340)[39] also originally adopted a six-week Lenten period before Easter (including Holy Week). However, with no fasting on either Saturdays or Sundays in this tradition, there was a total of only thirty fast days before the fast of Holy Saturday. As indicated above, a week was added to the beginning of this period, bringing the total to thirty-five days of fasting. Ultimately, even another week was added so that an actual forty-day fast, an eight-week inclusive Lent before Easter, resulted.[40]

While other liturgical sources for Jerusalem, Antioch, and Constantinople suggest a six-week Lent with five fast days in each week, concluding on the Friday before Lazarus Saturday and Palm Sunday, the Spanish pilgrim Egeria claims that Jerusalem knew a total eight-week pattern—a seven-week Lent and the six-day fast of Great Week—in the late fourth century.[41] Although her statement has often been dismissed as misinformation,[42] as "an experiment that did not last,"[43] or as reflecting the practice of an ascetical community in Jerusalem which began the Lenten fast one or two weeks before others did,[44] some comparative evidence has been provided by Frans van de Paverd, who argues in his recent study of John Chrysostom's *Homilies on the Statues* that fourth-century Antioch also knew a similar eight-week Lenten pattern.[45]

However Lent came to be calculated and organized in these various Christian traditions after Nicea, it is clear that this "forty days" was understood eventually as a time for the final preparation of catechumens for Easter baptism, for the preparation of those undergoing public penance for reconciliation on or before Easter (on the morning of Holy Thursday in Roman practice), and for the pre-paschal preparation of the whole Christian community in general. Basing his comments primarily upon the mid-fifth-century Lenten sermons of Leo I, Patrick Regan summarizes this focus in the following manner:

> The purpose and character of Lent are entirely derived from the great festival for which it prepares. The Pasch is not only an annual celebration of the passion and passage of Christ, but it is for Christians of the fourth and fifth centuries the yearly reminder of their own incorporation into the paschal event through baptism. Consequently the approach of the Pasch renews in the memory of all the faithful their commitment to live the new life of him who for their sake was crucified, buried, and raised. But it also accuses them of their failure to do so. . . . [46]

Only in the late fifth century and beyond, when infant initiation comes to replace that of adult, thus effectively bringing about the extinction of the catechumenate, and when the system of public penance is replaced by the form of repeatable individual confession and absolution, do the forty days then take on the sole character of preparation of the faithful for the events of Holy Week and the celebration of Easter. Such a focus—extremely penitential, and oriented in character and piety toward the "passion of Jesus," with little attention given to the period's baptismal and catechumenal origins—has tended to shape the interpretation and practice of the "forty days" of Lent until the present day.[47]

Conclusion: The Origins of Lent

The season of Lent as it developed into a pre-paschal preparation period of "forty days" for catechumens, pentitents, and Christian faithful within the fourth-century post-Nicene context has multiple and complicated origins. While the development of the six-day pre-paschal fast may have played some role in its initial formation, what evidence there is suggests that this particular fast, although important for the origins of Holy Week, is separate and distinct from that which came to be understood, properly speaking, as Lent. In other words, the traditional theory that the forty days of Lent merely reflect the historically-oriented backwards extension of the six-day pre-paschal fast in an attempt to closely assimilate those preparing for Easter baptism to Jesus' post-baptismal forty-day desert fast is highly questionable, if not clearly wrong. As we have seen, current scholarship argues that such historical assimilation of the forty days to the fast of Jesus was already present before Nicea within, at least, the Alexandrian liturgical tradition, although originally it had no relationship either to Pascha or to baptism at all. But as a fasting period already in place in this tradition, it suitably became pre-baptismal in orientation because baptismal preparation necessarily included fasting as one of its major components.[48] Then when paschal baptism, interpreted in the light of a Romans 6 baptismal theology, became the normative *ideal* after Nicea, this Alexandrian post-Epiphany pattern could become *the* pre-paschal Lenten pattern. It may be said, therefore, that the sudden emergence of the forty-day Lenten season after Nicea represents a harmonizing and standardizing combination of different, primarily *initiatory* practices in early, pre-Nicene Christianity. These practices consisted of:

1. an original forty-day post-*Epiphany* fast in the Alexandrian tradition, already associated with Jesus' own post-baptismal fast in the desert, which, as a fasting period already in place, became the suitable time for the pre-baptismal preparation of catechumens;
2. the three-week preparation of catechumens for *Easter* baptism in the Roman and North African traditions; and
3. the three-week preparation of catechumens for baptism elsewhere either on a different liturgical feast or on no specified occasion whatsoever.

After Nicea—and probably as the result of Nicea—these practices all became "paschalized" as the pre-Easter Lenten *Quadragesima,* although in Alexandria itself this paschalization process, as we have seen, was only partially successful and left the celebration of baptism itself separate from the celebration of Easter.

The conjectural nature of scholarship on Lent must be kept in mind and so received with due caution. However, if current scholarship, represented primarily by Talley, is correct, the origins of what becomes "Lent" have very little to do with Easter at all. Rather, those origins have to do both with early fasting practices in general and with the final preparation of baptismal candidates, whenever their baptisms might be celebrated. Greater awareness of these origins may serve today as a necessary corrective to the "passion" orientation, noted above, that still tends to characterize and shape contemporary Christian Lenten observance.

NOTES

1. See Adolf Adam, *The Liturgical Year: Its History and Meaning after the Reform of the Liturgy* (New York, 1981), pp. 91 ff.; Gregory Dix, *The Shape of the Liturgy* (London, 1945), pp. 347-60; Patrick Regan, "The Three Days and the Forty Days," *Worship* 54 (1980): 2-18; and Pierre Jounel, "The Year," in A.-G. Martimort, ed., *The Church at Prayer* vol. 4 (Collegeville, 1986), pp. 65-72.

2. Dix, *The Shape of the Liturgy,* p. 354.

3. Thomas Talley, *The Origins of the Liturgical Year,* 2d ed. (Collegeville, 1986); and "The Origin of Lent at Alexandria," in idem, *Worship: Reforming Tradition* (Washington, D.C., 1990), pp. 87–112.

4. See Talley, *Origins of the Liturgical Year,* and Paul F. Bradshaw, "The Origins of Easter," in volume 5 of this series.

5. Talley, *Origins of the Liturgical Year,* pp. 176–214. See also idem, "The Origin of Lent at Alexandria," pp. 97–108.

6. Although *Apostolic Tradition* 20 refers to a Friday and Saturday (?) fast for those who are to be baptized at the close of a Saturday night vigil, it does not specifically relate either the pre-baptismal fast, baptism, or the vigil to *Pascha.* Hippolytus of Rome himself certainly knew paschal baptism but there is no evidence that the compilers of *Apostolic Tradition,* whoever they may have been, did. On this, see Paul F. Bradshaw, *The Search for the Origins of Christian Worship* (New York, 1992), pp. 90, 174–78, and idem, "Re-dating the *Apostolic Tradition:* Some Preliminary Steps," in Nathan Mitchell and John Baldovin, eds., *Rule of Prayer, Rule of Faith: Essays in Honor of Aidan Kavanagh, O. S. B.* (Collegeville, 1996), pp. 3–17.

7. Dix, *The Shape of the Liturgy,* pp. 348–53.

8. Robert Taft, "Historicism Revisited," in idem, *Beyond East and West: Problems in Liturgical Understanding* (Washington, D.C., 1984), pp. 15–30; John Baldovin, *The Urban Character of Christian Worship* (Rome, 1987), pp. 90–93.

9. See Bradshaw, *Search for the Origins of Christian Worship,* pp. 65–67.

10. *Historia Ecclesiastica* 5.22.

11. *The Festal Letters of S. Athanasius* (Oxford, 1854), p. 100.

12. *Ep.* 24.4 (*PL* 22:428).

13. *PL* 13.1131–1147.

14. See Antoine Chavasse, "La structure du Carême et les lectures des messes quadragésimales dans la liturgie romaine," *La Maison-Dieu* 31 (1952): 76–120; "La préparation de la Pâque, à Rome, avant le Ve siècle. Jeûne et organisation liturgique," in *Memorial J. Chaine* (Lyon, 1950), pp. 61–80; and "Temps de préparation à la Pâque, d'après quelques livres liturgiques romains," *Recherches de Science religieuse* 37 (1950), pp. 125–45. For a more detailed summary and discussion of Chavasse's work, see M. E. Johnson, "From Three Weeks to Forty Days: Baptismal Preparation and the Origins of Lent," *Studia Liturgica* 20 (1990): 185–200; reprinted in idem, ed., *Living Water, Sealing Spirit: Readings on Christian Initiation* (Collegeville, 1995), pp. 118–36.

15. Chavasse noted that the series of Johannine readings during the last three weeks of Lent in early Roman lectionaries and in the Tridentine *Missale Romanum* began with John 4:5–32 on the Friday of Lent III. For some reason, however, it placed John 9:1–38 (Wednesday of Lent IV) and John 11:1–45 (Friday of Lent IV) *before* John 8:46–59 (Sunday of Lent V), and John 10:22–38 (Wednesday of Lent V), with the continuation of John 11 (47–54) on the Friday of Lent V. On this basis he attempted to reconstruct an earlier shape for this Johannine series, which he believed would have corresponded to the three *missae pro scrutiniis* in the Gelasian Sacramentary. According to his reconstruction, John 4:5–32, John 9:1–38, and John 11:1–54 would have been read, respectively, on the third, fourth, and fifth Sundays in Lent in the time of Leo the Great. Even so, at an earlier stage of development this would have constituted a short lectionary series for the Sundays of an original three-week Lenten period, including Holy Week. The reason that this series of readings appears in a different sequence in later Roman sources, according to Chavasse, is due to the fact that the baptismal scrutinies along with their readings became shifted to weekdays (ultimately, seven in number) in the later Roman tradition. Thanks to the work of Chavasse, this is precisely the sequence of Sunday gospel readings assigned to the third, fourth, and fifth Sundays in Lent in Series A of the current Roman Lectionary. To these Sundays have been attached the three scrutinies of adult catechumens in the current Roman *Rite of Christian Initiation of Adults.*

16. Talley, *Origins of the Liturgical Year,* p. 167.

17. M. F. Lages, "Étapes de l'evolution du Carême à Jérusalem avant le Ve siècle. Essai d'analyse structurale," *Revue des Études Arméniennes* 6 (1969): 67–102; and idem, "The Hierosolymitain Origin of the Catechetical Rites in the Armenian Liturgy," *Didaskalia* 1 (1967): 233–50. See also M. E. Johnson, "Reconciling Cyril and Egeria on the Catechetical Process in Fourth-Century Jerusalem," in Paul F. Bradshaw, ed., *Essays in Early Eastern Initiation* (Bramcote, Notts., 1988), pp. 24–26. For the Armenian Lectionary see Athanase Renoux, *Le Codex armenien Jérusalem 121,* vol. 2 (Turnhout, 1971).

18. E. C. Whitaker, *Documents of the Baptismal Liturgy* (London, 1970), p. 60 [emphasis added].

19. Michel Tarschnischvili, *Le grand lectionnaire de l'Église de Jérusalem,* vol. 1 (Louvain, 1959), p. 68.

20. See Johnson, "From Three Weeks to Forty Days," pp. 191–93.

21. Whitaker, *Documents of the Baptismal Liturgy,* p. 227.

22. Lawrence A. Hoffman, "The Great Sabbath and Lent: Jewish Origins?" in this volume.

23. Ibid., p. 29.

24. Talley, *Origins of the Liturgical Year,* p. 167.

25. See Gabriele Winkler, *Das armenische Initiationsrituale* (Rome, 1982), pp. 437–38; and idem, "The Original Meaning of the Prebaptismal Anointing and its Implications," *Worship* 52 (1978): 24–45.

26. See Talley, *Origins of the Liturgical Year,* pp. 189, 203–14.

27. Ibid., p. 167.

28. Paul F. Bradshaw, " 'Diem baptismo sollemniorem': Initiation and Easter in Christian Antiquity," in E. Carr, S. Parenti, and A. A. Thiermeyer, eds., *Eulogêma: Studies in Honor of Robert Taft, S. J.* (Rome, 1993), pp. 41–51; reprinted in Johnson, *Living Water, Sealing Spirit,* pp. 137–47.

29. Talley, *Origins of the Liturgical Year,* p. 168.

30. A. Baumstark, *Comparative Liturgy* (London, 1958), p. 194; R.-G. Coquin, "Une Réforme liturgique du concile de Nicée (325)?" in *Comptes Rendus, Académie des Inscriptions et Belles-lettres* (Paris, 1967), pp. 178–92.

31. English translation from Talley, *Origins of the Liturgical Year,* p. 192 [emphasis added].

32. English translation from Alexander Roberts and James Donaldson, *The Ante-Nicene Fathers,* vol. 6 (New York, 1925), p. 269 [emphasis added].

33. English translation from Paul Bradshaw, ed., *The Canons of Hippolytus* (Bramcote, Notts., 1987), p. 25 [emphasis added].

34. See Morton Smith, *Clement of Alexandria and a Secret Gospel of Mark* (Cambridge, 1973). The passage is between the canonical Mark 10:34 and 10:35.

35. In all fairness, it must be noted that Talley's theory is based less on available early Alexandrian evidence and more on a hypothetical reconstruction of early Alexandrian practice discerned from the Markan sequence of gospel readings for the Saturdays and Sundays of Lent in the later Byzantine Lenten lectionary. In the Byzantine lectionary this Markan sequence is followed until Lazarus Saturday, when the reading given is John 11, the "canonical" version, in Talley's opinion, of the account narrated between Mark 10:34 and 10:35 in the *Mar Saba Clementine Fragment.* See Talley, *Origins of the Liturgical Year,* pp. 194 ff..

36. Coquin, "Une Réforme liturgique du concile de Nicée (325)?" pp. 178–92.

37. See Paul F. Bradshaw, "Baptismal Practice in the Alexandrian Tradition: Eastern or Western?" in idem, *Essays in Early Eastern Initiation*, pp. 5–10; reprinted in Johnson, *Living Water, Sealing Spirit*, pp. 82–100.

38. See Regan, "The Three Days and the Forty Days," pp. 11–15.

39. *Festal Letters of S. Athanasius*, pp. 21, 100; as cited by Talley, *Origins of the Liturgical Year*, pp. 169–70.

40. See Talley, *Origins of the Liturgical Year*, p. 219.

41. *Peregrinatio Egeriae* 46:1–4.

42. A. A. Stephenson, "The Lenten Catechetical Syllabus in Fourth-Century Jerusalem," *Theological Studies* 15 (1954): 116.

43. Baldovin, *Urban Character of Christian Worship*, p. 92, n. 37.

44. See Talley, *Origins of the Liturgical Year*, p. 174.

45. F. Van De Paverd, *St. John Chrysostom, The Homilies on the Statues* (Rome, 1991), pp. xxiii, 210–16, 250–54, 358, 361.

46. Regan, "The Three Days and the Forty Days," pp. 6–7.

47. Among contemporary Roman Catholics and some Episcopalians, for example, the devotional exercise of the Stations of the Cross is frequently held on the Fridays during Lent. And among Lutherans, in my experience, the Lenten tradition of midweek worship often focuses on the medieval devotion of the so-called Seven Last Words of Jesus from the Cross or includes each week a partial reading of the Passion narrative, often from sources which harmonize the four Gospel accounts. Both practices can tend to turn Lent into a forty-day Passion Sunday or Good Friday.

48. That those preparing for baptism, as well as the whole community, were expected to fast as part of the immediate preparation for baptism is documented as early as *Didache* 7.4 (probably late first- or early second-century Syria).

This essay will appear in somewhat different form in *The Rites of Christian Initiation: Their Evolution and Interpretation* by Maxwell Johnson (forthcoming, The Liturgical Press).

Lent in Perspective: A Summary Dialogue

LAWRENCE A. HOFFMAN AND MAXWELL E. JOHNSON

Lawrence A. Hoffman:

Against my claim that Lent derives from the Jewish practice of pre-paschal preparation, Maxwell Johnson argues that only in the fourth century was Lent customarily associated with the Christian Pascha. Specifically, his claim is that: (1) With the exception of the practice remarked on by Socrates (fifth century), the three-week "Lent" is associated with baptism but not necessarily at Easter. (2) Prior to Nicea, baptism at Easter was at most a "preference" (to cite Bradshaw) generally limited to North Africa and Rome. (3) The three-week fast mentioned by Socrates was therefore likely not preparatory to Easter at all. Hence, (4) the Jewish model of preparing for Passover by cleaning oneself of leaven (that is, sin) is an improbable source for the Christian event called Lent, which had originally nothing to do with the Christian parallel to Passover (Easter).

On the other hand, Johnson notes several instances of a three-week fast beyond the ones of which I was aware, adding to the probability that the three-week Lenten system (which I claim to have been Jewish in origin) was central, not marginal, to early Christian custom. And as I have pointed out, the three-week fast was practiced (according to Lages) in Jerusalem, where we might anticipate the greatest degree of influence from the Palestinian rabbinic system.

Johnson observes, however, that Jerusalem aside (about which we have no certain evidence, after all, other than Lages' reconstruction of what was probable), the three-week period that we find in Rome and North Africa is connected to Easter—as my hypothesis would anticipate. Still, other lenten traditions were independent of Easter, so that the evidence against a direct takeover *universally* from the Jewish pre-Passover system seems hard to refute. It does seem more likely that the *wide-scale* connection of the three-week period leading up to Easter and its assignment of forty days occurred in the wake of the Nicean calendar. That would explain why only after Nicea we find a pre-paschal Lent that has become normative; and also why Socrates and others question the number forty with regard to the alternative counting traditions that the various churches observed. They were all fitting their accepted and inherited customs into a procrustean bed of "forty" mandated by . . . well, mandated by what?

Mandated by Nicea, presumably. But again, why forty? Let us summarize the situation.

There were churches (as in Egypt) that had a forty-day period before Nicea, and there were churches elsewhere that had a three-week period but did not name it "forty days." After Nicea everybody had a forty-day period and called it that, but the nature of the forty-day period varied. At first it included days that were not allowed to be fasts—in some places (chiefly in the West) Sundays only, in others (chiefly in the East) Saturdays and Sundays. Only later was the period extended to produce forty days of actual fasting. In addition, in some places (the East, mainly) the period preceded "Great Week" and in others (the West, mainly), where this week did not exist as a separate entity, it ran right up to Holy Thursday. This produced a situation where Lent appeared to be of differing duration. But the idea of forty days loomed as the ideal, and we should ask where that ideal came from.

The idea of forty days was related to Jesus' baptism and the forty days of temptation that followed. So say the texts collected by Johnson as the final statement of the scholarly tradition going back through Talley to Coquin and Baumstark. That does indeed explain the forty-day pre-baptismal but post-Epiphany fast in Alexandria and elsewhere. But it does not explain how or why the same figure was attached to the post-

Nicean fasts of various durations that preceded Easter, nor why forty days ought to be applied at all to the pre-paschal period.

In sum, I accept Johnson's point that at least some three-week catechumenate practices were associated not with Easter (as I mistakenly assumed) but with baptism at some other time. Still, he leaves unanswered two very important questions: (1) Why the three-week period to begin with? Why come up arbitrarily with three weeks out of nowhere? And (2) why then apply the number forty to it? As much as the number forty fits a post-baptismal fast that is patterned after the forty days of Jesus' own temptation, it has nothing whatever to do with a pre-baptismal period.

It is Talley who originally discusses the forty-day period in question, and he answers my second question implicitly by arguing that the scriptural model of Jesus' fast following his own baptism at Epiphany was already a liturgical norm; forty days were already in place anyway. Only the rearrangement of baptism at its end rather than its beginning was novel. So far so good, at least in Alexandria, where Talley's primary data emerge. Now Alexandrian Judaism had little impact upon Palestinian Judaism, as we see from the vast gulf separating Philonic Judaism from the rabbinic system that eventually prevailed. Alexandrian Christianity, on the other hand, was a dominant influence upon the mother-country of Palestine. We should assume, therefore, a two-fold and contradictory stream of influence: from Egypt and from Palestine. From Egypt, we get a forty-day Alexandrian pre-baptismal fast that spread elsewhere, including to Palestine. It influenced all church practice eventually, in that the idea of a forty-day fast to precede baptism would be applied everywhere and (after Nicea) would actually be moved to the period prior to Easter. But we should admit the other direction of influence also: customs that began in Palestine, and then spread elsewhere, sometimes to Alexandria, sometimes not.

Among these, I argue, is an elemental three-week preparatory period to Pascha-Passover. My original assumption was that the Christian community took this over immediately as its own introduction to Pascha. The process now seems more complex than that. But doing away with the necessary immediate transfer of a Jewish pre-paschal preparation period to a Christian pre-paschal parallel is not equivalent to solving the issue of the origin of Lent, for we still have to explain the Christian adoption of a three-week period, even a three-week fast that is originally unassociated calendrically with the occasion called Pascha but that did precede baptism.

I begin with a reconsideration of the kind of thinking entailed by the application of the number forty. What is striking is the way in which it is so readily transposed upon customs that did not number forty days. It is biblical, so the key may lie in the scriptural usage that church and synagogue inherited. On the face of it, forty is just a round number, perhaps a standard scriptural designation for the number of days or years entailed in a given paradigmatic experience. The spies take forty days to scout the land of Canaan, for instance (Num. 13:25); similarly, "the land had rest for forty years" between the time that Othniel conquered the Arameans and "the children of Israel again did what was evil in the sight of the Lord" (Judg. 3:11). The flood lasts forty days and forty nights as well (Gen. 7:17; 8:6). These may well just mean "a long time."

But elsewhere, forty measures the coming of age of a generation, in that it describes the time entailed in the formative event that makes the generation what it is. Most frequently cited in this regard is the generation of wandering precipitated by the desert rebellion against Moses; it lasts forty years (Num. 14:33; 32:13; Deut. 2:7, 8:2,4; Deut. 29:4; Josh. 5:6).

Forty is also the number of days Moses ascends the mountain (Exod. 24:18; 34:28) and the time he takes to entreat God to pardon the sin of the Golden Calf (Deut. 9:25). And it is the age of maturity, the time to grow up and take responsibility for life. Esau gets married when he turns forty (Gen. 26:34), as did Isaac (Gen 25:20), and Joshua was forty years old when Moses appointed him to spy out the Land (Josh. 14:10). Even after death occurs, it takes forty days to be embalmed and pass, as it were, into the land of the dead (Gen. 50:3).

There are other examples too, but they all have this in com-

mon. They are liminal events, betwixt and between periods of
passing from stage to stage or of preparing for a task or of taking time out of life to go into seclusion. The midrash (Lev. Rab.
23:12) even associates forty days with the length of time it takes
for the embryo to take on specific personality. We can say that
Jews and Christians of the first century inherited a tradition in
which the round number of forty functioned to signify a period of growth, decay, change, change-over, or preparation, for
individuals and for entire peoples or even humankind at large.

That Jesus would be tempted forty days after his baptism is
altogether appropriate, therefore: it is his liminal instance par
excellence, his own coming of age, if you like. He passes the
trials common to liminal events described in anthropological
literature the world over. That preparation *for* baptism would
be called forty days is likewise to be expected—regardless of
how many days people actually spent in fast and catechesis:
naming something forty and expecting the actual count to be
forty were two different things. Much ink has been spilled
wondering how diverse Lenten traditions that were not forty
days long could have been so labeled—as indeed, Socrates
himself wonders as early as the fifth century. We must imagine
that by Socrates' time, literalism had overcome the earlier
symbolic use of language, at least in Socrates' circle. We can
pardon him, however. It is a little harder to pardon us for expecting the same sort of literal tally between a term "forty"
and the actual number of days that made it up. It is fruitless
to search out an original period of forty days; and equally foolish to imagine that if we can find one fast of actually forty days
(or even named forty days), that fast must be the *Urfast* so to
speak, the original fast whence the others came into being. Far
more likely, any fast could be named a forty-day event; only
later, by the fifth century, and in Hellenistic circles where literalism of numerical computation ruled, did people insist on
coming up with an actual count that added to forty.

More important than the details of the forty-day Lent is the
principle of applying a numerical model to an actual event and
calling something forty when it is clearly more or less: this is
a kind of typology. We are accustomed to *theological* typology,

for example, the way theological models drawn from the Hebrew Bible frame later events in the Christian narrative. But the typological mode of thinking extends beyond theological bounds. It can be numerical. Forty is thus a numerical type, a number that means "getting ready" or "passing through trial." It can be applied to any event that is a preparation or a trial.

I argued in my original article that dates can work typologically. I see no way to avoid the conclusion that the Great Sabbath was such a date. According to John, Jesus died on it, so in Johannine tradition, it became the "date" on which martyrs ought to die. The martyrs Polycarp and Pionius die on the Great Sabbath, a hundred years apart and in the dead of winter, nowhere near the Passover season when the Jewish Great Sabbath occurs (if indeed there even was such a Sabbath in the first few Christian centuries—Israel Yuval argues that there was not). Dates like the Great Sabbath are like tallies of years (forty, in our case); they provide associational frames of reference in which to conceptualize experience. They do not necessarily record historical or numerical fact.

Johnson's detailed review of the fact that the pre-baptismal fast of three weeks occurred after Epiphany, not before Easter, implies that there is no connection between it and the three-week preparation for Passover only if one insists on a perfect agreement of dates, as numerical realism would demand. The real question ought to be whether any *typological* equivalence existed between baptism (whenever it occurred) and Passover—and of course there is. Christ is the Passover, for which baptism is the entry. It culminates in eucharistic communion that functions in the same way that a Passover seder does, in that the seder relives the saving event of the original paschal lamb. Rabbinic tradition demands preparatory cleansing for the latter; Christian tradition demands it for the former. In both cases we have a three-week period of liminal waiting and preparing.

I suggest, therefore, that the solution to the origin of Lent is indeed partly answered by Johnson: his data do indicate a forty-day count only after Nicea, and an earlier tradition in which baptismal preparation was not necessarily connected to Easter at all. But the origin of the "three weeks" remains elusive, even with Johnson's thesis said and done. Where did it come from? We know too little to say for sure, but we do know of a similar period in rabbinic tradition, alive and well in Jerusalem where the nascent church was taking root. Thus, at this stage of our knowledge, the most probable solution is still a direct borrowing from Judaism into Christianity, but along typological lines. Preparation for the Passover emerges as preparation for entry into the church and participation in Christ, the Passover for Christians.

We reconstruct events in the following way:

1. The scriptural tradition of a fast by Jesus *after* his own baptism developed into a liturgical fast *prior* to baptism. The number forty was borrowed from the scriptural model. In actual fact, however, two kinds of borrowing should be differentiated: *chronological* and *typological.* Since the liturgical fast occurred when the original one had taken place (both after Epiphany), it is a case of *chronological* borrowing—in this case, from the life of Jesus to the life of the church.

2. Altogether separately, in Palestine, Jews had adopted a custom of preparing for Passover by a lectionary cycle that emphasized approximately three weeks as a time of washing oneself clean of the leaven of sin. A second borrowing now occurred, first in Palestine and then elsewhere (albeit not, apparently, in Alexandria). Christians adopted the three-week period from Judaism, but they applied it *typologically,* not chronologically. As three weeks of preparation prepared the Jew for participation in the paschal meal, so three weeks of preparation prepared the Christian for baptism into the church and subsequent participation in the eucharistic meal of the faithful. Chronological borrowing was prohibited by the fact that baptism was already calendrically fixed according to criteria other than its having to occur at Passover time. But typology was still possible: a three-week cleansing period prior to the Christian ideational equivalent of Passover: baptism and eucharistic communion. It was simply celebrated at a time other than the original springtime period that Jews observed.

The three-week fast was therefore moved to whatever time a particular church customarily used for its catechetical culmination.

Socrates retains the three weeks, just as Johnson says, as does the Second Council of Braga in Spain, and the Georgian and Armenian lectionaries. But their respective fasts have been moved to the appropriate baptismal occasion of the church in question. The idea of three weeks is Jewish; the theology of their preparing the catechumen for entry into the mysteries of Christ is a Christianization of the Jewish idea that preparation is needed for the mysteries of Passover. Only the placement of the preparatory period is novel. The new calendration was *necessitated* by the prior fixing of baptism at other times; but what made it possible was the mode of thinking called typology.

3. A second level of typological interpretation was also occurring. If the adaptation of the Jewish preparatory three-week period to a Christian one is the first typological consideration, the second was the imposition of a forty-day schema upon a period that was not really forty days at all. No matter how long the period of catechesis really lasted, it was seen as taking forty days, because of the association of forty with the liminal transition to new status, especially given the model of Jesus' own forty-day fast.

4. Finally, we have the post-Nicea chronological culmination to the whole process. Chronology eventually matches typology: baptism is moved to Easter, and what is now Lent coincides calendrically with the Jewish preparation for Passover. The original three-week period is thus moved back to where it had begun, although by now, it had ceased being three weeks. The number forty would now be taken not only typologically but literally, so that Lent was now figured out to last forty days, one way or another.

Maxwell E. Johnson:

I am, indeed, most grateful to Lawrence Hoffman for his careful and critical response to my essay and for this opportunity to clarify some details and to pursue some of these questions further. As he seems to indicate toward the end of his response, it may be that both of us are basically correct in our approaches to the material, or that the truth lies more in a synthesis of our views. Alternatively, of course, it may be that both of us are completely wrong. Nevertheless, there are four points I wish to make by way of brief response in the hope that others might find from my essay, Hoffman's response, and this response, some kind of starting point for further research on the origins and evolution of Lent.

1. As I noted in my essay, since Rome (Hippolytus, but not *Apostolic Tradition*) and North Africa (Tertullian) did have a preference for Easter baptism from early on, the three-week period of preparation for baptism, witnessed to in the later liturgical sources from those traditions, certainly may be understood as a kind of primitive pre-paschal "Lent." And, if Mario F. Lages is correct in his analysis, three weeks of catechesis prior to Easter baptism may have been the practice also in Jerusalem. In this case, at least, Hoffman's claim that the three-week period of "washing oneself clean of the leaven of sin" prior to Passover in Palestinian Judaism may, indeed, be functioning as a source for Christian practice. I shall leave it up to Hoffman, however, to demonstrate just how formative and widespread these three weeks of preparation actually were within Palestinian Judaism itself. In other words, are these three weeks a well-known and documented ritual practice in early Judaism or a conjecture based on one textual reference in a lectionary coming from a much later time period?

2. As much as I think Hoffman is correct to point to typology in the calculation of Lent, I have a problem with his particular application of Passover typology in this context. It is well known that when Socrates refers to "three weeks" of preparation in the Roman tradition as the "forty days," he is wrong for his own fifth-century context. By that time Rome itself was keeping a Lent of six weeks. If Chavasse and Talley are correct, however, Socrates' three-week reference is important because it may reflect the remnant of an earlier Roman pattern of preparation. Similarly, it should be noted that, apart

from this text, there is no evidence to support the notion that Christians anywhere referred to this three-week period typologically as the "forty days." And, nowhere is it stated that the "pre-baptismal fast of three weeks occurred after Epiphany." Rather, the *only* liturgical tradition that seems to have known anything like a forty-day period for baptismal preparation before Nicea was in Egypt or Alexandria, and there it was connected *not* to Easter but to Epiphany! These "forty days," of course, were understood typologically, but the typological referent was not *Pascha.* In the Egyptian tradition this forty-day pre-baptismal fast was related not to Jesus' death and resurrection but rather to the forty-day temptation he underwent *after* the declaration of his identity at his baptism in the Jordan by John. As far as we can tell, the association of this "forty-day" period (already assimilated typologically in Egypt with Jesus' temptation) with pre-*paschal* preparation comes about only in the context of Nicea, after which we see throughout the East both "Lent" as a season before Easter and a marked preference for Easter baptism. At that point, Hoffman is absolutely correct in pointing to the typological use of "forty" in biblical texts and elsewhere as a way of explaining the divergent calculations of this "forty days" throughout the churches.

3. Closely related to my second point, it is important to underscore the theological diversity within the early Christian liturgical traditions. Hoffman says that "the real question ought to be whether any *typological* equivalence existed between baptism (whenever it occurred) and Passover—and of course there is. Christ is the Passover, for which baptism is the entry." As far as this goes, Hoffman is correct. But I should like to respond by saying that prior to Nicea, Paul's "Passover" theology of baptism as participation in the death and resurrection of Jesus (Romans 6:3–12) seems to have played a relatively minor role. As contemporary scholars (e.g., Georg Kretschmar, Gabriele Winkler, and Kilian McDonnell) have demonstrated, the dominant theological interpretation of Christian baptism throughout the Christian East came not from Paul but from the synoptic accounts of Jesus' own baptism by John and from

the imagery of John 3:5 (i.e., baptism as "new birth" in water and the Holy Spirit). Christian baptism, therefore, was not a paschal "death ritual" but a ritual of "new birth" and "adoption," a spiritual assimilation to the one who was declared the messianic "son" and "servant" at the Jordan and upon whom the Spirit descended. Such is clearly the theological interpretation of baptism within Egypt (cf. both Clement and Origen of Alexandria, who see Christian baptism as "crossing the Jordan") and among the early Semitic-speaking Christians of (East) Syria, and it is discernible within the later liturgical documents of the *non-Roman* western liturgical traditions of Gaul and Spain. Without a Passover or Easter interpretation of Christian baptism as we find in Romans 6, it is only logical to expect that Easter itself would *not* be the preferred occasion for baptism in these traditions. In other words, it is no surprise that if any annual feast were chosen as the prime occasion for baptism, it would be related to Epiphany, that is, the feast of Jesus' own baptism. For that matter, in spite of Lages, we simply do not know *when* the church at Jerusalem began to celebrate baptism at Easter. Prior to the catecheses of Cyril (or John) of Jerusalem in the mid- to late fourth century, we have absolutely no evidence upon which to build such a case. Nevertheless, these traditions, with the exception of Egypt, also seem to know of an early practice of a three-week period of preparation. But without a paschal understanding of baptism operating even within a Semitic group like the early Syrian Christians, why would a Jewish practice of three weeks of preparation for *Passover* even suggest itself as an option for a celebration unrelated to Passover? Again, the burden of proof for such an early Jewish connection or dependency would seem to depend on demonstrating that three-week preparation periods for feasts *in general* within Judaism were widely known and highly influential. While I would easily concede that three weeks of preparation for a feast in Judaism might lie somewhere behind Christian practice, I do not find the Passover argument theologically or typologically compelling.

4. Hoffman also wants to draw a close parallel between

Christian eucharistic celebration and the Passover seder. He writes: "It [baptism] culminates in eucharistic communion that functions in the same way that a Passover seder does, in that the seder relives the saving event of the original paschal lamb. Rabbinic tradition demands preparatory cleansing for the latter; Christian tradition demands it for the former. In both cases we have a three-week period of liminal waiting and preparing." Again, I find this to be a logical argument and conclusion in general. It should be noted, however, that Christian eucharistic celebration draws on much more than the important Passover connotations. In fact, interpreting the eucharist in a Passover context reflects the increasing paschalization of the meaning of Jesus within the early Christian communities, a paschalization best reflected, again, in Paul (i.e., "For our paschal lamb, Christ, has been sacrificed"; 1 Cor. 5:7). But other elements need to be taken into account. For one example, eucharist early on comes to be celebrated *weekly;* it is not a once-a-year meal. Eucharist, then, is not the Christian equivalent to Passover; Easter is. For another example, the Passover context of the Last Supper of Jesus and the twelve in the synoptic Gospels needs to be balanced by the whole range of narratives describing Jesus' meal-companionship with "tax collectors and sinners" during his ministry and within the New Testament meal-context descriptions of his resurrection appearances.

Hoffman's argument for direct dependency on Jewish liturgical tradition works best only if baptism is related—even if only typologically—to an annual Easter context from the very beginning. If the diversity of occasions for baptism throughout early Christianity rests on an original typological connection with Jewish preparation for the Passover, this makes Passover the *Urtype,* and hence, the *preferred* interpretative model for Christian baptism. Hoffman calls it, in fact, "the Christian ideational equivalent of Passover." But if the Jewish Passover and its preparation are the dominant *typologies* for understanding baptismal preparation, baptism, and its culmination in eucharistic communion, then it would be only logical to expect a marked preference for Easter baptism in the early churches from the very beginning as this "ideational equivalent" of Passover. The problem, however, is that there was no such early preference outside of third-century North Africa and Rome in the West and the late fourth century in the East (e.g., Cyril, John Chrysostom, and Theodore of Mopsuestia). Other early liturgical evidence we have from elsewhere seems to be based on a different baptismal typology, a different "ideational" focus altogether. Unless it can be demonstrated that this different baptismal typology is a corruption or aberration of an "original" Passover-Easter interpretative context, I simply cannot accept early Christian dependency upon a Jewish three-week period of preparation for Passover as *the* single answer to explain the diversity of baptismal practice and theology which is encountered.

This does not mean, however, that I am in complete disagreement with the overall developmental model of Lent that Hoffman offers at the conclusion of his response. He is certainly correct in pointing out that what becomes Lent after Nicea reflects a synthesis of various patterns and traditions: the forty-day post-Epiphany period of Egypt, already associated with Jesus' temptation in the desert; the typological association of "forty" to however this period was calculated within the different Christian traditions; and the final calculation of this period to equal a literal "forty days." What needs to be further developed, in my opinion, is his insistence on the Jewish origins of the three weeks of preparation for Easter *baptism,* and the implied "original" typological dominance of Passover-Easter within the baptismal theologies and practices of the early Christian communities. Indeed, such an original dominance is implied when he writes that after Nicea "the original three-week period is thus moved back to where it had begun." But had it ever moved away from this context in North Africa and Rome? And had it *ever* been there "originally" within other Christian traditions? North African, Roman, and, possibly, Jerusalem practice may support Hoffman's overall hypothesis. The diversity of early Christian practice and theology reflected elsewhere, where a three-week pattern of preparation is also discernable, however, calls this hypothesis into question. Passover-Easter typology may explain it in part for some churches. But it certainly does not explain the dominance of a Jordan-Epiphany typology in other places, even among those early Christians of strong Semitic background in Syria. Therefore, while I still find Hoffman's thesis appealing in that it provides *an* answer to "where" a three-week period of Christian baptismal or Easter preparation may have originated, I am not convinced that his is *the* answer or that the Jewish three-week period before Passover discerned by Hoffman is any more than a coincidence or conjecture.

PART 2

*The Aftermath of Sacred Time:
From Passover/Easter to
Shavuot/Pentecost*

From Passover to Shavuot

Efrat Zarren-Zohar

The seven-week period between Passover and Pentecost is known today in Judaism as the *S'firat Ha'omer* or the Days of the Counting of the Omer, "omer" being the biblical term for "sheaf." The period takes its name from the instructions in Leviticus 23:15 to count fifty days from the day when the first sheaf of barley is offered until the final celebration of the harvest, termed (in Deuteronomy 16:10) the Feast of Weeks (*shavu'ot*). Greek-speaking Jews called Shavuot Pentecost since it occurred fifty days after the offering of the barley sheaf.

It is hard to imagine a set of scholarly problems more complex than those occasioned by the *S'firat Ha'omer* season. The various biblical accounts regarding this interval display a maddening lack of clarity, which in turn, lead to multiple traditions concerning the exact date when Shavuot should be celebrated. The well-documented Pharisaic ritual of reaping the first fruits of the barley harvest and presenting them at the Temple in Jerusalem necessarily disappears after the Temple's destruction in 70 c.e. Yet its liturgical replacement in post-Temple times remains a question mark for more than a thousand years owing to a dearth of detail in our extant sources.

By the late Middle Ages, folk tradition had established many customs for the period, some of which have legitimate origins in antiquity and some of which do not. The difficulty, of course, is determining which are which. How and when did *S'firah* traditions arise? When did mourning customs begin to be associated with the season? And what is the role of Lag Ba'omer, the specially demarcated thirty-third day of the

71

Omer period? These are some of the tangled questions which
we will attempt to address below.

PASSOVER TO SHAVUOT IN
THE BIBLICAL PERIOD

The Ecological Context

In biblical Israel, seven main crops formed the basis for economic prosperity: wheat, barley, grapes, figs, pomegranates,
olives, and dates.[1] Wheat and barley were milled into flour for
bread. Fermented grapes produced wine, the main beverage of
the day. Olives were crushed for oil, to be used in cooking and
as a source of light. The syrup squeezed from ripe dates made
a sweet honey. But the fate of these crops depended upon a
complex set of climatic phenomena which occurred during the
critical period between Passover and Shavuot.[2]

From mid-April to mid-June, the flowers of the olive, grape,
pomegranate, and date open, and the embryonic figs begin to
develop. In addition, the kernels of wheat and barley fill with
starch. This season in the Land of Israel is distinguished by
contrasts in weather. Scorching southern winds alternate with
cold northern and western ones. The northern wind, which frequently brings rain, is most beneficial to wheat if it blows during the wheat's early stages of ripening, while it is still young.[3]
However, this same wind can wreak havoc on the olive crop if
the buds have already opened into flowers, since the flowers
may be blown away before pollination has begun. The same
danger threatens the grape, pomegranate, and date flowers.

By contrast, a prolonged southern/southeastern wind bringing days of dry heat is good for the olive, grape, date, and
pomegranate crops, but it can devastate the wheat and barley
if it comes before the kernels have filled with starch, for then
the grain will be scorched and the entire crop destroyed.[4] In
sum, while either wind can be a blessing to one set of crops, it
can spell disaster for the others if it blows too early or too late
and remains for too brief or too prolonged a time. Even if the

winds blow favorably, heavy rain after the wheat has ripened (i.e., during the harvest) can destroy the grain.[5]

The biblical farmer was no doubt aware of his dependence on the delicate balance of nature during this crucial interval between Passover and Shavuot. Once the sickle was put to the mature grain (Deut. 16:9), Nogah Hareuveni proposes, "it was natural that the farmers of the land of Israel should count off each day with great trepidation and with prayers to get through these fifty days without crop damage."[6]

Determining the Counting Period and the Subsequent Celebration of Shavuot

Shavuot (Pentecost) is the sole biblically ordained festival with no specific date affixed to it, but depending instead on counting from a prior date. All we know for certain about when the counting was supposed to commence is that there is no uniform agreement even in the Bible about its beginning.

H. Louis Ginsberg posits a three-stage development of the celebration of Shavuot.[7] In stage one, described in Exodus 23:14–19, the festival was called *Chag Hakatzir* or the Feast of Reaping. While no exact date is given for the celebration of this festival, it probably occurred when barley reaping started, sometime around the beginning of the month of Iyar (May). Unlike later stages in the development of the festival, no period of anticipatory counting is mentioned.

In Ginsberg's stage two, delineated in Exodus 34:18–22 and Deuteronomy 16:9–10, the festival is termed *Chag Hashavuot,* the Feast of Weeks. Since all worship during this stage was centralized in the Temple in Jerusalem, the holiday was postponed from the beginning of the barley harvest (when leaving the fields to journey to Jerusalem would have been impractical) to the subsequent reaping of the wheat (which ripens later than barley). Thus, in Exodus 34 (in contrast to Exodus 23), each farmer is commanded to observe the festival with the first fruits specifically of wheat. Additionally, in Deuteronomy 16:9–10, the farmer is further instructed to count seven weeks from the time when the sickle is first put to the standing grain (i.e.,

the barley) and then, following the counting period, to observe
the Feast of Weeks. Needless to say, since barley does not ripen
at the same time throughout the land of Israel,[8] this reckoning
does not provide for a standard beginning to the count and
thus, as in stage one, no uniform day for the observance of
Shavuot existed.

Only in stage three, illustrated in Leviticus 23:10–21, do we
detect an attempt to fix the day when counting should begin.
(Yet ironically, the very words intended to establish religious
order and uniformity of counting will produce the opposite
effect, engendering heated controversy among various Jewish
sects, as we shall see.) According to the priestly source of stage
three, liturgical traditions relating to the *S'firah* season are
combined from stages one and two to create a more harmoni-
ous whole. In Leviticus, the biblical farmer is instructed to con-
tribute two offerings from his grain crop. The first, the *omer* of
presentation, constitutes a rite of desacrilization, which gives
to God the first cuttings of the barley crop and thus releases
the rest of the crop for human use.[9] The second offering,
known as *bikkurim* (first fruits), was made on the fiftieth day
after the presentation of the barley and was given in the form
of bread, the "finished product," so to speak, of the wheat harvest. Technically speaking, this second offering was not part of
a pilgrimage, since it is called *mikra kodesh* ("a holy convoca-
tion") rather than *chag* ("pilgrimage") and since it was to be
celebrated *b'chol moshvoteichem* ("in all your settlements").

The Linking of Passover and Shavuot in Biblical Times

Hareuveni offers a novel approach to explain the need of
the biblical authors in Deuteronomy 16, Leviticus 23, and
Numbers 28 to link Passover and Shavuot through a season
of counting.[10] To his mind, since the fate of the major crops
and thus, the fate of Israelite society, depended upon the delicate balance and exact timing of opposing forces of nature (as
explained above), it is easy to see how these natural phenomena could logically have been viewed as the result of battles
between various deities, giving rise to polytheistic worship or

even worship of Baal, the god of rain. The intertwining of Passover, the festival commemorating the Exodus from Egypt, with Shavuot, the agricultural festival of first fruits, was meant to underscore for ancient Israelites that the God who delivered them from Egypt controlled also the forces that determine the fate of the grain, wine, and olive crops. Testimony for this hypothesis comes from Hosea 2:1–19, where the prophet complains that Israel does not acknowledge that it is Yahweh, the deliverer from Egyptian bondage, not Baal, who gives the grain, wine, and oil. Hareuveni opines:

> Why did a commandment which deals with an agricultural crop stipulate a single specific date for a variable event? The answer becomes apparent when we consider the custom that could have evolved in the absence of a clear mandatory obligation, laid equally on all the people of Israel, to come to Jerusalem on a duly appointed day. The *omer* offering would have been likely to develop as a purely agricultural observance on separate dates in different regions. . . . The commandment to bring the *omer* offering on one specific date . . . served as a tremendous unifying force. One people brought the same one crop on one date to the one Temple, as an offering to the one God in one city, Jerusalem."[11]

PASSOVER TO SHAVUOT FROM THE POST-BIBLICAL THROUGH THE GEONIC PERIOD

The Ecological Context As Seen by the Rabbis

The Rabbis were well aware of the impending danger to the food supply posed by the climatic conditions of the *S'firah* period. Leviticus Rabbah asks: How was the *omer* waved? R. Simon b. R. Joshua said, "The movements forward and backward were to counteract the effects of injurious winds, and the movements upward and downward were to counteract the effects of injurious dews."[12] Moreover, R. Eleazar taught: " 'The Lord our God . . . keeps for our benefit the weeks appointed for harvest' (Jer. 5:24); this means no scorching heat, no blasting winds, and no noxious dews for the seven full weeks between Passover and Pentecost."[13] The Rabbis see the *omer* as a quid pro quo for God's stewardship over the grain. R. Judah said in the name of R. Akiba: "Why did the Torah state that we should bring an *omer* on Passover? Because Passover is the season of grain. Therefore, the Holy One, blessed be He, said, 'Bring before me an *omer* on Passover so that your grain in the fields may be blessed.' "[14] R. Phinehas said: "The Holy One causes winds to blow, clouds to rise, rains to come down, dews to bespangle plants, plants to spring up, fruits to grow plump—and you are asked to give Him in return no more than the *omer* of barley!"[15]

Finally, the entire harvest season becomes known as a time of judgment, for "the world is judged at four periods in the year. . . . On Passover for grain, on Shavuot for the fruit of trees."[16] If pleased, God says, "I close [the heavens] before you at Passover [i.e., rain ceases], and you go out and reap and thresh and winnow and do all that is required in the field and find it rich in blessing."[17] But "If Nisan passes and rain falls, it is a sign of divine anger."[18] In rabbinic, as in biblical days, the period of the *S'firah* was filled with trepidation as human beings watched to see whether the grain harvest would lead to the proverbial "feast or famine."

The Counting Period, the Counting "Liturgy," and the Reinterpretation of Shavuot

The rabbinic fixing of the counting period derives from the Rabbis' reading of the Hebrew phrase *mimochorat hashabbat* in Leviticus 23:10–12.

> When you enter the land . . . and reap its harvest, you shall bring the first sheaf of your harvest to the priest. He shall elevate the sheaf before the Lord for acceptance on your behalf . . . on the day after the sabbath (*mimochorat hashabbat*). . . . Until that very day, until you have brought the offering of your God, you shall eat no bread or parched grain or fresh ears. . . . From the day on which you bring the sheaf of elevation offering—the day after

the sabbath (*mimochorat hashabbat*)—you shall count off seven
weeks.[19] They must be complete: you must count until the day
after the seventh week—fifty days. Then you shall bring an offering of new grain to the Lord ... two loaves of bread from fine
[wheat] flour ... as first fruits to the Lord. ... On that same day
you shall hold a celebration. ... "

The Hebrew phrase found twice here, *mimochorat hashabbat,* engendered controversy because it does not specify which
Sabbath is intended. *Shabbat* normally means "Sabbath day"
(i.e., Saturday), but some held that in context, it referred to a
festival day that has "Sabbath-like" qualities. Resolving this
issue mattered, because it determined (1) when to present the
omer (thus desacralizing the barley crop and freeing it for
consumption); (2) when to begin counting the fifty days; and
(3) when to celebrate the harvest festival of Shavuot.

Of all the possible interpretations of the word *shabbat*
here,[20] we need examine only the two that marked the original debate between the Pharisees and the Sadducees. The
Pharisees, whose interpretation became normative after the
destruction of the Second Temple (70 C.E.), interpreted *shabbat*
as referring not to any Sabbath at all, but to Nisan 15, the first
festival day in the week of Passover.[21] By contrast, the Boethusians, generally identified as Sadducees, interpreted *shabbat*
here to be the Sabbath day within the Passover week.[22] For
them, the counting of the *omer* began the day after (on Sunday) and Shavuot thus fell every year on a Sunday, fifty days
later. The Sadducean interpretation probably does reflect the
original meaning of Leviticus, since the word *shabbat* in the
Bible is never used by itself to refer to any festival or holy
day other than the Sabbath itself. Moreover, the Samaritans
and the Septuagint (in Lev. 23:15) understand *shabbat* as Saturday,[23] and even several Rabbis have difficulty explaining the
Pharisaic interpretation.[24]

Nevertheless, the Pharisees underscored their interpretation by prescribing a grand public ceremony around the *omer*-
cutting rite, the first testimony of a liturgy connected with the
S'firah season:

When it grew dark [the reaper] called out to them [the bystand-
ers], "Has the sun set?" and they replied, "Yes!" "Has the sun
set?" "Yes!" "Is this the sickle?" "Yes!" "Is this the sickle?" "Yes!"
"Is this the basket [to hold the *omer*]?" "Yes!" "Is this the basket?" "Yes!" "On this Sabbath?" "Yes!" "On this Sabbath?"
"Yes!" "Shall I reap?" "Reap!" "Shall I reap?" "Reap!" Three
times [the reaper called out] for every separate matter and they
would reply "Yes! Yes! Yes!" And why so much [pomp]? Because
of the Boethusians who used to claim that the *omer* should not
be reaped on the evening of the [first] Festival day [of Passover].[25]

Louis Finkelstein[26] posits several reasons for the controversy between the two groups but holds ultimately that the
dispute is really about the date of Shavuot, which only secondarily involved that of the *omer,* since the former was com-
puted by counting from the latter. The Pharisees identified
Shavuot as the day of Revelation at Mount Sinai, an event
whose date is not mentioned in the Bible.[27] The Sadducees, in
contrast, insisted upon regarding Shavuot as a simple agricultural festival, and stood to gain materially (thinks Finkelstein)
if the pilgrims were to arrive on Sundays.[28] Was this controversy purely politics then, with an overlay of economic interest? Was it honestly motivated by the historicizing of Shavuot?
Or was it a calendrical dispute that went back to two exegetical
traditions? We will probably never know for sure.

Even after the Temple's destruction, when the *omer* could
no longer be brought to the priest, the ritual of counting remained in force and various Rabbis attempted to bolster its
importance in the eyes of the people.[29]

QUASI-OMINOUS CHARACTERISTICS
LINKED TO THE *S'FIRAH* PERIOD

In time, the *S'firah* season became associated with mourning, and Jews were adjured to abstain from getting married,
working after sunset, and cutting their hair. But all of this is
post-talmudic.

The Prohibition Against Marriage

Natronai Gaon (853–858) was asked, "Why do we not allow weddings to take place between Passover and Shavuot? Is this due to a halakhic prohibition or not?"[30] We may infer that by Natronai's time, at least some Jews were already abstaining from marriage within the *S'firah* season, yet had no idea why they were doing so.[31] Natronai responds by classifying the restriction as a mere mourning custom, not an actual halakhic prohibition, and ascribes its origin to talmudic-midrashic reports that many students of Rabbi Akiba died during this time. But he adds, "From that time onwards [second century C.E.] the sages did not countenance weddings then."

There are no fewer than four accounts in rabbinic literature concerning the death of Rabbi Akiba's students. B. Yebamot 62b says that 12,000 pairs of disciples (24,000 all together) died between Passover and Shavuot because they did not treat each other with respect. Midrash Ecclesiastes Rabbah 11:6 attributes to Akiba himself the statement that 12,000 (not 24,000) of his disciples died during the period between Passover and Shavuot because they were envious of one another in knowledge of Torah. Genesis Rabbah 61:3 concurs: the number is 12,000; they died because of mutual envy. But the period in which they died is unspecified. Finally, Midrash Tanchuma (Chayei Sarah 6) cites the number of disciples who died as only 300, and knows nothing of why or when they perished.

None of the legends associates their death with national mourning, and in fact, since the students died as a result of their own sinful behavior, it seems odd that mourning customs would ever become attached to the event. Indeed, counting the *omer* begins on Nisan 16, but the Babylonian Talmud (Ta'anit 17b) actually forbids mourning from Nisan 8 to Nisan 21.

In sum, we know from geonic literature that the custom of not marrying during the *S'firah* period was common by the time of Natronai Gaon, but was post-talmudic in origin, and only retrospectively associated with earlier reports of the deaths of Rabbi Akiba's students.

Holding that the death of the students is a historical

rationalization of an earlier custom, Theodor Gaster posits a more ancient and primitive practice as the real origin for the ban on marriage after Passover.

> The true explanation is to be found in the universal custom of regarding the days or weeks preceding the harvest and the opening of the agricultural year as a time when the corporate life of the community is, so to speak, in eclipse, one lease of it now drawing to a close and the next being not yet assured. This state of suspended animation is expressed by fasts and austerities and by curtailment of all normal activities. Especially interesting in this connection is the ban on marriages—originally a method of showing that, at the time when the annual lease of life is running out, human increase also is arrested."[32]

Gaster's explanation accords with the anxiety concerning the health of the crops that we saw expressed above in rabbinic literature. The season of reaping was indeed thought to be a dangerous time, when God could wreak judgment upon the Israelites by afflicting the food that sustains them. Jews were not alone in their apprehension. Many ancient cultures consider the harvest period to be an especially critical time during which elaborate taboos and restrictions are imposed.[33]

There may, however, be a second source for the restrictions against marriage during this period. A theory going back to M. Landsberger explains it as borrowed from the Romans.[34] The ominous character of May and the first half of the month of June (roughly corresponding to the *S'firah* season) is recorded by Ovid and attributed to fear of the dead. Apparently, banning marriages during this time was connected with the celebration of Lemuria, a Roman festival during which, according to Plutarch, offerings were made to honor the dead.[35] Similarly, in his study of medieval Jewish life, Israel Abrahams opines, "The modern wedding customs of all races and creeds are largely indebted to heathen sources. . . . In Spain the Jews copied the Greek custom of marrying only on the new moon. . . . In fact, the Middle Ages encouraged a perfectly free trade in superstitions, and Jews and Christians borrowed terrors from one another with the utmost enthusiasm."[36]

We now have evidence specifically of a Roman prohibition of marriage during the harvest season. While it would not have greatly affected the Jews until approximately 63 B.C.E. (when the Land of Israel came under the Roman sphere of influence), the general anxiety rooted in an agricultural economy might have been prevalent centuries earlier. To be sure, the restriction is not mentioned in rabbinic literature of the time, but that may be because it was just a custom derived from generalized cultural apprehension, but not yet a halakhicly proscribed practice.

The practice of avoiding marriage from Passover to Shavuot was apparently passed down from generation to generation long after Jews ceased earning their livelihood primarily from agriculture and long after they ceased living under the influence of Roman culture. Knowing nothing of its real origins, Natronai Gaon explicitly links the custom of not getting married during the S'firah season to talmudic reports of the second-century death of Akiba's students. He felt compelled to seek out justification for what he knew to be an old custom and found it in the Rabbi Akiba account.

The Prohibition against Working after Sunset

The prohibition against working after sunset is first mentioned in our extant sources by Hai Gaon (998–1038), who explains that the disciples of Rabbi Akiba died during the daytime and were buried after sunset; people had been excused from work that evening in order to bury them. But even Hai suspects this line of reasoning and offers also a second explanation, based on the similarity of syntax between the instruction to count fifty days of the *omer* and the parallel instruction to count fifty years until the sabbatical year.

> The phrase (Lev. 23:15) regarding the counting of the *omer*, "You shall count seven complete weeks . . . " (*sheva shabbatot t'mimot*) implies rest from labor and the sabbatical year, because we read similarly [about the sabbatical year] (Lev. 25:8), "You shall count seven weeks of years" (*sheva shabbatot shanim*). Just as work in

the field is forbidden in the sabbatical year, so too when we count the *omer,* a liturgical rite that occurs at sunset, we rest from work also [in the period stipulated, namely, after sunset].[37]

Whatever its real origin, by the early fourteenth century the custom seems to have been rarely observed, if indeed, it ever had been. Jacob ben Asher records it in his law code, the *Tur,* along with the custom not to marry. But whereas for the latter, he says explicitly, "It is the custom everywhere . . . ," with regard to the cessation from work, he simply says, "I have found it written that it is customary not to do work. . . . " He then cites Hai's responsum with the additional explanation, "Moreover, women customarily did not work after nightfall then." He kept the ban on marriage, albeit still (like Natronai) as a mere custom, not a real legal prohibition; he did not keep the work regulation at all.[38]

The Prohibition against Haircuts

Unlike the prior two prohibitions, the ban on haircuts during this time period is not found among the geonim. It is most likely a later custom which originated in post-geonic times, probably after the time of Rashi (1040–1105), who seems not to know of it. The next generation mentions it, however; it turns up in several of the legal manuals of Spain and Provence.[39] Not cutting hair was already a well-known custom related to mourning in general, so that its observance in connection with the *S'firah* season is not a surprising evolution, once mourning and the *S'firah* were firmly linked.[40]

THE ORIGIN OF AND CUSTOMS
SURROUNDING LAG BA'OMER

On the thirty-third day of the counting of the *omer,* known in Hebrew as Lag Ba'omer,[41] the restrictions discussed above are relaxed, and in many communities, the day is even celebrated as a semi-holiday. Lag Ba'omer is shrouded in mystery;

scholars are unsure of the reason for its celebration, and traditional Jewish sources, if they mention it at all, disagree over how to observe it. It is not mentioned in the Talmud or geonic sources and liturgically, no special ritual is practiced on it.

Lag Ba'omer in Traditional Sources

There are two approaches to the question of how the date of Lag Ba'omer is to be determined, which in turn explain the divergent estimates of the period of time when the mourning restrictions are believed to be in force. One school of thought views Lag Ba'omer as the day when the plague that killed Akiba's disciples ended. Our first extant witness, Abraham Hayarchi (1155–1215) of Provence, attests, "It is the custom in France and Provence to marry from Lag Ba'omer on; and I have heard in the name of R. Zerachiah Halevi from Gerona [1125–1186] that it has been found written in an [unidentified] old Spanish manuscript that the disciples of Rabbi Akiba died from Passover until . . . fifteen days before Shavuot, and that is Lag Ba'omer."[42] The talmudic tradition knew nothing of the plague ending midway in the *omer* period; but by the twelfth century, a new holiday called Lag Ba'omer had arisen and had been connected to a new tradition regarding the plague's early cessation.

Hayarchi does not attach any special significance to Lag Ba'omer, however. It is merely a day like all days, but historically significant because on it the plague ended; from Lag Ba'omer onwards, therefore, the period of mourning ceased.

But should Lag Ba'omer be included in the period of leniency, or is it the end of the mourning period, so that weddings are permitted only the day after? In keeping with the idea that the day itself is unimportant, later Spanish commentators interpreted Hayarchi to mean that mourning should end on the day following Lag Ba'omer, not on Lag Ba'omer itself, which is merely the final day of restrictions.[43]

In the second school of thought, Lag Ba'omer is not just the anniversary of the day the plague ended. Rather, the thirty-third day of counting the *omer* was determined by subtracting the number of festive days during the *S'firah* period (i.e., the days of Passover, Sabbaths, and new moons) from the total number of days (forty-nine).[44] According to this approach, the total number of days on which mourning is appropriate turns out arithmetically to be thirty-two, and thus the day following must be a day of celebration in itself, which just happens to coincide with the historical accident of the end of the disciples' deaths. Mourning therefore ceases on that day and is accompanied by celebration. Commentators from Germany and Poland, in contrast to Spain, take this latter approach, designating Lag Ba'omer as a day of celebration and rejoicing.[45]

The notion that there is something sacrosanct about the number thirty-two gave rise to three different customs regarding the mourning period. Some communities observed it for the thirty-two days from Passover to Shavuot except for the special festive days themselves (the days of Passover, Sabbaths, and new moons); others kept the thirty-two days from Passover to Lag Ba'omer and celebrated on Lag Ba'omer, the thirty-third day in the cycle. Still others counted thirty-two days backward from Shavuot, skipping Lag Ba'omer, and therefore beginning their fast, purely by mathematical accident, on the first day of the month of Iyar.

In sum, there are two very different ways of viewing the nature of Lag Ba'omer according to the traditional sources. One perceives it as the last day in the mourning period while the other sees it as a day of celebration following the end of the mourning period. In any case, the day is certainly a medieval addition to the *S'firah* period.

Customs Practiced on Lag Ba'omer

Because the death of Rabbi Akiba's students was believed to have ceased on Lag Ba'omer, it became known traditionally as the "Scholar's Festival." It is customary to give children a holiday from school and take them on excursions to the forest and fields where they play with bows and arrows, run races, sing, dance, and light bonfires. The custom of playing with bows and arrows is sometimes explained by allusions to reenacting the war against Rome from the days of Rabbi Akiba.[46] Mystics believe that the bow with which children play symbolizes the rainbow that, according to the Zohar, will appear in the sky before the coming of the Messiah.[47] However, according to folklorist Theodor Gaster, playing with bows and arrows, excursions into the forest, singing, dancing, and lighting bonfires are more likely "the last lingering survival of the typical May Day ceremony. For the fact is, it is customary in many parts of the world to kindle bonfires at the end of April or the beginning of May as a means of forefending demons and witches."[48] Lag Ba'omer began, therefore, as a Jewish May Day.

For many Sephardic and Chasidic Jews, Lag Ba'omer is associated with another death: not of the students of Akiba but of Rabbi Shimon Bar Yochai, also a student of Rabbi Akiba but more importantly, the putative author of the Zohar. The day of Bar Yochai's death is termed a *hillula* ("festivity")[49] and is marked by pilgrimages to his tomb in the village of Meron in the Galilee. At these pilgrimages, huge bonfires are lit, young boys receive their first haircut, and the Torah scrolls are brought with great ceremony from Tsfat, the closest city to Meron. Until recently, scholarship has tried to find the origin of these customs in incidents from Bar Yochai's life or from statements of his quoted in the Zohar.

There is, however, no reason even to believe that Bar Yochai died on Lag Ba'omer. Moreover, scholars have had to assume, along with tradition, that Lag Ba'omer is indeed the day upon which he died, since no written source makes reference to such a date, including the Zohar itself.

Recently, Avraham Ya'ari has thoroughly researched how the date of Bar Yochai's death was fixed on Lag Ba'omer, as well as (1) why and how the *hillula* celebration originated, and (2) why the customs practiced during it are associated with the sage at all. A close reading of the historical sources, including diaries written by pilgrims in the late Middle Ages, reveals that *hillula* customs practiced at Bar Yochai's gravesite were originally observed at the reputed tomb of the prophet Samuel in Ramah (Nebi Samwil).[50]

During the twelfth century, a tall hill not far from Jerusalem came to be considered the burial site of Samuel the prophet. Already by the thirteenth century, a pilgrimage was observed by Jews from as far away as Syria, Egypt, and Babylonia on the 28th of Iyar, which was said to have been the day that Samuel died. A letter written in 1489 recounts that the number of pilgrims was large and that they "lit large torches or bonfires." Another letter from 1537 mentions the custom of processing with a Torah scroll from Jerusalem to the site of Samuel's tomb, during which participants would sing and recite prayers. According to a third account from the mid-sixteenth century, young boys received their first haircuts there, and an amount of money equal in weight to the hair was given towards the upkeep of the site. These contributions supported the poor and most of the public institutions in Israel, including the academies where the rabbis in charge of religious regulations studied.

All this changed sometime between 1565 and 1570, when Muslim authorities forbade Jews to enter the tomb area. In one stroke, Jews lost a popular yearly pilgrimage from the nearby Diaspora, as well as the main source of income for the poor of Jerusalem, the public institutions of the Land, and especially, the academies of learning on which the rabbis relied. The grave of Shimon Bar Yochai was therefore selected as an alternative pilgrimage site. It offered the advantage of being situated in Galilee and of already being the site for celebrations on Lag Ba'omer, the 18th of Iyar, just ten days prior to the annual visits to the tomb of Samuel. All of the customs originally celebrated in Ramah at the tomb of Samuel were thus transferred to the gravesite of Shimon Bar Yochai in Meron.[51]

Theories concerning the Origin of Lag Ba'omer
among Scholars

Few scholars accept the explanation given by Avraham Hayarchi in the name of Zerachyah Halevi that the death of

Rabbi Akiba's students stopped at Lag Ba'omer. How then did the day come to be associated with scholars?

Gaster, as we have seen, perceives Lag Ba'omer as akin to a "Jewish May Day."[52] Gustav Dalman speculates that Lag Ba'omer originally may have been the celebration of the actual beginning of the summer, which was marked by the early rising of the constellation Pleiades between the thirteenth and the twenty-fifth of May.[53] Some scholars posit even more fanciful interpretations.[54] A particularly intriguing theory comes from Joseph Derenbourg, who compares Lag Ba'omer to "mi-carême," a day observed midway through Lent when mourning practices are relaxed.[55] His theory is supported by the observation that in certain communities (as we saw), the mourning period was counted not from the second day of Passover counting forward, but from Shavuot backward, with the mourning practices commencing at Rosh Hodesh Iyar; under this system, it happens that Lag Ba'omer falls exactly midway within the mourning period. Thus, perhaps Lag Ba'omer is indeed a "mid-Lenten" relaxation of mourning within the *S'firah* season as counted from Rosh Hodesh Iyar until Shavuot.

THE *S'FIRAT HA'OMER* RITUAL TODAY

After the destruction of the Second Temple, it was impossible to perform the commandment of reaping and bringing the *omer* as an offering. But unlike other commandments dependent upon the land and the sacrificial system, rituals connected with the *omer* were not on that account discontinued. The actual offering was transformed into a synagogue ritual: every evening as part of the statutory worship, the days are counted aloud, along with a benediction affirming the intention of performing the commandment of counting the *omer.*

In the Talmud, Amemar views the counting ritual as a means of remembering the destruction of the Temple,[56] but most commentators take a more positive approach by attempting to understand the counting as a means of linking Passover to Shavuot. In his *Guide of the Perplexed,* Maimonides perceives the counting as an expression of yearning for the revelation of Torah on Shavuot:

> The Feast of Shavuot is the anniversary of the Revelation on Mount Sinai. In order to increase the importance of this day, we count the days that pass since the preceding festival, just as one who expects his most intimate friend on a certain day counts the days and even the hours. This is the reason why we count the *omer* from the day of the Exodus until the day of the Giving of the Law. Indeed, the latter was the aim and object of the Exodus from Egypt.[57]

Similarly, in *Sefer Hachinukh* (anonymous, prior to 1313) we find the idea that "we were commanded to count in order to imprint in our souls the great yearning towards the honored and longed-for day, just as a slave yearns for a bit of shade."[58]

As one might expect, Kabbalists saw the *S'firah* as a time of purification towards mystical union with God on Shavuot. Each day of counting was a further ascension from the impurities of Egypt to the spiritual heights of Mount Sinai. Each day brought further transformation of self from impurity to purity, from evil to good, from Pharoah to God.[59]

Most North American Reform congregations have abandoned the practice of counting the *omer,* though some are reclaiming it, at least in part. But modern Conservative Judaism still includes it officially, as does Orthodoxy, and commentators today continue to find new meaning in it. Following Amemar's understanding of the counting as an expression of yearning for the restoration of Zion, the Conservative authority Isaac Klein proposes, "Today we translate [counting the *omer*] into a means of strengthening our resolve to reclaim the soil of the Holy Land and to work for the rebuilding of Zion as a homeland for the exiled and as a center of spiritual life for our people."[60] Adopting the Maimonidean perspective, Klein adds that counting indicates "we want not only freedom from bondage but also freedom for a purpose, i.e., to receive the moral law at Mount Sinai and to practice it."[61] Underscoring the difference between the physical experience of freedom at the Exodus versus the metaphysical experience of freedom at Sinai, Orthodox Rabbi Irving Greenberg states, "Counting the days becomes the bridge from the social liberation that occurred on Passover to the constitution of freedom accepted and ratified at Sinai. Through the act of counting the *omer,* traditional Jews affirm that the purpose of freedom (Passover) is to live the holy life and ethical regimen of the Torah."[62] Reform rabbis Elyse Frishman and Sandy Levine [Kinneret Shiryon] suggest that the period of the *omer* finds its parallel in the human stages of development from childhood through adolescence to adulthood. On Passover, we recall our slavery and childhood as a people; during the *omer* period, our wandering and adolescence lead us to Shavuot, when we achieve full-fledged adulthood through the receipt of freedom with responsibility.[63] And finally, counting the *omer* has returned as a means of marking personal spiritual growth—a Jewish reflection of the more general turn to spirituality in the 1990s.[64]

NOTES

1. Deut. 8:7–10.

2. Nogah Hareuveni, *Nature in Our Biblical Heritage* (Kiryat Ono, Israel, 1980), pp. 28–64.

3. B. B. B. 147a.

4. Cf. Pharoah's dream, Gen. 41:6, and P. T. Shek. 5:1: "Once the whole world was scorched and they did not know from where to bring the grain offering."

5. See, e.g., 1 Sam. 12:17–19.

6. Hareuveni, *Nature,* p. 60. Cf. Jer. 5:24.

7. H. Louis Ginsberg, "The Grain Harvest Laws of Leviticus 23:9–22 and Numbers 28:26–31," *PAAJR* 46–47 (Jubilee Volume, 1980): 141–54, and idem, *The Israelian Heritage of Judaism,* Texts and Studies of the Jewish Theological Seminary of America 24 (New York, 1982), pp. 42–83.

8. Hareuveni, *Nature,* p. 52; Ginsberg, *The Israelian Heritage,* p. 49.

9. Baruch Levine, *JPS Torah Commentary: Leviticus* (Philadelphia, 1989), p. 158.

10. Hareuveni, *Nature,* pp. 30–43. Cf. Jacob Licht, *Encyclopedia Mikra'it,* s.v. "omer," col. 300, tracing the Israelite *omer to* an Ugaritic ritual for Baal. Licht cites R. De Vaux, *Revue Biblique* 46 (1937): 526, and T. Worden, *Vetus Testamentum* 3 (1953): 292–95.

11. Hareuveni, *Nature,* pp. 53–54.

12. Lev. Rab. 27:5. Cf. Pesikta Rabbati, Piska 18, 4/5 (Braude, p. 386).

13. Pesikta Rabbati, Piska 18, 2 (Braude, p. 381). Cf. Ecc. Rab. 1:3,1, and Pesikta d'Rav Kahana, Piska 8 (Buber, p. 59b).

14. B. R. H. 16a; cf Ecc. Rab. 1:3,1; 5:15,1. Song of Songs Rab. 4:4,1; 7:2,2.

15. Pesikta Rabbati, Piska 18, 1 (Braude, p. 380). Cf. Ecc. Rab. 1:3,1; Pesikta d'Rav Kahana, Piska 8 (Buber, 59a).

16. M. R. H. 1:2.

17. Song of Songs Rab. 7:2,2.

18. Taan. 12b.

19. That "shabbatot" in verse 15b refers to "weeks" is clear. Whether sabbatical week (Sunday to Saturday) or non-sabbatical week is in question. If it refers to a sabbatical week, "shabbat" in the preceding verse might mean Saturday and the S'firah period would begin on Sunday. If a non-sabbatical week, it could begin on any day. Jeffrey H. Tigay, "Notes on the Development of the Jewish Week," *Eretz Israel,* vol. 14 (Jerusalem, 1978), suspends judgment for lack of biblical evidence, but notes Deuteronomy 16:9, where *sheva shabbatot shavuot* decidedly refers to seven non-sabbatical weeks.

20. Menachem Haran, *Encyclopedia Mikra'it,* vol. 8, s.v. *Shabbat—Mimochorat Hashabbat,* cols. 517–21. For further examples in which "shabbat" was taken to mean the last (festival) day of the Passover week, see J. Van Goudoever, *Biblical Calendars* (Netherlands, 1959). For instances where it meant the first Saturday after the week of Passover, see Baruch Levine, "The Temple Scroll: Aspects of Its Historical Provenance and Literary Character," *Bulletin of the American School for Oriental Research* 232 (Fall 1978). For "shabbat" as the first Saturday after the harvest began, see Ginsberg "Grain Harvest Laws," p. 146. But see his later view, in *Israelian Heritage,* pp. 74–75. On "shabbat" as a replacement term for the old Assyrian *sapattum* and the pentacontad calendar, see Hildegard and Julius Lewy, "The Origin of the Week and the Oldest West Asiatic Calendar," *HUCA* 17 (1942–1943): 1–152.

21. Sifra Emor 23:11,15, M. Hag. 2:4, M. Men. 10:3; B. Men 65b. Cf. Targum Jerushalmi "after the first festal day of Passover" and Onkelos "from the day after the festival day." Also cf. Philo. All cited in Van Goudoever, *Biblical Calendars*, p. 19. See also Josephus, Ant. 3:10:5. For modern commentary which supports the Pharisaic view, see Louis Finkelstein, *The Pharisees: The Sociological Background of Their Faith*, vol. 2 (Philadelphia, 1938), pp. 643–48.

22. Boethuseans may have followed the calendar of Jubilees. See *Encyclopedia Mikra'it*, s.v. *Shabbat–Mimochorat Hashabbat*, p. 518, and Ginsberg, "Grain Harvest Laws," pp. 145–46.

23. Van Goudoever, *Biblical Calendars*, pp. 19–21.

24. B. Men 65b; Pesikta de Rav Kahana, Piska 8.

25. M. Men. 10:3.

26. Finkelstein, *Pharisees*, pp. 115–18, 641–54.

27. Neither Josephus (Ant. 3:10:6) nor Philo (*De Septenario*, 21) hint that Shavuot memorializes Sinai. The earliest reference to the Ten Commandments being given on the sixth day of Sivan is in Yoma 4b. The earliest reference to the Torah being given on Shavuot is attributed to R. Meir (Ex. Rab. 31:16). Some scholars point to 2 Chronicles 15:10–15 and Jubilees 6:1–21 as earlier references, but the evidence is unclear.

28. Finkelstein, *Pharisees*, pp. 643–44.

29. Cf. B. Men. 65b, 66a; Lev. Rab. 28:4–6, Pesikta Rabbati, Piska 18 (Braude), Pesikta d'Rav Kahana, Piska 8 (Buber).

30. *Otsar Hageonim*, ed. B. M. Lewin, vol. 7 (Jerusalem, 1936), Yeb. 327, p. 141.

31. See Abraham Block, *The Biblical and Historical Background of the Jewish Holy Days* (New York, 1978), pp. 168–75, who actually credits later geonim (esp. Hai, d. 1038) with creating the S'firah restrictions to link the death of Rabbi Akiba's students to the Bar Kochba rebellion.

32. Theodor H. Gaster, *Festivals of the Jewish Year* (New York, 1953), p. 52.

33. A. E. Crawley, *Encyclopedia of Religion and Ethics*, vol. 8 (New York, 1928), s.v. "May, Midsummer," p. 501.

34. Lou Silberman, "The S'firah Season: A Study in Folklore," *HUCA* 22 (1949): 224–27.

35. Jewish literature also connects the dead with this time period. R. Akiba maintained that the judgment of the wicked in Gehinnom endures twelve months, whereas R. Yochanan ben Nuri contended "From Passover to Shavuot" (M. Eduyot 2:10).

36. Israel Abrahams, *Jewish Life in the Middle Ages* (New York, 1985), pp. 184–85.

37. *Otsar* Hageonim, ed. Lewin, Yeb. 328.

38. *Tur,* O. H. 493.

39. Cf. Zerachiah HaLevi (1125–1186, Spain/Provence) and Abraham Ibn HaYarchi (1155–1215, Provence/Spain), possibly the first to report the practice.

40. Silberman ("S'firah Season") connects the custom to ancient Rome, where cutting hair was said to cause storms. His reconstruction seems inadequate in light of its late appearance in our sources.

41. "Lag" is a word made up of the letters *lamed* and *gimel,* which have the numerical value of 33.

42. Hamanhig 91b.

43. See commentaries to *Tur,* O. H. 493.

44. Traced to an anonymous tosafist and cited by Joel Sirkes, *BaCH to Tur,* O. H. 493.

45. See commentaries to *Tur,* O. H. 493.

46. J. D. Eisenstein, *Otzar Dinim Uminhagim* (New York, 1917), s.v. "Lag Ba'omer," p. 188.

47. *Jewish Encyclopedia,* s.v. *Omer,* p. 400.

48. Gaster, *Festivals of the Jewish Year,* p. 58.

49. Zohar, Idra Zuta, p. 296b. On the *hillula* (in English), see Julian Morgenstern, "Lag Ba'omer—Its Origins and Import," *HUCA* 39 (1968): 82–83.

50. Avraham Ya'ari, "Toldot Hahillula Bameron," *Tarbiz* 31 (1965): 79–84.

51. Received wisdom is that the mystics of Tsfat sanctioned these practices, but the opposite was the case; Isaac Luria forbade merriment and celebration on Lag Ba'omer, preferring to make a pilgrimage to Bar Yochai's grave on the ten days before Shavuot. See Ya'ari, "Toldot Hahillula Bameron," pp. 83–90.

52. Gaster, *Festivals of the Jewish Year,* pp. 51–58.

53. Silberman, "Sefirah Season," p. 236, citing Gustaf Dalman, *Arbeit und Sitte in Palastina* (Hildesheim, 1964), vol. 1, part 2, pp. 294 and 460–61.

54. Silberman, "Sefirah Season," p. 236, cites Hubert Grimme (*Das israelitische Pfingstfeste und der Plejandenkult* [Paderborn, 1907]), to the effect that Lag Ba'omer is reminiscent of an ancient Babylonian celebration in honor of the victory of Marduk. Julian Morgenstern sees Lag Ba'omer as a celebration of the day on which manna fell in the wilderness of Sinai ("Lag Ba'omer: Its Origin and

Import," pp. 82–83). However, according to a more accurate reading of the Bible, manna fell not on the eighteenth of Iyar but rather on the seventeenth.

55. Derenbourg, "Le 33e de l'Omer," *REJ* 29 (1894): 149.

56. Men. 66a.

57. Moses Maimonides, *The Guide of the Perplexed,* trans. M. Friedlander (New York, 1881), Part 3, chap. 43, p. 211.

58. Cited in Yom Tov Levinsky, *Sefer Hamo'adim,* vol. 6 (Tel Aviv, 1955), p. 328.

59. Ibid. Cf. Arthur Waskow, *Seasons of Our Joy* (New York, 1982), pp. 168-9.

60. Isaac Klein, *A Guide to Jewish Religious Practice* (New York, 1979), p. 135.

61. Ibid.

62. Irving Greenberg, *The Jewish Way: Living the Holidays* (New York, 1988), p. 59.

63. Elyse Frishman and Sandy Levine, Untitled term paper (widely circulated in the 1980s), Hebrew Union College–Jewish Institute of Religion (1980).

64. Kerry M. Olitzky, with Rachel Smookler, *Anticipating Revelation, Counting Our Way through the Desert: An Omer Calendar for the Spirit* (New York, 1998).

was, therefore, not a season which merely "filled in" the time between the festival bookends of Easter and Pentecost; rather, the season itself *was* the celebration, a continuous observance of the paschal mystery.

Although the evidence for a distinctively Christian marking of Pentecost does begin to appear in the late second century, the witnesses to this protracted celebration are not many. There are indications in the Asian *Acts of Paul* and an indirect reference from Irenaeus of Lyons, as well as references by Hippolytus of Rome and Origen in Alexandria.[2] But it is Tertullian, in North Africa, who provides the fullest of the early testimony for the fifty-day period. After emphasizing the appropriateness of Easter for the administration of baptism, he goes on to say: "After this Pentecost is a most joyful period (*laetissimum spatium*) for preparing baptisms, in which also the resurrection of the Lord was frequently made known to the disciples, the grace of the Holy Spirit established, and the hope of the coming of the Lord was revealed."[3] The season, as Tertullian describes it, embraces the post-resurrection appearances and the ascension of the Lord, the gift of the Spirit, and the eschatological anticipation of the Lord's second coming. Thus, even though it is a season of paschal celebration, the span focuses not only on the resurrection but also on many manifestations of the paschal mystery, including the sending of the Spirit.

In another place, Tertullian compares Christian feasts to pagan feasts: "Call out the individual solemnities of the nations, and set them in a row, they will not be able to make up a Pentecost," again attesting to the fifty-day season.[4] His characterization of this time witnesses to its closeness to Sunday in significance and liturgical observances.

We need to remember that the "paschal mystery" of the late second century was quite different from what was generally observed from the fourth century onwards and from what is still observed in Christian communities today. Easter was then typologically centered on the narrative of the immolation of the lamb, as in Exodus 12, and on the narrative of the death of Jesus, the New Lamb, which was the heart of the feast.[5] The

triduum of Good Friday, Holy Saturday, and Easter Sunday
had not developed, and so the Easter celebration, as a fifty-day
season, did not highlight the mysteries of death and resurrection in mutually exclusive ways. As the end of the fourth century witnessed the gradual separation of the paschal "moments" before the celebration of Easter (Palm Sunday, Holy
Thursday, Good Friday, etc.), it was inevitable that this separation of the discrete narratives of the paschal events before the
feast of Easter would influence the shape of the fifty days after
Easter in a similar way.

While it is commonplace to acknowledge that the integrity
of the fifty-day season began to break down in the course of
the fourth century, this disintegration was not universal. The
churches of Egypt, for example, seem to have been most faithful in maintaining the uninterrupted continuity of the fifty
days. The *Canons of Hippolytus,* an Egyptian church order dating from just before the middle of the fourth century, prescribes fasting after the "fifty days."[6] The festal letters of
Athanasius of Alexandria from 329 to 373, in which the bishop
would announce the dates of the paschal celebrations for the
coming year, testify to the "seven weeks" of paschal solemnity. Such letters testifying to the seven weeks survive also
from Theophilus, Patriarch of Alexandria from 385 to 412, and
his successor, Cyril, who wrote the letters from 414 to 442.
While the content of Cyril's missives are far more preoccupied
with the Egyptian churches' struggles against heresies, particularly Nestorianism, he occasionally speaks of the "days of
Pentecost." Moreover, the rules of the Egyptian desert monks,
whose lives were spent on the margins of society and at a re-
move therefore from the liturgical practices of the major
Christian communities, advocated rigorous fasting, but the
rules also make it clear that this rigorism was suspended during the period between Easter and Pentecost.[7]

The Egyptian faithfulness to the earliest configuration,
through the fourth and fifth centuries at least, may have been
unique, for we learn from two other witnesses, one eastern and
one western, that the span of the Easter season, *quinquagesima,* was disintegrating elsewhere. These two complicate

the picture somewhat, for the texts arising from their worshiping communities—the churches of Jerusalem and of Turin in northern Italy—witness to a period of transition from the fifty-day span to the celebration of Pentecost as a single day of observance.

Jerusalem

In her daily chronicle of the liturgical events taking place in Jerusalem, the pilgrim Egeria details the liturgies which happen *quinquagesimarum autem die*, "on the fiftieth day." Describing everything that "is done exactly according to custom," she says that the vigil of Pentecost "is held in the Anastasis [church of the resurrection], so that the bishop may read the passage from the gospel which is always read on Sundays, that of the resurrection of the Lord." In the morning all the people assemble in the major church at the Martyrium, where "the sacrifice [i.e., the eucharist] is offered in the manner in which it is customarily done on Sundays." She says that this day is ritually unique in that the dismissal is moved up "so that it is given before the third hour [about 9 a.m.]." Her narrative continues with the rite immediately following the eucharist:

> All the people without exception, singing hymns, lead the bishop to Sion, but in such a manner that they are in Sion at precisely the third hour. When they arrive, there is read from the Acts of the Apostles that passage in which the Holy Spirit came down so that all tongues might be heard and all might understand what was being said.[8]

The "sacrifice" is again offered, and afterwards the people return to their homes, rest, eat lunch, and then ascend the Mount of Olives "with the result that not a single Christian remains in the city, for they have all gone." The faithful go first to the Imbomon, "that is, to the place from which the Lord ascended into heaven. . . . Then the passage from the gospel is read which speaks of the ascension of the Lord; then there is a reading from the Acts of the Apostles which speaks of the ascension of the Lord into heaven after the resurrection."[9]

From Egeria's account here, it is apparent that the character of the fifty days was still operative, for the day commemorated the major narratives of the paschal season: the resurrection, the descent of the Holy Spirit, and the ascension of the Lord.[10] That this day marked the end of the season is further confirmed by Egeria's mention the following day that "everyone again observes the fast that prevails throughout the year,"[11] signaling the end of the sacred paschal time by the resumption of fasting. By itself, this text suggests that in the Holy Land at the end of the fourth century, the observance of *quinquagesima* still persisted. Yet Egeria's attestation in this case, as in quite a few others, is not so simple.

Just before her description of the fiftieth day is a brief account of two rites celebrated on "the fortieth day after Easter, which is a Thursday." While later Christian observance of the ascension on the fortieth day after Easter might lead us to think that these rites in Jerusalem were similar, the evidence is far from clear. The first celebration is the vigil, while the other is on Thursday, the fortieth day itself:

> The vigil is held in the church of Bethlehem, the church where the grotto in which the Lord was born is located. On the following day, this is, on Thursday, the feast of the fortieth day, the divine service is celebrated in the prescribed manner, and as a result the priests and the bishop preach, delivering sermons appropriate to the day and the place.[12]

While those to whom Egeria wrote undoubtedly recognized what she meant when she wrote about the "prescribed manner" and the narratives "appropriate" to the fortieth day after Easter, this remains an enigma for us. But it is certainly possible that this second liturgy, on Thursday, commemorated the ascension of the Lord on the fortieth day, as chronicled in the Acts of the Apostles. Thomas Talley has argued persuasively that the church of Jerusalem had to maintain two separate ritual tracts for its attending faithful, the local obser-

vances for the native worshipers, as well as the rites expected
by pilgrims, nurtured in faith with traditions different from
those of Jerusalem, who came to visit the historical sites of the
life of Jesus in the Holy City.[13] Might Egeria's chronicle have
captured a time when two observances of the ascension were
taking place, one which marked it as one of the paschal mysteries observed in the fifty-day season and another which
marked the feast according to the Lukan chronology, i.e., on
the fortieth day after Easter? If the latter were what was in
fact occurring, this would signal the imminent dissolution of
the paschal season.

Turin

Gennadius of Marseilles is the only external witness to
the northern Italian episcopate of Maximus of Turin, and—at
the end of a long paragraph in which he lists the topics of the
Torinese bishop's sermons—he tells us that Maximus "died
during the reign of Honorius and the younger Theodosius,"[14]
which would be between 408 and 423 c. e., just a few decades
after Egeria's eastward journey in 383. Maximus's sermons
provide a western document which, like Egeria's, presents two
conflicting views of the post-Easter time.

Sermon 44 of Maximus clearly points to a *quinquagesima,*
the season of paschal joy, or, in his words, "a continual and uninterrupted festival" (*iugis et continuata festiuitas*). He elabo-
rates further:

> The whole course of 50 days is celebrated on the model of Sunday,
> then, and all these days are counted as Sundays, since the resur-
> rection is a Sunday. . . . For the Lord arranged it that, just as we
> mourned over His suffering with the fasts of a 40-day period, so
> we would rejoice over His resurrection during the festivals of a
> 50-day period. . . . But when He ascends to heaven after these days
> we fast again, as the Savior says: *But the days will come when the
> bridegroom will be taken from them, and then they will fast in those
> days.*[15]

While this sermon indicates that the paschal mysteries were all part of the fifty-day season, "all counted as Sundays," another sermon from the Torinese bishop, sermon 40, indicates that the season was not being observed:

> I believe that you know, brethren, why we celebrate this venerable day of Pentecost with no less joy than we accorded the holy Pasch, and why we observe this solemnity with the same devotion that we gave to that feast. For then, as we have done now, we fasted on the Sabbath, kept vigils, and prayed earnestly through the night. It is necessary, therefore, that a like joy follow a like observance.[16]

Obviously, there was some change in the observance of the Easter season in Turin during the bishop's tenure, for there would have been no fasting and vigil-keeping, as described in sermon 40, during the "continual and uninterrupted festival" described in sermon 44. Because the period of Maximus's episcopate cannot be more tightly dated, one does not know how quickly the change took place.

Egeria's travelogue may suggest that there were two liturgical customs for celebrating the narrative of the ascension, one according to the Lukan tradition which placed the occasion on the fortieth day after the resurrection, and the other which linked it with the end of the season on the fiftieth day. Maximus's western attestation reveals two liturgical configurations, one marking it as a season, the other seeing it as a feast *day* only, preceded by a fast and a vigil. This seems to indicate a breakdown of the original schema in late antiquity, though not yet universal if the Egyptian testimony is kept in mind.

After Egeria and Maximus, signs of the dissolution of the integrity of the "fifty days" appear in abundance. Instead of finding all the paschal mysteries celebrated together during *quinquagesima* as parts of the one paschal mystery, evidence of the discrete celebration of each of these "moments" arises, particularly of the ascension of the Lord on the fortieth day after Easter and the descent of the Holy Spirit on the fiftieth day.

The Feast of the Ascension on the Fortieth Day

The gospel text in which Jesus says that the friends of the bridegroom do not fast while the groom is still with them[17] was used to explain the absence of fasting during the span of the fifty-day season. While the risen Savior was with the community during this paschal season, the community did not mourn, but celebrated. Yet once the Lukan chronology of the life of Jesus began to be observed and to shape the liturgical year, the absence of the Savior was assumed to have begun on the fortieth day rather than on the fiftieth. In Spain a canon from the early-fourth-century Council of Elvira indicates that some churches, unfamiliar with Greek and thus not knowing that the very word for the feast indicated its placement on the fiftieth day, were celebrating Pentecost on the fortieth day after Easter. There are other indications from the fourth century—the Council of Nicea and *Apostolic Constitutions,* for example—that Spain was not the only place where this practice occurred.[18]

Since the narrative content of the liturgy of the fortieth day after Easter as described by Egeria cannot be determined, one must look elsewhere for the first appearance of a distinct day commemorating the narrative of the ascension. The feast appears in the preaching of John Chrysostom in Antioch and of Gregory of Nyssa, both at the end of the fourth century.[19] In the West the feast is found first in the preaching of Chromatius of Aquileia, bishop of that northern Italian city on the Adriatic from 388 to 407.[20] This feast, then, is known to communities in both Greek and Latin Christianity by the end of the fourth century.

A puzzling additional piece of evidence appears in the *Diversarum hereseon liber* of Filastrius of Brescia, a bishop, like Chromatius, of northern Italy. This heresiology was written between 383 and 391, and in it Filastrius states:

> Through the year four fasts are celebrated by the Church: the first at Christmas, then at Easter, the third at the Ascension, the fourth

at Pentecost. In effect, we should fast at the birth of the Savior and Lord, then during the forty days leading up to Easter, likewise at his Ascension into heaven on the fortieth day after Easter, then for the ten days until Pentecost, or later.[21]

As difficult as this piece is to integrate into the development, it is clear here that the ascension was celebrated on the fortieth day and that it was preceded and succeeded by fasting! Because there is no earlier evidence from Brescia, one does not know if *quinquagesima* had been the norm before this time and then broken up, or if the fifty-day season had never been the norm there.

The Feast of Pentecost on the Fiftieth Day

As the practice of observing a fifty-day paschal season was being eroded, an odd reversal was taking place in the translation of the New Testament text of Acts 2:1 from Greek into Latin. While in the celebration of the liturgical year the fifty *days* were tending to become a fiftieth *day,* the fourth-century translations of the New Testament were rendering Acts 2:1 in a way that seemed to favor the opposite. According to the original Greek, the verse reads "On the day of Pentecost, each went to his own home." Yet some Old Latin versions, including Jerome's Vulgate of the late fourth century (which would be incomparably influential for a millenium and a half), changed the Greek singular "day" into the plural, *cum complerentur dies pentecostes,* "when the days of Pentecost were fulfilled." Had the language shift gone from the Greek plural to a Latin singular noun in the fourth-century translations, this would have accompanied the liturgical shift from the "fifty days" to the "fiftieth day." But the Latin mistranslation actually reflects the opposite of the evolution of the liturgical year. As the Latin biblical text moved to have "Pentecost" reflect the season, i.e., "the days of Pentecost," the season was becoming a feast *day* only, and in most Christian churches it has remained so since that early time.

The Octave of Easter

The final element that influences the dissolution of the season is the highlighting of the octave of Easter, the first week after Easter during which mystagogical catecheses were delivered to the newly baptized. The week was traditionally called the octave *in albis*, i.e., when the newly initiated were dressed in white garments.

Egeria is among the earliest witnesses to the rise of the paschal octave, and her diary leads one to think that the practice was already fairly common at the time of her sojourn in Jerusalem:

> The eight days of Easter are observed just as at home with us. The liturgy is celebrated in the prescribed manner throughout the eight days of Easter just as it is celebrated everywhere from Easter Sunday to its octave. . . . During the eight days of Easter, every day after lunch, in the company of all the clergy and the neophytes—I mean those who have just been baptized—and of all the *aputactitae*, both men and women, and of as many of the people as wish to come, the bishop goes up to the Eleona.[22]

This octave, while attentive to the initiation rites, is but one more nail in *quinquagesima*'s coffin.

The Feast of Mid-Pentecost

While the discrete celebrations of the ascension on the fortieth day, the descent of the Spirit on the fiftieth, and the octave for the initiates point to the imminent dissolution of the fifty-day season, there is evidence in the same period of another feast which suggests that the *laetissimum spatium* was still maintained in some communities. The celebration of "Mid-Pentecost" on the twenty-fifth day of the season points to the integrity of the earliest stratum of the *quinquagesima*. In the East the feast is found at the end of the fourth century, some time earlier than its mid-fifth-century appearance in the West.

Amphiloque, late-fourth-century bishop of Iconium, is the earliest witness to it, and he claimed that the celebration was "situated at the mid-point between the resurrection and Pentecost; it recalls the resurrection, points to Pentecost, and announces the ascension, like the trumpet of a herald." A century later Severus of Antioch attests to the existence of the feast, and a Syriac hymn celebrating Christ the Mediator likewise survives in the eastern tradition regarding this liturgical midway point. The pericope for the feast, according to Severus's homily, was John 7:14—"about the middle of the festival Jesus went up into the temple and began to teach"—the same text which is attached to the feast when it is first found in a Latin tradition.[23]

This Latin attestation comes in two homilies of Peter Chrysologus, bishop of the church of Ravenna in northern Italy in the second quarter of the fifth century. Peter's rhetoric defends the celebration of Mid-Pentecost, indicating that it had been part of the Ravennese tradition for some time but that the faithful there did not appreciate its importance:

> Even though some things seem hidden in their own deep mystery, nevertheless no solemnity in the church's worship is without benefit. The divine feast is not to be solemnized by our will but is to be kept for its own miracles. . . . We have made our way so that we might arrive at the middle of this great solemnity, for Jesus, God and our Lord, consecrator of every feast, journeyed in the middle of the feast to enter Jerusalem.[24]

Perhaps the Christians in Ravenna had begun to tire of the maintenance of this feast when they knew that other churches were beginning to observe the feast of the ascension on the fortieth day, i.e., according to the Lukan chronology, as we have seen in northern Italy already in the churches of Aquileia and Brescia. While we do not find the feast of Mid-Pentecost subsequently in the church of Ravenna, its later survival is evident in the medieval Milanese sacramentaries of Aribert and Bergamo.[25] Aquileian codices of the sixth and seventh centuries list John 7:14 as the pericope in the fourth week after Easter, when the feast of Mid-Pentecost would have occurred.

Conclusion

The span of the first five or six centuries of the Christian faith seems to indicate a general movement from the integrity of *quinquagesima* to its dissolution in late antiquity and the early Middle Ages, perhaps as a result of the same tendency to historicize the life of Jesus of Nazareth in liturgical celebration that also brought Holy Week into being. From a continuous celebration of the paschal mystery that held together the resurrection, the post-resurrection appearances, the ascension, the descent of the Holy Spirit, and the mission of the disciples, the season began to break up from the late fourth century onwards into a series of discrete festal observances, with the days in between becoming less and less significant.

NOTES

1. The apostle Paul, in his closing remarks in the First Letter to the Corinthians, writes, "I will stay in Ephesus until Pentecost" (16:8, NRSV). Again as a marker of time, the evangelist Luke writes in Acts, "When the day of Pentecost had come" (2:1), and, later in the same book, that Paul "was eager to be in Jerusalem, if possible, on the feast of Pentecost" (20:16).

2. See Robert Cabié, *La Pentecôte. L'évolution de la Cinquantaine pascale au cours des cinq premiers siècles* (Tournai, Belgium, 1965), pp. 37–45.

3. *De baptismo* 19.2.

4. *De idolatria* 14.7.

5. See Christine Mohrmann, "Pascha, passio, transitus," *Ephemerides liturgicae* 66 (1952): 37–52; and Paul Bradshaw's "The Origins of Easter," in volume 5 of this series.

6. Canon 22; see Paul F. Bradshaw, ed., *The Canons of Hippolytus* (Bramcote, Notts., 1987), p. 27.

7. See Cabié, *La Pentecôte,* pp. 61–76.

8. *Itinerarium Aetheriae* 43.1–3.

9. Ibid. 43.4–5.

10. Here I have recounted only those elements of the liturgical day which are relevant to the present discussion. According to Egeria's account, the day continued with various rites, including the

blessing of the catechumens; a ceremony with candles at the city gate; another rite in the Martyrium, with hymns, antiphons, blessings, and prayers; and lastly, another liturgy at Sion, with scripture readings, psalms, antiphons, prayers, a blessing, and dismissal. At the end all come forward "to the bishop's hand," and return home around midnight.

11. *Itinerarium Aetheriae* 44.1.

12. Ibid. 42.

13. Thomas J. Talley, *The Origins of the Liturgical Year* (New York, 1986), pp. 177–83.

14. Boniface Ramsey, *The Sermons of St. Maximus of Turin*, Ancient Christian Writers 50 (New York, 1989), p. 2.

15. Ibid., p. 110.

16. Ibid., p. 99.

17. Matt. 9:14–15; Mark 2:18–20; Luke 5:33–35.

18. See Cabié, *La Pentecôte*, pp. 181–85.

19. Ibid.

20. Chromatius of Aquileia, *Opera*, Corpus Christianorum, series Latina 9a (Turnholt, 1974), pp. 32–37.

21. Filastrius of Brescia, *Diversarum hereseon liber*, Corpus Christianorum, series Latina 9 (Turnholt, 1957), p. 312.

22. *Itinerarium Aetheriae* 39.1,3.

23. See Cabié, *La Pentecôte*, pp. 100–101.

24. *Sermo* 85.1; see also *Sermo* 85bis.

25. Cabié, *La Pentecôte*, p. 103.

PART 3

*Symbols and the Arts
in Sacred Celebration*

A Symbol of Salvation in
the Passover Seder

Lawrence A. Hoffman

This essay is intended as another contribution to our understanding of the growth of the seder ritual. The subject of in-
quiry, however, is not the liturgical text itself, but the symbolic
importance attributed to that text by those who recited it in
the first two centuries of the common era. More specifically,
my interest here is a particular type of symbol which I shall
call salvational, and define as words and actions understood by
ancient worshipers to represent deliverance.

How people are saved, what they are saved from, and, therefore, what salvation means, are central questions in religious
debate. Both Judaism and Christianity provide wide-ranging
spectrums of possible answers. So we must not confuse a general human desire for deliverance with any particular dog-
matic description thereof. "Salvation" is used here, then, in its
generalized sense with no necessary connotations of either
this or that, Jewish or Christian, theological system. As our
study proceeds, we shall encounter evidence pointing to a particular system, of course, but I leave it to the theologian to ex-
plicate this data. My liturgical perspective obliges me to recognize the fact that participants in a ritual are usually not
conscious of the experience itself. Ritual words and actions
that awaken this experience are, by definition, "salvational,"
and I propose here to treat a certain class of words and actions,
those which accompany the use of *matsah* at the Passover seder, to see if they are salvational in this general sense and if,
therefore, *matsah* once functioned as a salvational symbol.

That the salvational symbolism of *matsah* was widely assumed

at an early date is indicated by almost unanimous agreement
of post-Talmudic authorities on the subject. Though they do
not always speak explicitly of deliverance, they generally do
refer to a common tradition identifying *matsah* as a replacement for the *pesach,* or Passover offering, and according to
Exodus 12:27, this offering was the symbol par excellence of
salvation. "It is the Passover sacrifice to the Lord, because He
passed over the houses of the Israelites, when He smote the
Egyptians, and He *saved* our houses." *Shibbolei Haleket,* for
example, calls it "a remembrance of the *pesach*" (*zekher lape-
sach*),[1] as does the *Tur,* which says also, "comparable to the
pesach" (*dumia d'pesach*).[2] Earlier still, Sherira Gaon (d. 969)
explains why technical use of the bread of affliction (that is,
matsah) is forbidden on Passover Day: "the bread of affliction
comes at the time of eating *pesach,* and the *pesach* is eaten
only at night";[3] and his son, Hai (d. 1038), while discussing the
pesach, makes a conceptual jump to *matsah* as if he were discussing one and the same thing.[4] To this day the Sefardic rite
prefaces the eating of *afikoman-matsah* with the words, *zekher
l'korban pesach hane'ekhal al hasova,* "a remembrance of the
Passover offering, eaten while full." Not all these authorities
recognize the salvational symbolism inherent in the "*matsah* =
pesach" equation, but that is because the symbolic identification was made long before their time. They accepted it along
with the rest of rabbinic lore, even though the emotive content within it had already lapsed.[5] We shall see that the expansion of the symbolic denotation of *matsah* to refer to the de-
funct Passover offering, and hence to the deliverance inherent
in that offering, was complete by the second century.

Since Passover is known biblically as the festival of *matsah*
(*chag hamatzot*), it is to be expected that *matsah* would play a
large role in the seder. Exactly where and how it would be included, however, could not be determined by the simple process of biblical exegesis, since the institution of the seder was
postbiblical. While proof texts, always desirable from the Rabbis' perspective, were frequently found, it cannot be denied
that the elaborate complex of seder rituals revolving about

matsah derived ultimately from rabbinic creativity, not biblical prototype.

To begin with, although of course anyone could eat unleavened bread at any time during Passover, eating it to satisfy the commandment to do so was limited to seder eve,[6] while consuming it earlier that day was actually prohibited.[7] R. Levi, a direct disciple of Judah Hanasi, indicates the severity of the prohibition by comparing the breaching thereof to someone who has intercourse with his betrothed, since he cannot wait for the proper moment of marriage (*nisu'in*).[8] Other regulations that we shall have to return to later were that the consumption of *matsah* was to cease at midnight, that one was to eat it while one was full, and that a certain minimum quantity known technically as *k'zayit* ("the size of an olive") was necessary.[9]

Nor were the occasions and manner of eating *matsah* during the seder left to chance. So successful were the tannaim in laying down the succession of events by which the commandment was to be carried out, that we accept them as obvious today. The evening's proceedings were surrounded by *matsah,* as the recitation of *ha lachma anya* ("Behold the bread of affliction") initiated the festivities, and the eating of the *afikoman,* now redefined as a piece of *matsah,* concluded them. In the interim, the *matsah* was apportioned for its various uses, according to an elaborate system; the *matsah shel mitzvah,* the piece eaten to fulfill the commandment, was introduced with the proper benediction; and Hillel, for one, chose to consume his *matsah* in a unique fashion that became traditional for generations.

How are we to account for all these ritual requirements? We could say, of course, that they were accidental developments having no consequence whatever; or even that some were connected in one manner or other, but that most were simply haphazard customs. But clearly, it would be improper to rule out the possibility of an overriding concern from which all the above-mentioned laws and rituals derived.

One such unifying concern is at hand. The development of all this ceremony can be explained by the assumption that by the first century, *matsah* had acquired a symbolic value that went far beyond the role allotted to it in the biblical narrative. From a historical recollection of the Exodus of the past, it had been transmuted into a symbol of salvation for the future.[10] Our task now must be to trace that novel adaptation and to explain the numerous rules and rituals related to it.

An ideal starting point is the *afikoman*. Though the rationale behind the well-known ordinance, *ein maftirin achar hapesach afikoman,*[11] may never be unearthed—indeed, syntactically, the sentence defies translation—there seems to be sufficient evidence to posit at least the general direction which investigation should take. The widespread diversity of rabbinic interpretation of *afikoman* stemming from the first amoraic generation[12] lends credence to the belief that by the third century the institution was already so old as to have its origins shrouded in mystery. The Babli quotes Rav as interpreting it to be *shelo y'akru meichaburah l'chaburah,* participants should not move from group to group on seder night, an opinion echoed anonymously in the Yerushalmi.[13] Samuel, on the other hand, refers the term to after-dinner eating, a view paralleled by Hananiah bar Shila and R. Yochanan.[14] R. Sisi's son thinks the prohibited entity is *mini zemer,* the playing of music.[15]

As diverse as these views may seem, they all do, in fact, converge in the usual explanation of *afikoman* as after-dinner revelry.[16] This would explain why the Mishnah felt obliged to ban drinking extra wine between the mandatory third and fourth cups, and why the ban is mentioned precisely before the phrase regarding *afikoman*. Fearing that after-dinner carousing would detract from the religiosity due that night, especially in this early period, when dinner preceded the recitation of the Haggadah and the temptation to escape a lengthy religious ceremony may have been great, the Mishnah first bans too much drinking at the end of the night and then, *immediately after,* prohibits revelry itself by the phrase, *ein maftirin. . . .* [17] The Tosefta makes the same contextual link in even clearer terms, as does the Yerushalmi. The former interprets *ein maftirin* as after-dinner eating, and then adds by way of explanation, "One should occupy oneself with the laws of Passover all night."[18] The latter explains that the ban on extra drinking is limited to after dinner, because "wine after dinner leads to drunkenness while wine before dinner does not," and then, knowing both laws to be related, turns immediately to the regulation of *ein maftirin*.[19] That carousing was general at occasions like our seder can be gathered from a study of the symposia literature[20] and even, perhaps, from the New Testament, where Paul berates the Corinthians for celebrating the Lord's Supper unworthily.[21]

We cannot go far wrong, then, if we summarize the initial conception of *afikoman* as follows. By the first century there was a home ceremony which marked the advent of Passover. Though it contained very little of the ritual and prayer now associated with the seder—Josephus has practically nothing to say about it—it can still be considered the seminal institution from which the later seder evolved. The paschal lamb, which had been slaughtered that afternoon, was now consumed according to well-established regulations, and a rather unstructured recounting of the Exodus and related lore took place. To avoid the possiblity of drunken revelry, it became customary to forbid too much drinking after dinner; for similar reasons, dropping in on various households all night, and enjoying such accoutrements of revelry as music and after-dinner gorging on delicacies, were forbidden. This latter sort of activity was encapsulated in the concise phrase, *ein maftirin achar hapesach afikoman,* the word *afikoman* being derived from the Greek.[22] At this early date, the term *afikoman* had absolutely nothing to do with *matsah*.

How different the matter was only one century later. We suddenly discover a novel symbolic value adhering to *matsah*. Though our tannaitic sources make no overt reference to this additional feature, the first-generation amoraim (third century) assume it in such a way as to place its earlier existence beyond doubt:

> "After the *pesach* [is consumed] one may not pursue revelry" [that is, *ein maftirin achar hapesach afikoman*] . . . Rav Judah said in Samuel's name. . . . The Mishnah teaches, "One may not pursue

revelry after the *pesach*"; [therefore] the prohibition applies to
"after the pesach." But "after the *matsah*" one may pursue revelry.... Mar Zutra taught it this way: Rav Joseph said in the name
of Samuel, "After the *matsah* one may pursue revelry."[23]

The issue before these amoraim was whether the ban
against pursuing revelry (*ein maftirin afikoman*) after the
pesach (*achar hapesach*) applies also to after *matsah* (*achar
hamatzah*), a question that makes no sense whatever, unless we
assume that by the third century, *matsah* was equated with the
pesach. The same question could conceivably have been asked
about wine, *charoset, maror,* or anything else on the seder plate,
but it was not. The only questionable item was *matsah,* because
matsah alone had taken on the additional significance of symbolizing the *pesach*.

The evidence for the existence of this symbolic transformation is overwhelming. We need only recall the regulations that
grew up regarding the eating of *matsah*. All are legal parallels to laws regarding the *pesach*. With the latter, too, nothing
was eaten either before nightfall or after midnight.[24] With the
pesach, as with *matsah, k'zayit* (an olive's bulk) was the accepted minimum quantity.[25] And, as with *matsah,* the *pesach*
was to cap off the meal, being eaten while one was full.[26]

No wonder, as we saw above, that post-Talmudic rabbinic
literature simply assumes the equation of these two entities.
To the sampling of geonic and post-geonic opinion already
given,[27] a citation should be added to indicate the continuation
of this novel symbolism in the Palestinian as well as the Babylonian tradition. In two places, the Yerushalmi asks whether
the Passover offering of a servant or a woman overrides the
Sabbath "work" regulations which might be construed as pre-
venting such a sacrifice on the Sabbath. Immediately thereafter, the Talmud inquiries, *matzatan mah hi?* "What about their
matsah?"[28] As with the Babli's discussion of *afikoman,* so here,
in the Yerushalmi, the link between *matsah* and *pesach* is
manifest. The discussion of one leads automatically to a consideration of the other.

This identity of symbolic denotation was at hand in Samuel's

day, that is, in the first half of the third century. That its origin
was earlier still can be argued on both logical and documentary ground: logical because the amoraim treat the equation
of *matsah* and *pesach* as a given, assumed by one and all; and
documentary because the Tosefta already prescribes that the
k'zayit matsah be eaten last.[29] As for the exact point in time
within the tannaitic period when we would assume such a nov-
elty to appear, the most obvious impetus would seem to be
the destruction of the Temple cult, when in fact the Passover
offering ceased. Evidence from the New Testament, however,
raises the possibility of an even earlier origin:

> For the tradition that I handed to you came to me from the Lord
> himself: that the Lord Jesus on the night of his arrest took bread
> and after giving thanks to God broke it, and said, "This is my
> body which is for you. Do this as a memorial of me." In the same
> way he took the cup after supper and said, "This cup is the new
> covenant sealed by my blood. Whenever you drink it do this as a
> memorial of me." For every time you eat this bread and drink this
> cup, you proclaim the death of the Lord until he comes."[30]

If Paul understood the Lord's Supper to have been a seder,
then he was already using *matsah* as a redemptive symbol by
the sixth decade of the first century. It is of course true that,
as many scholars have noted, the notion of a seder is not yet
manifestly present; the seder aspect may, therefore, be an addition of the evangelists, and we could then say that whereas
bread itself was symbolic of salvation in Paul's time, *matsah*
was so only tangentially, by virtue of its being a form of bread.
There can be no doubt about Paul's use of bread as a salvational symbol, and as we shall see, such a conception of bread
was common to Jewish circles in Paul's time. In fact, this prior
equation of bread, generally, with salvation may account for
the choice of *matsah* to fill the vacuum left by the *pesach*. The
paschal lamb was, above all, a symbol of deliverance, specifically, the deliverance from Egypt, and it would have been natural to elect something which already had salvational overtones
to fill its place.

Whether or not one posits the identity of *matsah* with

pesach by Paul's time depends on how one understands Paul's words to the Corinthians. In any event, the link existed by the time of the Gospels, for there the Last Supper is definitely a seder, where bread (*matsah*) is Jesus' body, and Jesus' body, in turn, is the paschal lamb.[31] Even if, however, the symbolic link is already present in Paul's writing, we are probably justified in concluding that the spiritual vacuum created by the end of the Temple cult set the stamp of finality on the development. Whereas Jews previously had celebrated deliverance with a Passover offering, it was now the *matsah* that harbored this emotional appeal.

Both Christian and Jew now had a cohesive system of salvational symbols. For the Jew, this meal, characterized originally by the *pesach* and now by *matsah,* recalled the deliverance of Egypt. For the Christian, it marked the salvation of the new covenant under the saving grace of the new paschal lamb, whose body was the *matsah.*[32]

The Talmud understands this novel symbolic value of *matsah* as being derived from the application of hermeneutic principles to the biblical commandment to eat *matsah* along with the paschal lamb.[33] The amoraim quoted in the discussion, however, lived three centuries later than the event in question, and, while the scriptural proximity of the words *matsah* and *pesach* may not be entirely beside the point, we are surely justified in looking elsewhere for the prime motivation behind this symbolic connection. As mentioned above, the missing link may be the general salvational symbolism already assumed to lie within bread itself. Such a rabbinic utilization of bread has been described by Eugene Mihaly.[34]

Among the midrashim adduced by Mihaly are those selections which picture the garden of Eden as replete with bread trees "as large as the cedars of Lebanon."[35] Such texts should be viewed together with the rabbinic argument over the proper term for the benediction over bread, *motsi* or *hamotsi.* Though there are two recensions of the latter discussion, each with its own version of the protagonists' positions, both agree in the end that *motsi lechem min ha'arets,* "brings forth bread from the earth," implies *shehu atid lehotsi lechem min ha'arets,* "that *in the future* He will bring forth bread from the earth."[36] In other words, the blissful state of the Garden of Eden will some day be replicated, and once more bread will grow from the ground. Were it not for the potential error of merging the final *mem* of *ha'olam* (the word preceding *motsi* in the benediction) with the initial *mem* of *motsi*—our text concludes—we would indeed be duty-bound to omit the definite article and use that form which anticipates future deliverance.

Further evidence for the salvational usage assigned to bread comes from the Lord's Prayer. Though it is beyond the scope of this paper to deal fully with the relationship of this early Christian prayer to its Jewish equivalent, the *Kaddish*, our purposes require our spending a moment on the phrase, "Give us this day our daily bread."[37] Scholars have noted that the initial paragraph of the *Kaddish* parallels the opening of the Lord's Prayer, both being prayers for the speedy coming of the Kingdom.[38] But the Lord's Prayer then apparently diverges from this central eschatological theme by adding a number of additional petitions: daily bread, forgiveness, and freedom from temptation. The last two petitions, however, are clearly related to deliverance, since sin is the stumbling block to salvation. We are left, then, with the request for daily bread as the sole divergence from the main theme. But once it is realized that bread is salvational in overtone, even this apparently irrelevant insertion in the prayer is revealed as an actual restatement of the basic idea itself. And, as a matter of fact, this is exactly how the early church understood it. The Greek, *epiousion,* is rendered by the *Didache* as "supernatural bread";[39] Jerome calls it "bread for the morrow";[40] Ambrose calls it "bread for the kingdom," and adds, "that is not the bread that enters the body, but the bread of eternal life."[41] So our Christian sources agree with the Jewish counterparts in identifying bread as a symbol of deliverance.

We can summarize the matter so far by saying that sometime in the first century this symbolic attribute of bread was transferred to *matsah,* and when the *pesach,* itself an age-old deliverance symbol, ceased, *matsah* took its place. The laws regulating the eating of the *pesach* were accordingly applied to the consuming of *matsah,* and, since one such law was that a piece of the *pesach* be eaten last, it was decided that a piece of *matsah, k'zayit* in bulk, be consumed at the end of the meal. This now became known as the *afikoman.*

With this background in mind, the other rituals and prayers connected with *matsah* fall into place. They too relate to the new understanding of *matsah* as a symbol of deliverance.

Consider, for example, the distribution of *matsah* during the seder. Though tradition is by no means unanimous on the subject,[42] our customary ritual specifies the utilization of three *matsot* to be divided in a specific way. At the beginning of the evening, one piece is broken in two, one half being set aside for the *afikoman,* and the other being returned to the plate. Of the two and one-half pieces now remaining on the plate, a whole one, or *sh'lemah,* is used for the *motsi,* the benediction over bread; the half, or *p'rusah,* is accompanied by the blessing over *matsah;* and the remaining whole one is generally used for *korekh,* the "Hillel sandwich." Both the number of *matsot*—three—and the allotment of them during the seder constituted with some minor differences the old Babylonian custom.[43] The Palestinians differed in that they used only two pieces of *matsah* to begin with.[44] The origin of the "Hillel sandwich" is generally explained by the story of Hillel, who, we are told, took literally the biblical commandment to eat the *pesach* together with the *matsah* and *maror,*[45] and therefore "used to combine all three of them together and eat them."[46] But the sages differed with him, so it became customary to follow both the sages' habit of eating each food separately (along with the blessings involved), and also Hillel's habit of eating them all together (though without a repetition of the benedictions). So today, after we eat *matsah* and *maror* individually, we then combine them in a sandwich.

But whence the custom of a sandwich? Hillel had none. Of his two *matsot*—he followed the Palestinian practice, of course—he must have used one piece for the *motsi,* and then— since no *matsah* was used as *afikoman* in his day—he put a slice of *pesach* together with some *maror* on the second piece, to fulfill the commandment of eating *matsah*. But he did not combine two pieces of *matsah* to make a sandwich, as we do. How then did the practice of making a sandwich arise?

The mystery disappears when one realizes that *matsah*, as a symbol of deliverance, took the place of the *pesach* after 70. Whereas Hillel could combine *pesach, matsah*, and *maror*, Jews after 70 had only *matsah* and *maror* available to them. So they took an extra piece of *matsah*, and now, with *maror, matsah* qua *matsah*, and *matsah* qua *pesach*, they had a sandwich. Ultimately, when the Babylonian practice of including a third piece of *matsah* on the seder plate became usual, this extra piece came to be reserved for the purpose.[47]

We can now turn to the seder's introductory reference to *matsah*, the recitation of *ha lachma anya*, "Behold the bread of affliction." Scholarly opinion on this prayer is summarized by Goldschmidt, who concludes that although the prayer in its present form is obviously a late combination of three—and in some rituals, four—independent formulas, an original prototypical introduction forming the nucleus of our version can be posited for the period of the second commonwealth.[48] The existence of a pre-70 version is predicated both on linguistic grounds and on the inclusion in the penultimate line of what appears to be an invitation to join in offering a genuine paschal lamb (*yifsach*).[49]

Strangely enough, this scholarly consensus on the existence of such an early original version exists despite the fact that the prayer is found in no tannaitic sources, nor even in the Yerushalmi. The earliest possible reference to it is the Babli's recollection of Rav Huna's custom of opening the door "when he wrapped bread and inviting wayfarers to dine with him by saying *kol man dits'rikh leitei v'yeikhul*, "Let all who are in need come and eat";[50] and even this is by no means a direct citation of *ha lachma anya*, at least not any version known to us, unless one assumes that Rav Huna deliberately transposed the verbs and changed the dialect from the Palestinian to the Babylonian.[51] Scholars, however, have generally assumed that Rav Huna was referring to our *ha lachma anya*, and, partly

because he used it regularly as an invitation to the poor, they
have further assumed that such an invitation was the prayer's
original function on Passover.[52]

But let us analyze the incident of Rav Huna more closely.
As to the date of our prayer's origin, what evidence is there
that Rav Huna was quoting an already existent prayer? Perhaps it was the other way around, Rav Huna's good deed being
drawn on as a paradigm for a later prayer. Given the absence
of evidence in Palestinian sources, and the uncertain nature
of the Babli narrative, the assumption of a tannaitic *ha lachma
anya* is at least open to question and ought to require further
evidence of another nature before being taken as certain. Secondly, as to the function of the prayer, even if we grant that
Rav Huna was quoting an earlier prayer which he understood
to be an invitation to the poor, it still does not follow that the
prayer was composed for that original purpose.

Regarding the first question, I am inclined, nevertheless, to
accept a theory of first-century composition. I do so because
of external evidence from what we may consider unofficial liturgical sources. Students of ritual have long been aware that
the actual extent of available custom is not represented in
the Mishnah, say, or even the Tosefta or the Yerushalmi. These
books represent only an isolated segment of contemporary usage. To judge by the Babli, for example, we would have no idea
of the actual art of the synagogue, as archaeology has revealed
it. Similarly, none of the official tannaitic or amoraic texts give
us a true estimate of the *merkavah* mystics or the range of
popular superstition. It may be that official ritual did not contain a *ha lachma anya;* but unofficial ritual did, even though—
as with the fifth cup of wine which was championed by a
certain segment of rabbinic opinion, but omitted from the
Mishnah—the *ha lachma anya* was not accepted into the
official liturgy of the seder.[53] Unfortunately, we lack an abundance of unofficial liturgical texts from the tannaitic period,
but we do have evidence from a later time which, in this case,
is almost as good: the genizah fragments.

In the Haggadah texts published by Abrahams, *ha lachma
anya* is to be found in fragments two and twelve.[54] Though it

is true that fragment twelve may reflect Babylonian usage, and may theoretically be viewed as an outgrowth of the Rav Huna narrative from the Babli, fragment two follows the threefold division of "Four" Questions typical of the Palestinian recension of the Mishnah, and thus indicates that in at least some Palestinian congregations *ha lachma anya* was recited. It therefore formed part of the Haggadah in both Palestine and Babylon. Now, it is unlikely that either of these two communities borrowed a prayer belonging to the ritual of the other, since the known cases of this are few and are generally accompanied by polemical literature of the parties involved.[55] We must, therefore, posit the passage's origins in a period that antedates the development of two alternative rites. Though this need not be as early as the first century, it is at least sometime in the tannaitic age, and we may certainly conclude that the absence of *ha lachma anya* in pre-geonic Palestinian sources in no way demonstrates a late Babylonian dating. So we have no reason to reject early dating, particularly, as we must now demonstrate, since such an early origin accords well with the theory that *matsah* was a symbol of salvation at the time.

The assumption that *ha lachma anya* was merely an invitation to the poor, devoid of further symbolism, entails some problems. Why the poor should have been singled out, aside from obvious humanitarian reasons, is not clear, since we do not invite the poor to share in all the other *mitzvot*. And even if we assume the seder to have been of such monumental significance that the poor had to be included, as the Mishnah itself may suggest (Pes. 10:1), the use of the word *v'yifsach* (literally, "let him offer a Passover sacrifice" or *pesach*) remains problematic. If the invitation dates from cultic times, we have the problem that it should have been recited before the *pesach* was slaughtered, since the law obligated those who ate it as a group to have already constituted a group at the time of its sacrifice. And, if it was composed after 70, and the word *v'yifsach* was taken metaphorically as an allusion to the whole Passover meal to which the poor were being invited, why was it inserted in the proceedings after the *Kiddush* (the opening prayer that inaugurates the day's sanctity) instead of before?[56]

In other words, not only must we explain why such an invitation to the poor existed at all, we must also explain its rather strange location in the Haggadah text. Again, the assumption that the *matsah* was by now a salvational symbol equivalent to the *pesach* alleviates these difficulties, since it allows us to arrive at an altogether different notion of how this passage functioned in the first place.

We know from both Josephus and the Rabbis that the paschal lamb was sacrificed in companies and then eaten by those who offered it.[57] The Tosefta states clearly that only those who were numbered among the original company could participate in the feast.[58] Because original ownership of the animal was vital, the Mishnah even records a legal formula meant to facilitate joint participation in a single offering of debated ownership.[59] Since the seder was a feast of celebrants organized into companies, we can imagine the care that was taken to ensure that those present were legally entitled to consider themselves members of the fellowship.

Ha lachma anya is not an invitation to outsiders to enter the group, but a formula of inclusion by which all those already present—not just the poor—were made to constitute a company. We may date it just after the destruction of the Temple, and understand it as an inclusionary formula adopted as a replacement of the one which would have been said were the cult still a living reality. Thus, just as before, those present were invited to consider themselves a legal company. Though there was no *pesach* any more, there was *matsah,* and *matsah* was the equivalent of the *pesach.* So the leader began the passage with a reference to the *matsah,* perhaps holding it aloft. Since the whole point of the seder was a recollection of the Egyptian deliverance, both in itself and in its role of paradigmatic salvation for the future, the term for *matsah* used in the relevant biblical narrative, *lechem oni* ("bread of affliction"), was employed. The meal was still held first, and our formula was placed at that juncture where the *pesach* would have been eaten, but not before *Kiddush,* since no new guests were being invited. Those who were already present were simply being asked to formulate themselves as a company in the presence of *matsah,* the surrogate for the *pesach.* And since, moreover, this was a formula, not a prayer per se, it was spoken in the vernacular, Aramaic.

The absence of early texts does not enable us to say for sure which of the several lines in our prayer were there from the beginning. However, there is no reason to doubt that, aside from the reference to a return from exile, which is an obvious later expansion of the theme, the passage was not much different than it is today. We have (1) a reference (in the Yemenite rite, and going back at least as far as Maimonides) to the deliverance of old;[60] (2) a reference to the *lechem oni* which our ancestors ate; (3) an invitation to constitute a company, with an explicit mention of the *pesach;* and (4) a prayer for deliverance anew. In this collection of interdependent lines, whatever their original order, we have all the links in the new symbolism: recollection of the old deliverance and anticipation of the new; the *pesach* as the original symbol of salvation, and its novel surrogate, *matsah.*

Thus, *matsah* was used as a salvational symbol. It was held aloft as the seder began, precisely at that point where the lamb had been brought; and around it participants were constituted as a legal company, just as would have been required for a paschal lamb. Just as a piece of *matsah* here took the place of the lamb, so, elsewhere, it was selected to replace the *pesach* in the fashioning of the Hillel "sandwich." And when the ritual concluded, it was *matsah* in place of the paschal offering that was eaten last.

That *matsah* took the place of the *pesach* and was surrounded by legalities hitherto applicable only to that offering is, I think, easily established by the evidence I have put forward. But I have argued further that the choice of *matsah* rather than some other item on the seder plate was not a haphazard event. It followed from the fact that bread was already a salvational symbol in the common imagination. The use of bread as a symbol in both the Lord's Supper and in the early seder should be seen as two sides of the same coin. Jesus spoke directly to the Jewish context of his listeners. What else should symbolize the body of the new Lamb if not bread?

Moreover, I think we err in over-rationalizing the symbolic suggestions of *matsah* in those formative years. Scholarship has been too willing to paint a picture of a normative Jewish community that was spiritually stultified, congenitally unable to appreciate the religious moment. This would be a Jewish community that did not take the promise of deliverance seriously. That may indeed be the problem of secularized twentieth-century Americans, but it surely was not a difficulty for the tannaim. The Mishnah is full of rituals which make no sense at all if we assume Jews approached their religious life with serene philosophical detachment. Only the contrary assumption, that Jews believed the Temple cult operated with necessary cosmic implications, can explain such matters as the intense preoccupation with the proper order of cultic minutiae,[61] the preparation of the High Priest on Yom Kippur,[62] and the care taken by him to say only a short prayer in the Holy of Holies, "lest he terrify Israel."[63] It is similarly difficult to attach only metaphorical importance to such matters as criteria governing the choice of a precentor for the fast day prayers,[64] the activity of Honi Ham'agel,[65] and rituals like the red heifer and the *eglah arufah*.[66] So, with the *matsah,* there seems no reason to deny that its redemptive symbolism was experienced immediately and deeply by those present.

We should see *ha lachma anya,* "Behold the bread of affliction," as an obvious Jewish parallel to the institution of the Lord's Supper. If Christians could hold up the bread of redemption that was the body of Christ, their own paschal lamb, why should it be so hard to picture Jews doing the same thing with the bread that was simultaneously their own *pesach* and declaring *kol dikhfin yeitei v'yeikhul; kol ditsrikh yeitei v'yifsach:* that is, "Let all who hunger come and eat; all who are in need [of salvation] come and offer a *pesach*"? Perhaps their very action of constituting a sacrificial company would hasten the day of deliverance. As Rabbi Joshua himself said of Passover eve, "On that night they were redeemed, and on that night they will be redeemed in the future."[67]

So the seder, from its very inception, was imbued with the

hope of imminent deliverance. *Matsah* as a surrogate for the *pesach* recalled the past and pointed to the future. Eventually its salvational symbolism lost its immediacy, while other symbols were adopted in its place. What has been demonstrated here with regard to *matsah* could be shown to be the case in later ages with such novel rituals as opening the door for Elijah, concluding the seder with "Next year in Jerusalem," reciting *piyyutim* which glorify the historic role of *leil shimurim,* "the night of watching," and even reviving the fifth cup and associating it with Elijah. But the first such symbol of salvation was *matsah,* and it set the salvational tone of the seder for generations to come.

NOTES

This essay was published originally as "A Symbol of Salvation in the Passover Haggadah," *Worship* 53, no. 6 (1979): 519–37.

1. *Shibbolei Haleket,* ed. Solomon Buber (1887; reprint ed., Jerusalem, 1962), p. 188.

2. *Tur,* O. H., #472, 477, 478.

3. *Sha'arei T'shuvah,* ed. W. Leiter (New York, 1946), #222.

4. *T'shuvot Hageonim,* ed. S. Assaf (Jerusalem, 1942), #37.

5. The Ashkenazim continued to see the Haggadah as salvational, but by their time the symbolism was different. Their interest became *leil shimurim,* the cup of Elijah, and an imminent return from exile. Cf. *Rokeach, Hilkhot Pesach,* #291; and references by Eugene Mihaly, "The Passover Haggadah as PaRaDiSe," *CCAR Journal* 13, no. 5 (April 1960): 26–27, n. 118. For evidence of this preponderant concern from the fourteenth to the sixteenth centuries, see especially the art of the medieval illuminated manuscripts. Cf. Joseph Gutmann, "The Illuminated Medieval Passover Haggadah: Investigations and Research Problems," *Studies in Bibliography and Booklore* 7 (1965): 3–26; Mendel Metzger, *La Haggada Enluminée* (Leiden, 1973).

6. *Mekhilta,* ed. Horowitz (Jerusalem, 1960), *Bo,* p. 64. "The first night it is obligatory; the rest of the days it is a matter of choice."

7. M. Pes. 10:1. The source here does not explicitly state that *matsah* was the object of the prohibition, but we may assume that to be

the case, since if ordinary leavened food were the issue, the law would have stated the point at which eating must cease, not when it might commence.

8. P. Pes. 10:1.

9. Though not all these laws are specified in tannaitic texts, they are all assumed by the amoraim and by authorities thereafter. As such, they have become an integral part of the codes and of our seder today. The Mishnah's failure to stipulate them is due in part to the fact that much of this symbolic development occurred on a popular level and was not immediately stamped with authoritative approval. But no amora ever questions the validity of these customs, and statements of them go unchallenged just as if they were based on official recensions of tannaitic law.

10. Cf. Mihaly, "The Passover Haggadah," p. 26; and Solomon Zeitlin, "The Liturgy of the First Night of Passover," *JQR,* n.s., 38 (1947 / 1948): 456. Both authors discuss this salvational symbolism, but Zeitlin understands it as referring specifically to physical deliverance, while Mihaly calls *matsah* "the food of inner spiritual liberation."

11. M. Pes. 10:8.

12. Pes. 119b; P. Pes. 10:4, 6.

13. Pes. 119b; P. Pes. 10:4. The Yerushalmi cites this as an explanatory note to the answer given the foolish son. The *Mekhilta* lacks it. Cf. *Mekhilta,* ed. Horowitz, *Bo,* p. 73.

14. Pes. 119b. Bahr thinks it means simply dessert, but does not account for other interpretations in rabbinic literature. See "The Seder of Passover and the Eucharistic Words," *Novum Testamentum* 12 (1970).

15. P. Pes. 10:6.

16. See, for example, Ben Yehudah, *Thesaurus* 1:348, n. 5.

17. M. Pes. 10:7, 8.

18. T. Pes. 10:11.

19. P. Pes. 10:6.

20. S. Stein, "The Influence of Symposia Literature on the Literary Form of the Pesach Haggadah," *JJS* 8 (1957): 21.

21. 1 Cor. 11:20, 27.

22. Perhaps *epi komon.* See Ben Yehudah, *Thesaurus* 1:348. Daube (*He That Cometh* [London, 1966]) takes issue with this etymology and suggests instead *afikomenos* = "the coming one," a messianic symbol (p. 14). The alternative, *epi komon,* meaning "off to a crawl," he argues, is absurd (p. 8). But on purely etymological grounds neither is

preferable, and *epi komon* need not mean simply "off to a crawl." Daube prefers *afikomenos* because, primarily, the *matsah* as *afikoman* is *tsafun* = hidden away, and this implies the doctrine of a hidden messiah whom we await. I prefer translating *afikoman* as after-dinner carousing since (a) this accounts for *all* the Talmudic interpretations: music, dessert, and going from house to house; (b) such carousing is documented in Jewish, Christian, and pagan sources of the time; (c) it need not imply that the *ein maftirin* phrase of the Mishnah is an "arcane pronouncement" intended for the wise, as Daube would have it (p. 9); this is a doubtful hypothesis, since the parallel text in the Palestinian Talmud utilizes this as an answer to the simple, not the wise! and (d) it allows an interpretation of the *afikoman* before the time when the word became equivalent to a piece of *matsah*, whereas emphasizing *tsafun* ("hidden away") does not.

23. Pes. 119b / 120a.

24. T. Pes. 5:2, 13.

25. M. Pes. 8:7; T. Pes. 7:6. Cf. P. Pes. 5:3 where, regarding the *pesach*, the Mishnah's phrase, *shelo l'okhlav*, is interpreted as *she'einan y'kholin le'ekhol k'zayit.*

26. T. Pes. 5:3.

27. See notes 1–4 above.

28. P. Pes. 8:1; P. Kid. 1:7.

29. T. Pes. 1:32. The Tosefta already equated *afikoman* with *matsah*, not revelry. The amoraic search for an interpretation of *ein maftirin . . . afikoman* is no evidence that they did not know of a final piece of *matsah* as *afikoman*. Their concern was not the final piece of *matsah* which they took for granted, but the original intent of the mishnaic ordinance, which might have carried additional consequence for them. In fact, that so many of them interpret the clause as a prohibition against additional eating is a clear indication that by their time *afikoman* was *matsah*, something one ate.

30. 1 Cor. 11: 23–26.

31. There is no need here to enter extensively into the perennial complex of questions regarding the relationship of Mark 14 to 1 Corinthians 11; the debate as to whether or not the Last Supper was originally a seder; the stage of development of the theological identification of Jesus as the Lamb of God, and so on. For our purposes it is enough to note that, in his letter to the Corinthians, Paul neither specifies a seder nor uses the word for *matsah*. On the other hand, in 1 Corinthians 5:7, Christ is already called "our Passover, sacrificed for us," and verse 8 specifically connects the feast with the ideas of

'unleaven'ment. So the salvational link between Jesus' body and the
pesach is present in Paul, as is the prior connection between Jesus'
body and bread, though the specification of a seder and the notion
that Jesus would have used *matsah* may or may not have been so
early. The scholarship on the question is vast, but see the bibliography in the International Dictionary of the Bible, s.v. "Lamb," "Last
Supper," and "Lord's Supper," and especially, Joachim Jeremias, *The
Eucharistic Words of Jesus* (New York, 1966). The view that Jesus is
the *pesach* reaches its zenith in John, where the date of the crucifixion is given as the 14th of Nisan, the date when the *pesach* would
have been offered. From then on, the church fathers seem to assume
Jesus' death to be functionally equivalent to the Passover sacrifice.
See, for example, Justin Martyr, *Apology 1,* 66:3, cited in Zeitlin,
"The Liturgy of the First Night of Passover," p. 446. "For the Pascha
was Christ afterward sacrificed. . . . As the blood of the Passover
saved us who were in Egypt, so also the blood of Christ will deliver
those who have believed from death."

32. Though the symbol of wine is technically outside the scope
of this paper, mention should be made of its role in the symbolic
system. Rabbi Tarfon's fifth cup may have already been viewed as a
reference to future redemption, and a parallel redemptive role can
be seen in the wine mentioned in the Lord's Supper narrative (1 Cor.
11:25; Mark 14:24). The New Testament's connection between wine
and blood is echoed by the Yerushalmi's statement that *charoset,*
made with wine, is *zecher ledam* (P. Pes. 10:3), and even by the Bible,
where wine is *dam anavim* (Gen. 49:11). Cf. Zeitlin, "The Liturgy of
the First Night of Passover," pp. 437–38, where this aspect of *charoset*
is discussed. Note, too, that it was the blood of the paschal lamb,
smeared on the doorposts, that saved, and the blood of Christ that
marks the new salvation for Christians. Even the instruction, "Do
this in remembrance of me" (1 Cor. 11:24), may have a parallel in the
usual phrase from the *kiddush, zekher litzi'at mitzrayim* ("in remembrance of the Exodus from Egypt"), the latter pointing to the paradigmatic redemptive event for Jews, the former to that for Christians.
A study of the rabbinic use of the word *zekher,* as in the halakhic
technical term *zekher ladavar,* certainly indicates a symbolic "pointing towards" rather than mere remembrance. For a perspective linking Jesus' words with Hillel's practice, see Jakob Petuchowski, "Do
This In Remembrance of Me," *JBL* 76 (1957): 293–98.

33. Pes. 120a. The biblical verse is Num. 9:11.

34. Mihaly, "The Passover Haggadah," pp. 26–27.

35. B. R. 15:7.

36. B. R. 15:7, Ber. 38a / b.

37. Matt. 6:11; Luke 11:3.

38. See David de Sola Pool, *The Kaddish* (New York, 1929), appendix D, pp. 111–12.

39. *Didache,* chap 8.

40. Jerome, *Commentary on Matthew* 6:11.

41. Ambrose, *Sacraments* 4:5.

42. The *rishonim,* trying to harmonize a variety of legal considerations culled from both Babylonian and Palestinian tradition, invented several options in the utilization of *matsah.* See the lengthy discussion in the *Tur,* O. H., #475 / 476. But these variations in no way prevent our reconstruction of earlier practice, which emerges as being basically identical to our custom today.

43. Cf. responsa by Moses Gaon in *Otsar Hageonim,* ed. B. M. Lewin (Pes. #340; Natronai Gaon in *Sha'arei T'shuvah,* ed. W. Leiter, #280; and Amram Gaon in *Seder Rav Amram,* ed. Daniel Goldschmidt (Jerusalem, 1971), p. 116. See also an attempt to justify the Babylonia custom vis-à-vis the Palestinian counterpart in *Otsar Hageonim,* Pes. #326. They insisted on following Rav Papa's precedent (Ber. 39a) of saying the *motsi* with both *p'rusah* and *sh'lemah* in hand, though the *p'rusah* was referred to the second benediction, so nothing was eaten until after both blessings had been recited. Cf. Louis Ginzberg, *Geonica* (New York, 1909), 2:179, and references there, especially, *Shaarei Simchah,* ed. Bamberger (Furth, 1961), 2:103.

44. Cf. *Otsar Chilluf Minhagim bein Anshei Mizrach uv'nei Erets Yisrael,* ed. B. M. Lewin (Jerusalem, 1942), #21; *Haggadah Sh'lemah,* ed. M. Kasher (Jerusalem, 1961), pp. 61–62.

45. Num. 9:11.

46. T. Pes. 2:14.

47. The geonim do not seem to have specified this use for the third *matsah* yet. Sherira, the only gaon who devotes some space to what he does with it, says that he reserves it for *birkat hamazon* (the after-dinner Grace) because of the Talmudic adage (San. 92a), "One who leaves no bread on his table will never see a sign of blessing." So he, like his predecessors, used the same *matsah* both for the majority practice and for Hillel's *korekh.* Sherira's explanation is part of his justification of the Babylonian usage of the *matsot,* in the face

of Kairuwan Jewry's recognition that Palestinian Jewry used only two. Alfasi, coming from a similar North African environment, later ruled with the Palestinians that two were sufficient.

48. Daniel Goldschmidt, *Haggadah Shel Pesach V'toldoteha* (Jerusalem, 1960), pp. 7–9.

49. Cf. Leopold Zunz, *Had'rashot B'yisrael*, 1892, trans. Chanoch Albeck (Jerusalem, 1947), p. 61; *The Passover Haggadah*, ed. N. Glatzer (New York, 1953), p. 20.

50. Tann. 20b. The next source, chronologically, is a geonic responsum of the ninth century, which, however, described the prayer as ancient, *minhag avot.* (*Otsar Hageonim*, ed. Lewin, Pes. #304).

51. Stein, "The Influence of Symposia Literature," p. 30.

52. Stein, ibid., p. 31, for example, assuming that the prayer was an invitation to the poor, is led to celebrate "the popular element (within Judaism) represented by the wide opening of doors, as expressed in the *kol dikhfin.* . . . " But he himself says that the Greco-Roman banquets from which the seder evolved knew no such invitation to the masses. The hypothesis that the Jewish equivalent, the seder, adopted such a democratic character, is pure speculation.

53. Goldschmidt is aware of this unofficial origin, and labels the passage "the custom of the people, not a legal decision of the sages." See Goldschmidt, *Haggadah Shel Pesach V'toldoteha*, p. 9.

54. Israel Abrahams, "Some Egyptian Fragments of the Passover Haggada," *JQR* 10 (1898): 44, 50. The evidence from other fragments is not unanimous, but this is to be expected, since our passage was at most an unofficial option. Thus, fragment ten (p. 49), though not complete, seems as it stands to lack *ha lachma anya*, as does the fragment published by Goldschmidt, *Haggadah Shel Pesach V'toldoteha*, p. 77. The other fragments do not begin until midway through the Haggadah, and thus offer no evidence either way.

55. The *K'dushah* and the problem of *payyetanic* insertions in the *t'fillah* are cases in point. Cf. Louis Ginzberg, *Ginze Schechter* (New York, 1923), 2:552–55, and *Otsar Hageonim*, ed. Lewin, Ber. #169.

56. See discussion by Goldschmidt, *Haggadah Shel Pesach V'toldoteha*, pp. 8–9.

57. Josephus, *Ant.* 3:10; *Mekhilta*, ed. Horowitz, *Bo*, p. 254.

58. T. Pes. 5:2.

59. M. Pes. 1:9, 10.

60. Cf. Goldschmidt, *Haggadah Shel Pesach V'toldoteha*, p. 8; Kasher, *Haggadah Sh'lemah*, introduction, p. 106, and Haggadah text, p. 4.

61. M. Yoma 5:7. "If the actions were performed out of order, it is as if nothing had been done at all."

62. M. Yoma, chap. 1.

63. M. Yoma, 5:1.

64. M. Taan. 2:2.

65. M. Taan. 3:8.

66. M. Parah, chap. 3; M. Sotah, chap. 9

67. *Mekhilta,* ed. Horowitz, *Bo,* p. 52.

Haggadah Art

Joseph Gutmann

Three distinct traditions of Haggadah illumination had developed by the early fourteenth century in Latin Europe: the Sefardi (Spain and Southern France), the Ashkenazi (Germany, Northern France, and Northern Italy), and the Italian. Before the fourteenth century only stylized symbolic sketches of the *maror* leaf and *matsah* are encountered, in eleventh- to twelfth-century manuscript pages from the Cairo Genizah. As a rule, Haggadahs produced in Islamic countries were not illustrated.

The Haggadah as an independent illustrated book may have been stimulated by the contemporary emergence of private Latin liturgical books such as the Psalter and Breviary. By the thirteenth century monasteries no longer had a monopoly on book production. The social and economic growth of town life in Europe, the rise of universities, and the emergence of a new burgher class spurred an increasing demand for private Christian illuminated books, a demand met by lay artists in the newly established craft guilds. The Haggadah, along with the Bible and Machzor, became for Jews in contemporary Europe a favorite text for illustration.

The Haggadah illustrations form a visual accompaniment to the recitation of the Passover seder liturgy. The picture cycle is in some sense a sacred repetition, a visual reenactment, of the Jewish communal past, present, and future. The Haggadah, in most periods, was not intended for the synagogue but for the assembled family participating in the seder. The medieval Haggadah was often commissioned by wealthy individuals and made for their private use. Often the Haggadah manuscripts shared the fate of their Jewish owners, wandering from land to land, frequently far removed from their place of origin. They became the property of private Judaica collectors and at times were acquired by Christian monasteries and private Christian collections. Today, many outstanding Haggadah manuscripts are found in great Judaica collections like the British Library in London, the Bodleian Library in Oxford, and the Biblioteca Palatina in Parma, Italy.

For the most part, the extant Haggadah manuscripts were decorated by Christians, as the craft guilds were generally closed to Jews, who, with few exceptions, were unable to obtain the requisite artistic training. Thus it is not surprising that the format of the Haggadah is similar to that of Christian service books and that their decorations follow the Christian artistic conventions of the late Romanesque, Gothic, and Renaissance styles. Distinctly Christian motifs such as halos, female angels, and hands bestowing the Christian benediction also appear. The very Hebrew script itself at times takes on the contours of the Gothic and Renaissance scripts. In spite of the brutal persecutions of Jews, the illustrations unmistakably spell out the intimate bond between Jewish and Christian societies in Europe, and reveal the strong impress of the Christian milieu.

Over fifty fourteenth- and fifteenth-century illustrated Haggadah manuscripts are extant. Many of the Spanish and Ashkenazi Haggadah manuscripts have appeared in facsimile editions.[1] In addition, a catalogue raisonné of Spanish Haggadah manuscripts in the British Library and a catalogue raisonné of most liturgical and biblical images have been published,[2] but in this article, I have avoided using names assigned to Haggadah manuscripts in the British Library catalogue and in recent publications. Such labels as "Sister of the Golden Haggadah," "Brother" to the Rylands Spanish Haggadah, and "Dragon Haggadah" are largely misleading and somewhat arbitrary.[3] Despite these extensive publications, many research problems remain, as very few Haggadah manuscripts are dated. In order conclusively to determine the artist, the locale, and the date of the miniatures in Haggadah manuscripts, it is necessary to examine contemporary Christian manuscript illuminations.

Other vital questions, too, await satisfactory solutions. We are not altogether sure, for instance, even of when, where, and why the illustrated Haggadah first emerged in Christian Western Europe, and how the production of Christian private books influenced the appearance of private Jewish ones.

As a summary statement of what we do know and what we do not, I will isolate several major issues that have exercised researchers since the study of illustrated manuscripts began.

1. *Were the medieval Haggadah miniatures dependent on ancient, but now lost Jewish manuscripts?*

This issue has been much debated in recent years. Some scholars have claimed that medieval Haggadah illustrations may be based on now lost illustrated Jewish manuscripts from Greco-Roman antiquity. This attractive theory was tenaciously advocated by the late Kurt Weitzmann and his disciples, but the possibility that illustrated Septuagint scrolls and/or illustrated Josephus manuscripts existed and were employed as models by Jews and later by Christians is, at the present state of our knowledge, no more than an *argumentum ex silentio,* with little actual evidence to substantiate it. We have yet to find an ancient Greco-Roman manuscript that contains a full cycle of illustrations to accompany a literary text. Ancient textual sources make no mention of extensive illustrated classical texts. While it is true that illustrated Christian manuscripts served as significant sources of inspiration for medieval church cycles, whether executed in stone, mosaic, or paint, nothing parallel is known in Greco-Roman antiquity.

Books, it must be pointed out, played a different role in the Jewish and Christian traditions from what had obtained in the Greco-Roman world. No Greco-Roman book, to the best of my knowledge, was ever canonized or considered a divinely inspired spiritual vehicle. Thus no book similar to the canonized Bible of the Jewish and Christian worlds ever emerged. The book in the Greco-Roman civilization was primarily a utilitarian object, not a conveyor of holy words. Since it served a practical purpose, writing and/or reading the book was not considered an act of religious merit and could be assigned to slaves and others of low status. Rhetoric, not reading or writing, was praised as the preferred mode of communication for people of high status. Fresco painting rather than manuscript illustration was very popular in the Greco-Roman period, as is certainly evident in the amazing painting cycle which appears in the Dura-Europos synagogue. To argue, however, that the depictions are based on lost manuscript illustrations by drawing superficial comparisons with medieval depictions has not proven convincing.

Let me cite one instance of an assumed relationship between the Dura synagogue and medieval Haggadah manuscript illustration. In the Dura synagogue scene as well as in Spanish Haggadah manuscripts, a nude female figure is depicted standing in a river. In both cases, the illustrations refer to Moses' rescue from the Nile river by the Egyptian princess. Close examination of the Dura scene and the Spanish Haggadah illustrations quickly dissolves the apparent similarity. In the third-century Dura synagogue, the princess is holding the child Moses and appears to be passing the child to Miriam and Jochebed. In the Spanish Haggadah manuscripts of the fourteenth century, no baby is being handed to another figure and usually three nude female figures are in the water. Aside from the fact that these illustrations are separated in time by over a thousand years, we find that they are based on different literary traditions. The Dura scene appears to illustrate the Targum rendering of the story, which recounts that the princess, suffering from leprosy, was divinely persuaded to bathe in the Nile. She was miraculously cured of her affliction when she touched the basket containing Moses.

The medieval depictions bear little resemblance to the Dura scene, but are closely modeled on earlier Spanish Christian illustrations. Although the Christian artistic models are on hand, I have been unable to find Christian or Jewish medieval literary sources to explain the renderings. What is clear, however, is that the medieval Haggadah scenes are based on Christian models and in fact have little in common with the Dura synagogue painting. On the basis of this scene and others, no convincing claim of an unbroken artistic tradition can be established that would not only link the Jewish and Christian depictions to the Dura synagogue, but prove the existence of ancient Jewish manuscripts that served as vehicles of transmission. Most likely the artists at Dura and in other Greco-Roman places worked from pictorial guides and not from manuscript illustrations.[4]

2. What are some remaining problems of those Haggadah manuscripts that are already researched?

The earliest extant Ashkenazi Haggadah appears to be the Bird's Head Haggadah, probably made in the Rhineland region around 1300. The scribe was Menachem, but the artist is unknown. The illustrations are for the most part located in the margins—a practice found in earlier Greek manuscripts and one that will continue in later Ashkenazi Haggadahs. The illustrations can roughly be arranged in three groups: (1) those that deal with historical events centering on the Exodus from Egypt; (2) those which depict ceremonial scenes such as the preparations for the Passover celebration, the baking of *matsah,* the washing of hands, the consumption of the symbolic foods, and the *Kiddush* blessings and drinking of the wine; and (3) a few illustrations that have eschatological significance. There are anomalies, however. Depictions common in later Ashkenazi Haggadah manuscripts such as the rescue of Moses and the Ten Plagues are absent. Some scenes are very unusual, such as carrying the dough during the Exodus, and Moses handing the Israelites five tablets (alluding perhaps to the five books of Moses) instead of the customary two tablets of the Commandments. Whether some illustrations reveal indirect influence by Byzantine models, or whether these Byzantine elements had already been absorbed in Latin manuscripts and thus entered our Haggadah directly from these Latin sources, deserves investigation.

This Haggadah also contains such eschatological scenes as the "Entry of the Righteous into Paradise." Three bearded men are led by an angel through a gate, probably illustrating the verse, "This is the gate of the Lord, the righteous may enter it" (Psalm 118:20). Another scene shows a Gothic building labeled Jerusalem with a figure standing within it and others pointing to it. The meaning of this depiction is not certain, but it may allude to the New Jerusalem or the Heavenly Jerusalem.[5]

Our Haggadah is one of many manuscripts made in Germany between 1250 and 1350 which feature people with the faces of animals or birds. These zoocephalic figures have yet to be satisfactorily explained. We note that Christian manuscripts show the four evangelists with human bodies and the heads of their respective symbolic animals. The meaning of these figures in Hebrew manuscripts is not clear, and the theories offered to date are not convincing. To what extent legal proscription or fear of the image, imitation of Christian practices, or Jewish caricature and self-deprecation are involved, or whether the practice is rooted in mystical Judeo-German pietism or a combination of the above, is worthy of in-depth investigation.[6]

The Darmstadt Passover Haggadah, one of the best known German manuscripts, has been reproduced twice in facsimile editions. It is a unique Haggadah manuscript in that its miniatures reveal few iconographic parallels to other extant pictorial cycles found in both earlier and later Haggadah manuscripts from medieval Germany. We look in vain for scenes depicting the preparations for the seder, the symbolic foods, or the baking of the *matsah;* not even an illustration as common as the four sons—the wise son, the wicked son, the simple son, and the son unable to ask—appears next to the Hebrew words describing the sons.[7] The Exodus from Egypt and the building of the store-cities Pithom and Raamses are also absent. Were it not for the fine Hebrew script, we would be hard put to identify this manuscript as distinctly Jewish. A full-page illustration surrounding the text beginning with the words "pour out Your wrath" from Psalm 79:6 is shown.

Many German Haggadah manuscripts customarily depict the arrival of Elijah and/or the Messiah, but in the Darmstadt Haggadah we find a puzzling seder scene with nine men, only one of whom wears a pointed Jew's hat. The books on the table are closed. Flanking the seder in a rib-vaulted architectural setting are women, each with an open book on her lap. The many interpretations given this and such other scenes as the Fountain of Youth and the Stag Hunt are not persuasive. All we know is that the Haggadah was written by Israel ben Meir of Heidelberg; its miniatures were probably made in an Upper Rhenish Christian workshop during the second quarter of the fifteenth century. In 1391 Jews were driven from Heidelberg, and the Haggadah text may have fallen into Christian hands. It is apparent that the illuminator had little or no knowledge of the Hebrew text and was unacquainted with any tradition of Haggadah illustration. Thus the Darmstadt Haggadah remains a fascinating and enigmatic manuscript.[8]

The Erna Michael Haggadah in the Israel Museum is paleographically related to the Darmstadt Haggadah. Like several other Ashkenazi Haggadah manuscripts of the fifteenth century, it is large in format. Its text dates from early fifteenth-century Germany, but I agree with the Metzgers that the "illuminations were either painted or heavily repainted in the nineteenth century in a medieval style which is rather vague where architecture, figures and costume are concerned."[9]

The Washington Haggadah is probably a German manuscript made around 1478 and linked with Joel ben Simeon, a Jewish scribe-artist who may have been born in Germany and who settled in northern Italy. He may have had a workshop where over fifteen manuscripts were produced during the second half of the fifteenth century. Joel is extremely important. We know the names of many centers of medieval Christian manuscript production and are familiar with the names of many medieval Jewish scribes, but we have little information about centers of Hebrew manuscript production. Many medieval Jewish scribes are known to have sometimes traveled. Of Jewish artist-scribes, however, we have scant and disputable information. Only the enigmatic Joel ben Simeon stands out. Yet we cannot completely account for the many variations in the signatures of his manuscripts. Sometimes Joel refers to himself as a scribe (*sofer*), at other times as a copyist (*lavlar*) or an artist (*zayyar*). We cannot fully explain why some manuscripts obviously not written by Joel or his workshop still contain colored pen drawings that seem either to belong to his workshop or to have been influenced by his manuscripts. The different artistic styles and models used in some of his signed manuscripts have not been completely identified.[10]

Several Haggadahs of the second half of the fifteenth century are not sumptuous codices like the Darmstadt Haggadah or Spanish Haggadah manuscripts. They contain many colored marginal illustrations that reveal an unpretentious, lively folk character and humor. These unusual illustrations have yet to be compared with the religious and secular manuscripts made for the Christian burgher class. The folk humor and naive literalness reflect a practice common in contemporary Christian manuscripts. The rhymed verses that accompany the Haggadah illustrations follow a fashion also current in contemporary Christian manuscripts. Furthermore, the wine-spattered Ashkenazi Haggadahs with their unsophisticated folk drawings testify that they, like their contemporary Christian counterparts, were not intended for display so much as to be read and used.[11]

To give some examples: At the point in the seder when the display of bitter herbs is called for, we sometimes find a man humorously pointing to his wife, in allusion to the verse in Ecclesiastes 7:26 that a bad woman "is more bitter than death." To accompany the words in the Passover Haggadah, "you open [the conversation] for him" in reference to the fourth child who is unable to ask the prescribed questions, we find at times a literal representation of an adult who pries open the incompetent son's mouth with his hands. Next to the text, "in every generation one must look upon himself as if he personally had come forth from Egypt," artists in these Ashkenazi Haggadahs of the fifteenth century sometimes literally depicted a man "looking at himself" in a mirror.[12]

Many of the surviving Spanish Haggadah manuscripts come from fourteenth-century Catalonia. One of the early extant Catalonian manuscripts from the first quarter of the fourteenth century is the so-called Golden Haggadah. It has fourteen full-page, framed illustrations, divided into four panels. Like most Spanish Haggadahs (as opposed to the Ashkenazi ones, where the illustrations embellish the words and appear side by side with them), the illustrations precede the text proper and are largely unrelated to it, and include or even feature a cycle of biblical scenes. This practice is similar to what we find in contemporary Latin Psalters. The Golden Haggadah especially, with its splendid Gothic illuminations, reflects the circumstance that Spanish Jewish aristocrats had access to Christian courtly circles and imitated a Christian practice of having private liturgical books beautifully illuminated. The Golden Haggadah contains biblical illustrations from Genesis and Exodus, while most other Spanish Haggadahs are confined to Exodus scenes. The biblical scenes also have Jewish legendary depictions, such as Abraham in the fiery furnace, Joseph being shown the way to Dothan by an angel, and the Israelites coming out of Egypt with hands raised. Among the ritual scenes found in the Haggadah text are the customary large green leaf, the *maror,* and a large, decorative, geometric roundel symbolizing the *matsah.*[13]

The best known illustrated Spanish Haggadah is the Sarajevo Haggadah. Made in the third quarter of the fourteenth century in Catalonia, it has been reproduced in facsimile editions three times—the earliest in 1898. Its sixty-nine miniatures prefacing the text range over the entire Pentateuch from Creation to the death of Moses. Most unusual in this Haggadah is the fact that a Jew is shown resting on the Sabbath, whereas in Christian art it is God who rests on the seventh day of Creation. Also the faces of the angels are covered by their wings. Although these miniatures have been researched, there are still many aspects of their iconography that demand investigation.[14]

The earliest Italian-rite Haggadah has recently been identified and dated to the first quarter of the fourteenth century. Its stylized figures are intermingled with dragons and grotesqueries. Its marginal illustrations reveal both ritual and biblical scenes.[15]

Another late-fourteenth-century Haggadah from Lombardy has recently been analyzed. The theory that the producer of the so-called Schocken Haggadah had access to Spanish Haggadah manuscripts is not entirely convincing. The Binding of Isaac scene, for instance, is based on well-known Italian Christian models and bears little resemblance to Spanish Haggadah illustrations.[16]

3. Are unique Jewish customs depicted in Haggadah manuscripts?

In Spain we find a number of distinctly Spanish-Jewish customs depicted. A fourteenth-century Spanish miniature[17] reveals a Passover seder at which the paterfamilias places a cloth-covered basket (sal) containing symbolic foods like matsah on the head of the child seated next to him as Ha lachma anya ("This is the bread of affliction . . . ") is recited. The basket is placed successively on the head of each person at the table. One of the many explanations given is that it is a symbolic reminder of the Exodus from Egypt where, in their haste to leave, the Israelites "took their dough before it was leavened, their kneading bowls wrapped in their cloaks upon their shoulder" (Exod. 12:34).[18]

We also find an illustration of the Spanish custom of public distribution of the matsah and charoset. One miniature shows the Haggadah being recited in the synagogue—a practice intended for the benefit of those who were unable to read the text.[19] It may also be that the large number of piyyutim (additional poetry) included in the surviving Spanish Haggadahs were intended to be read in the synagogue. Unique, too, in Spanish Haggadah manuscripts is the depiction of a winged angel or simply a hand pouring a cup full of blood on the assembled group below. This scene is next to Sh'fokh ("Pour out your wrath . . . "), and Spanish commentators explain that God will pour out four cups of wrath over idolators.[20]

In fifteenth-century Ashkenazi manuscripts it became customary to depict the arrival of the messianic guest. Sometimes the head of the household is seen opening the door as Sh'fokh is recited, and holding the prescribed cup of wine. He greets the messianic visitor—a bearded old man seated on a richly adorned ass, while several people, perhaps symbolic of the household of Israel, are shown riding with the Messiah to redemption in the land of Israel. These images may, in part, serve as a theological response to the Christian Palm Sunday practice of having Christ, the messianic redeemer, seated on his *Palmesel,* the messianic ass. These life-size Christ figures were wheeled on carts in liturgical procession through the town roads to the church interior—an evocation of Christ's triumphal entry into Jerusalem. The Ashkenazi images were perhaps meant to deny the Christian messianic claim that the Messiah had already appeared and to emphasize the Jewish belief that the Messiah has not yet come.[21]

Frequently, Ashkenazi Haggadahs have illustrations of the head of the house, who holds a cup in his left hand, curving the fingers of his right hand inward toward the palm as he raises this hand toward the flames of the so-called *Judenstern,* an oil-burning, star-shaped Sabbath lamp. These depictions reflect the prevalent Ashkenazi custom of holding the right hand up to the light to look at the fingernails when reciting the blessing over light at the *Havdalah* ceremony, performed Saturday evening at the conclusion of the Sabbath, and intended to mark the separation between Sabbath and weekdays as well as between light and darkness.[22]

In Italian-rite Haggadah manuscripts we find that at *Ha lachma anya* ("This is the bread of affliction . . . ") it was customary for all participants at the seder to raise a basket (*k'arah*),[23] which contained those symbolic foods still common today (like *matsah* and *maror*), but also some we no longer use which were staples long ago: meat, fish, and an egg, standing for mythic messianic monsters. The egg was symbolic of Ziz (a bird), the meat was symbolic of Behemoth (a beast of the fields), and the fish stood for Leviathan. These three messianic beasts had been stored away for the righteous in the world to come. On the night of Redemption, when Jewry anxiously awaited the ushering-in of the messianic age, how appropriate that these symbols in the seder basket should have reminded all present of the delights of the messianic banquet they would enjoy in the world to come.[24]

The height of Haggadah manuscript illustrations occurred in fourteenth- and fifteenth-century Europe. With the inven-

tion of the printing press, however, printed editions with illustrations gradually began to appear from the sixteenth century
on, and the illustrated manuscript began to disappear. It was
only in the eighteenth century in central Europe that Court
Jews and other wealthy Jews again commissioned illustrated
Haggadah manuscripts, most of whose creators copied the illustrations in printed Haggadahs.[25]

NOTES

I am grateful to Prof. Stanley F. Chyet for reading this article
and making valuable suggestions for its improvement.

1. Spanish facsimiles: B. Narkiss, *The Golden Haggadah* (Lon-
don, 1970); E. Werber, *The Sarajevo Haggadah* (Beograd, 1985);
R. Loewe, *The Rylands Haggadah* (London, 1988); G. Sed-Rajna, *The
Kaufmann Haggadah* (Budapest, 1990); E. Cohen et al., *The Barce-
lona Haggadah* (London, 1992). Ashkenazi facsimiles: M. Spitzer
et al., *The Bird's Head Haggada* (Jerusalem, 1957); J. Gutmann et al.,
Die Darmstädter Pessach-Haggadah (Berlin, 1972); D. Goldstein, *The
Ashkenazi Haggadah* (New York, 1985); M. M. Weinstein et al.,
The Washington Haggadah (Washington, 1991).

2. B. Narkiss, *Hebrew Illuminated Manuscripts in the British Isles:
A Catalogue Raisonné. The Spanish and Portuguese Manuscripts,* vol.
1 (New York, 1982). See reviews by D. Sperber in *Biblioteca Orientalis*
41 (1984): 158–62, and T. Metzger, *Cahiers de civilisation médiévale* 29
(1986): 393–95. See also M. Metzger, *La Haggada enluminée* (Leiden,
1973), and review by J. Gutmann, *Art Bulletin* 58 (1976): 440–42. Cf.
also J. Gutmann, *Hebrew Manuscript Painting* (New York, 1978);
B. Narkiss, *Hebrew Illuminated Manuscripts* (Jerusalem, 1969); T. and
M. Metzger, *Jewish Life in the Middle Ages* (New York, 1982); J. Gutmann, "The Illuminated Medieval Passover Haggadah: Investigations and Research Problems," *Studies in Bibliography and Booklore*
7 (1965): 3–25.

3. Metzger, *Jewish Life,* p. 299.

4. J. Gutmann, ed., *The Dura-Europos Synagogue: A Re-evaluat-
ion (1932–1992)* (Atlanta, 1992). J. Gutmann, "Josephus' Jewish An-
tiquities in Twelfth-Century Art: Renovatio or Creatio?" in Gutmann, *Sacred Images: Studies in Jewish Art from Antiquity to the
Middle Ages* (Northampton, 1979), IX, pp. 434–41.

5. Spitzer, *Bird's Head Haggadah.*

6. B. Narkiss, "On the Zoocephalic Phenomenon in Medieval Ashkenazi Manuscripts," in L. Sleptzoff et al., eds., *Norms and Variations in Art: Essays in Honor of Moshe Barash* (Jerusalem, 1983), pp. 49–62.

7. M. Friedman, "The Four Sons of the Haggadah and the Ages of Man," *Jewish Art* 11 (1985): 16–40. In Christian art these figures do not appear separately, as in Haggadah manuscripts, but on one page, linked with the ages of man and the temperaments.

8. Gutmann, *Darmstädter Pessach-Haggadah.*

9. Metzger, *Jewish Life,* p. 299. Narkiss, *Hebrew Illuminated Manuscripts,* pp. 116–17.

10. Weinstein, *Washington Haggadah.*

11. B. Narkiss and G. Sed-Rajna, *Index of Jewish Art* (Munich, 1981), 2:1–3—Yahuda Haggadah, The Hileq and Bileq Haggadah, The Second Nuremberg Haggadah. Cf. K. Kogman-Appel, "The Second Nuremberg Haggadah and the Yahudah Haggadah: Are They Made by the Same Artist?" *Eleventh Congress of Jewish Studies,* Division D, vol. 2 (Jerusalem, 1994): 25–32.

12. Gutmann, "Illuminated Medieval Passover Haggadah," p. 18.

13. Narkiss, *Golden Haggadah.* K. Kogman-Appel, "Die Modelle des Exoduszyklus der Goldenen Haggada," in C. Thoma et al., *Judentum—Ausblicke und Einsichten. Festgabe fuer Kurt Schubert zum siebzigsten Geburtstag* (Frankfurt/Main, 1993), pp. 269–300.

14. Werber, *Sarajevo Haggadah.* J. Kogman-Appel, "Der Exoduszyklus der Sarajevo Haggada: Bemerkungen zur Arbeitsweise spaetmittelalterliche juedischer Illuminatoren und ihrem Umgang mit Vorlagen," *Gesta* 35 (1996): 111–27.

15. M. Metzger, "Two Centuries (13th–14th) of Hebrew Manuscript Illumination in Italy," in A. Ebenbauer and K. Zatloukal, eds., *Die Juden in ihrer mittelalterlichen Umwelt* (Vienna, 1990), pp. 131–46. Mendel Metzger is preparing a major study, *The Rite and Iconography of the Haggadah in Italy.*

16. Y. Zirlin, "The Schocken Italian Haggadah of c.1400 and Its Origin," *Jewish Art* 12/13 (1986/87): 55–72.

17. Metzger, *Jewish Life,* p. 262, ill. 378.

18. T. Preschel, "A Strange Seder Custom and Its Origin," in V. D. Sanua, ed., *Fields of Offerings. Studies in Honor of Raphael Patai* (London and Toronto, 1983), pp. xvii–xx (in Hebrew).

19. Gutmann, "Illuminated Medieval Passover Haggadah," p. 18.

20. J. Gutmann, "The Messiah at the Seder: A Fifteenth-Century

Motif in Jewish Art," in Sh. Yeivin, ed., *Studies in Jewish History Presented to Professor Raphael Mahler on His Seventy-Fifth Birthday* (Merhavia, 1974), p. 36.

21. J. Gutmann, "Return in Mercy to Zion: A Messianic Dream in Jewish Art," in Gutmann, *Sacred Images,* XVII, pp. 240–41; and E. Lipsmayer, "Devotion and Decorum: Intention and Quality in Medieval German Scripture," *Gesta* 34 (1995): 20–27.

22. Gutmann, "The Illuminated Medieval Passover Haggadah," p. 18.

23. Metzger, *Jewish Life,* pp. 137, 139.

24. Hamburg Staats- und Universitätsbibliothek, Cod. Hebr. 155, fol. 10, and J. Gutmann, "Leviathan, Behemoth and Ziz: Jewish Messianic Symbols in Art," in Gutmann, *Sacred Images,* XVIII, pp. 219 ff.

25. Y. H. Yerushalmi, *Haggadah and History* (Philadelphia, 1975); H. Friedberg, "The Unwritten Message—Visual Commentary in Twentieth-Century Haggadah Illustration," *Jewish Art* 16/17 (1990/91): 157–71; H. Peled-Carmeli, *Illustrated Haggadot of the Eighteenth Century* (Jerusalem, 1983).

Passiontide Music

Robin A. Leaver

LITURGICAL ORIGINS OF MUSIC FOR HOLY WEEK

The practice of the fourth-century eastern church would seem to confirm an earlier usage in which all the passion narratives (Matt. 26–27; Mark 14–15; Luke 22–23; John 18–19) were read on Good Friday. The Spanish abbess or nun, Egeria (or Etheria), described the observance of Good Friday in Jerusalem. At midday the following meditation began:

> First, whichever Psalms speak of the Passion are read. Next, there are readings from the Apostles . . . wherever they speak of the Passion of the Lord. Next, the texts of the Passion from the Gospels are read. Then there are readings from the prophets, where they said that the Lord would suffer; and then they read from the Gospels where He foretells the Passion. And so, from the sixth to the ninth hour, passages from Scripture are continuously read and hymns are sung, to show the people that whatever the prophets had said would come to pass concerning the Passion of the Lord can be shown . . . to have taken place.[1]

The earliest evidence of the liturgical use of the passion narratives therefore suggests that the context was musical, with the cantillation of the scriptures and the singing of psalms and hymns.

The essentially commemorative nature of the use of the passion narratives in the Good Friday liturgy of the eastern church gave place to more pedagogical concerns in the West. Instead of all being associated with the Good Friday liturgy, the passion narratives were separated from each other by the mid-fifth century and became gospel lections at mass throughout Holy Week. But even separately they were also sung in the West, along with other scripture, psalms,[2] and hymns.

CATHOLIC PASSION MUSIC BEFORE THE NINETEENTH CENTURY[3]

Monophonic Passion

The *Ordines Romani,* the ancient collections of ceremonial directions of the Roman rite that antedate the *Caeremoniale Romanum,* indicate that the passion narratives were chanted by the single voice of the deacon, who customarily sang the gospel at mass.[4] The individual voices of the evangelist and Jesus, and the corporate voices of the disciples, were distinguished by different pitches of the basic reciting tone. The voice of the evangelist was pitched in the tenor range, and the voice of Jesus was usually a fifth lower, establishing the model that became almost universal later, when the words of the evangelist were sung by a tenor and the words of Jesus by a bass. But at this earlier period the different "speakers" were conveyed by alternate pitches and various melodic punctuation formulae for each person or group, sung by the deacon alone.[5]

Manuscripts of these monophonic passions dating from the ninth century begin to exhibit additional markings, the *litterae significativae* (significative letters), to designate pitch and dynamics (tempo and volume). The earliest appearances of these significative letters have been taken as indications that the passion was sung by several voices, a practice for which there is no reliable evidence until the thirteenth century. Nevertheless they do mark a change from a pedagogy to dramaturgy that would eventually lead to the singing of the passion by different voices representing the *dramatis personae* of the passion narrative. Manuscripts from the tenth century, for instance, display c (= celeriter = quickly) to designate the evangelist. Later the evangelist was indicated by m (media = tenor voice) or C (= Chronista), or, in southern Italian sources, l or lec (= lectio). The voice of Christ is marked t (= tenere or tarde = slowly), later transformed into a cross †, or replaced by b (bassa = bass voice) or I (= J = Jesus). The turba (crowd) was indicated either by a (= altus = high voice) or s (sursum = high voice), or later by S (= Synagoga).[6]

The earliest datable distribution of the passion narrative among several singers is found in a Dominican manuscript of 1254. A late thirteenth-century Sarum Gradual divides it among five singers, but in the fourteenth and fifteenth centuries the widespread practice was to use three. A significant contributory factor in the rise of a heightened dramatic interpretation of the passion story[7] was the flourishing of medieval monasticism: the Cistercians rooted in the mysticism of suffering as taught by Bernard of Clairvaux; the Franciscans and Dominicans with their intense piety; and the Augustinians, whose spirituality was invigorated by the Brethren of the Common Life and the piety of Thomas à Kempis's De Imitatione Christi.

The chant of the monophonic passions was given its final authorized form by Giovanni Guidetti, a pupil of Palestrina and chaplain to Pope Gregory XIII, in Cantus ecclesiastici passionis (Rome, 1586). These plainsong passions were in continuous use in Roman Catholicism at mass during Holy Week[8] until the reforms of Vatican II effectively displaced Latin, together with the associated chant, by its promotion of vernacular forms. The passion narratives are no longer required as gospels at mass throughout Holy Week. The gospel for Palm Sunday remains a passion narrative, but the once invariable St. Matthew Passion has been replaced by a three-year lectionary sequence (A = Matthew; B = Mark; C = Luke). The St. John Passion remains for Good Friday. In American Catholicism these are all commonly spoken rather than sung, though some churches still chant their vernacular forms to the traditional monophonic passion tones.[9]

Polyphonic Passion

Polyphonic passions did not develop independently but as part of the broader concern to give a greater prominence to the biblical lections at mass, principally at major festivals such as Christmas, Epiphany, Easter, Marian feasts, and so forth.[10] Since their subject matter dealt with the crucifixion, the very heart of western Christianity, polyphonic passions received special emphasis, without, however, entirely eclipsing polyphonic settings of the Christmas and Easter histories. There were two main types of polyphonic passion: (a) the responsorial passion[11] and (b) the through-composed passion.[12]

A. Responsorial Passion

In the responsorial passion the gospel narrative, that is, the words of the evangelist, is chanted monophonically, while the *turba* are sung polyphonically by two or more voices. There was some variety of practice. For example, in some responsorial settings only the words of groups of people, the *turba,* were treated polyphonically; in others only the voices of the evangelist and Christ were sung monophonically, with all other speech being treated polyphonically. From the middle of the fourteenth century it was customary for the passion to begin with a polyphonic *exordium,* the title of the passion beginning with the words *Passio domini nostri . . . ,* and later a *conclusio* at the end.

An extremely important two-page treatise on polyphonic settings of the *turba* is bound into a manuscript *Passionale* from Füssen, south Germany, dating from the middle of the fifteenth century.[13] It offers a full description of how the three-voice *turba* are to be created from the three reciting tones of the individual voices of the passion narrative:

Note first that in a passion three voices are divided as follows:
Primo, which is the octave above—f'
Secundo, which is the fifth in the middle—c'
Tertio, which is the octave below—f

And the first is the voice of the Jews or Pilate or Caiaphas . . . ,
the second is the voice of the evangelist or disciples,
the third is the voice of Jesus the Christ and Savior. . . .

Also know that when Jesus or an apostle, Pilate, Caiaphas, or the
maid of Annas, etc., speak, as denoted by the significative letters [*singularis numerus*], then it is sung by a single voice. But
when it comes to the violent clamor of the fearful and tumul-
tuous Jews, then they must continue together and certainly
sound together. . . .

The voice of the Jews at the cadence must descend a half-step, that
is, from f' to e'.

The voice of an apostle at the cadence must remain at the fifth,
that is, on c'.

The voice of the Savior at the cadence at the same time descends
a fourth, that is, from f to c.

Thus at the cadence the bass is in concord with the tenor at the
octave and with the discant at the tenth, which are perfect
sounds [*perfectissime voces*].[14]

The "Füssener Traktat" epitomizes a long-lasting tradition
that influenced not only later Catholic passions but also Lutheran responsorial passions, especially those attributed to
Johann Walter (see further below).

B. Through-Composed Passion

Through-composed settings of the passion, the so-called
motet passions,[15] in which the complete narrative of the passion is set polyphonically, began to appear in the early sixteenth century. As with settings of the *turba* in early responsorial passions, the early through-composed passions were
similarly harmonic elaborations of the chant formulae. Later
through-composed passions explored a more developed coun-
terpoint in a motet style. One of the earlier passions, formally
attributed to Obrecht but now usually thought to be the work
of Antoine de Longueval, employs an abbreviated text made
up from all four passion narratives. This means that it cannot have been intended for the mass during Holy Week. How-

ever, since its three main sections approximate the sequence of the Stations of the Cross, it may well have been sung at these devotions in Holy Week. Later passions that also employ the Longueval text include four probably written for use in the court chapel in Prague: one by Jacob Regnart (*c.* 1590), and three by Jacob Handl (Gallus) (1587),[16] whose passion music was also used by Lutherans. One notable through-composed passion, remarkable for its economy and intensity, is William Byrd's St. John Passion for three voices that first appeared in the first part of the composer's anthology of Catholic liturgical music, *Gradualia ac Cantiones sacrae* (London, 1607).

With the development of the oratorio in the later seventeenth century, the passion story was occasionally treated more expansively and operatically for performance outside the regular liturgy, especially in Vienna.[17]

PROTESTANT PASSION MUSIC BEFORE
THE NINETEENTH CENTURY[18]

The heart of Martin Luther's theology and liturgical action is to be found in his understanding of the theology of the cross.[19] In his sermon of 1519 on the passion of Christ he wrote: "We say without hesitation that he who contemplates God's sufferings for a day, an hour, yes, only a quarter of an hour, does better than to fast a whole year, pray a psalm daily, yes, better than to hear a hundred masses. This meditation changes man's being and, almost like baptism, gives him a new birth."[20] The sermon was later incorporated into Luther's *Betbüchlein* (Little Prayer Book) of 1522, and expanded in 1529 to include the *Passional,* a devotional aid for layfolk displaying in woodcuts and brief summaries the scope of the salvation history that centers on the cross of Christ. His 1519 sermon epitomizes the Lutheran understanding of the cross, from which a particularly rich tradition of passion music developed.

The Lutheran Liturgical Context for Passion Music

The observance of Holy Week was much simplified in Lutheran usage. In the *Formula missae* of 1523 Luther directed: "In church we do not want to quench the spirit of the faithful with tedium. Nor is it proper to distinguish Lent, Holy Week, or Good Friday from other days, lest we seem to mock and ridicule Christ with half a mass and one part of the sacrament [a reference to the Good Friday *Missa praesanctificata*]."[21] Three years later, in the *Deutsche Messe* (1526), he was more explicit:

> Lent, Palm Sunday and Holy Week shall be retained, not to force anyone to fast, but to preserve the passion history and the gospels appointed for that season. This, however, does not include the Lenten veil, throwing of palms, veiling of pictures . . . nor chanting the four passions,[22] nor preaching on the passion for eight hours on Good Friday. Holy Week shall be like any other week save that the passion history be explained every day for an hour throughout the week or on as many days as may be desirable, and that the sacrament be given to everyone who desires it. For among Christians the whole service should center in the word and sacrament.[23]

Luther's emphasis was on the passion narrative itself, which was to be the focus for worship and preaching during Holy Week. As the Reformation was established across Germany, various church orders included provisions for the observance of Holy Week, especially Palm Sunday and Good Friday. But there was no uniformity of practice: indeed, some Lutheran church orders made no provisions at all for Holy Week in general or Good Friday in particular. However, in many areas the St. Matthew Passion was retained as the gospel for Palm Sunday and the St. John Passion as the gospel for Good Friday, but passion narratives were also heard on other Sundays during Lent. On each of the days of Holy Week, including Good Friday, the usual daily vesper service included passion chorales, readings from the passion narratives, and preaching.

The same year that Luther published the *Deutsche Messe*,

Johannes Bugenhagen issued, clearly with Luther's approval, *Die Historia des leydens vnd der Aufferstehung vnsers Herrn Jhesu Christi* [History of the Passion and Resurrection of our Savior Jesus Christ] (Wittenberg, 1526), a conflation of the narratives from all four Gospels. Thereafter it was frequently included in the church orders of the regional Lutheran churches of Germany, as well as in numerous hymnals. Later other conflated histories of the birth and ascension of Jesus were also produced. This in turn led to the establishment of the Lutheran tradition of musical settings of these Christological *Historia,* especially the passion history.[24]

Responsorial Passion

Luther's primary concern for Lent and Holy Week was therefore the continued use of the traditional Gospels, especially the passion narratives, which should still be chanted.[25] In the *Deutsche Messe* Luther gave his own version of traditional lectionary tones,[26] which were almost certainly used for the singing of the passion in early Lutheran liturgy. Another solution was to adapt older responsorial settings, based on the old Latin passion tones, to Luther's German text of the New Testament. Of this type are the St. Matthew and St. John Passions attributed to Johann Walter, Luther's musical collaborator and Kantor in Torgau from c. 1529. The two passions are found in five of the six so-called Torgau-Walter manuscripts.[27] Since the German text is based on Luther's 1522/27 New Testament rather than the 1534 German Bible,[28] these vernacular passions were probably created in the early 1530s when Walter was establishing himself as Kantor in Torgau. The so-called Gotha manuscript (c. 1539), like the earlier manuscripts of Latin responsorial passions, gives only the *turba*;[29] the passion tones of the remaining narrative had to be supplied from elsewhere. The same manuscript clearly indicates the liturgical function of these two passions: the St. Matthew Passion is described as "Die deutsche Passion auf dem Palmensontag" [The German Passion for Palm Sunday], and the St. John Passion as "Die ander deutsche Passion auf den folgenden Freitag der marterwoche" [The other German Passion for the following Friday in Holy Week].

Although Walter can be considered the probable editor of these passions, he can by no means be designated their composer, since they utilize traditional passion tones, and the *turba* are adaptations of the mid-fifteenth-century "Füssener Traktat" passion, by the addition of a' to the three-part f-c'-f'.[30]

These Walter passions were enormously influential and became the primary responsorial passions sung in the Lutheran liturgy from the middle of the sixteenth century until well into the eighteenth century.[31] They also served as models for other similar responsorial passions. The three passions of Heinrich Schütz, St. Matthew, St. Luke, and St. John[32] (1665–1666; SWV 479–481) and Marco Gioseppe Peranda's St. Mark Passion (1668)[33]—formerly attributed to Schütz—were the last important responsorial passions to be composed in Lutheran Germany.[34] Their austerity underlines their liturgical function in the Dresden court chapel and the solemnity surrounding the observances of Lent and Holy Week. Nevertheless, these passions stand in stark contrast to the more usual Italianate style of music then being performed in the Dresden court chapel at other times during the church year, notably the music of Peranda (his St. Mark Passion is atypical) and Vincenzo Albrici. These *a cappella* passions also contrast with concerted and figured-bass passions being composed elsewhere in Germany at that time, especially in Hamburg, the center for German opera.

Through-Composed Passion

In 1538 the musician, composer, and publisher Georg Rhau issued his first substantial collection of polyphonic liturgical music for Lutheran use. Significantly, he began not with music for Advent, but with passion motets, *Selectae harmoniae qvatvor vocvm de passione domine* (Wittenberg, 1538), underlining the *theologia crucis* focus of Luther's reforms. The first two items in the set of part-books are Latin passions.[35] The first is designated "Passio Domini nostri Jesu Christi secun-

dum Marcum," and the second " ... secundum Matthaeum,"
although in fact both texts are very similar. The second setting
is the Longueval passion (see above), though in Rhau's collection it is attributed to Obrecht, the earliest source to do so.
Its appearance in Rhau's *Selectae harmoniae* ensured its continued use among Lutherans.[36] In 1568 Joachim à Burck reported, in the preface to his own passion: "the Latin Passion
of the famous musician Jakob Obrecht [*sic*] was composed by
a splendid mind and is being sung everywhere."[37] It also served
as the basic model for later through-composed passions in
Germany.

Settings of the passion in German eventually became the
norm. Later through-composed passions include the St. John
Passions of Joachim à Burck (Moller) (Wittenberg 1568)[38] and
Johann Steuerlein (Erfurt, 1576), and the St. Matthew Passion
of Johann Machold (Erfurt, 1593), which was influenced by
à Burck's passion. The high point of this passion genre was
reached in the St. John Passion of Leonhard Lechner, first performed in Stuttgart in 1593.[39] In this highly characterized and
dramatically intense passion there is no hint of the traditional
passion tones. In some respects it can be seen as the forerunner
of the dramatic treatment of the passion narrative that was
characteristic in the later oratorio passion that developed in
the second half of the seventeenth century.

Oratorio Passion

The basic characteristics of both the responsorial and
through-composed passions are the largely unadorned biblical
narrative and an *a cappella* performance. The oratorio passion[40] that eventually emerged at the end of the seventeenth
century, and flourished during the eighteenth century, differed by its use of accompanying instruments and the addition
of non-biblical, reflective, or meditational texts. The earliest
known example is the St. John Passion of Thomas Selle, written in Hamburg in 1643.

It was customary for motets and other polyphonic liturgical
music to be accompanied by various instruments *colla parte*

(with the voice-parts). One can therefore conceive of the possibility that some of the through-composed, motet-like passions in the *stile antico* were performed with instrumental accompaniment, especially in those churches and chapels which customarily employed instruments at other times and seasons of the church year. But this would have been exceptional, because churches that customarily used instruments generally did not do so (apart from the use of the organ) during the penitential seasons of Advent and Lent. Despite this hesitation, passions in the new *stile concertato* were both written and performed during the seventeenth century.[41] But their use was restricted, occurring only in churches in cities where opera was dominant, such as Hamburg, or in court chapels, such as Weißenfels, where there were fewer restrictions than in ordinary parish churches that tended to be more conservative. The introduction of the oratorio passion came late to many city and town churches. For example, the earliest known concerted or oratorio passion to be heard in Leipzig was the St. Mark Passion of Johann Kuhnau, first performed in the New Church on March 26, 1721, but at Good Friday vespers rather than at the morning service, at which the Walter St. John Passion continued to be sung as the gospel.

From the beginning, the Lutheran passion, whatever its type, had been associated with the chorale because it was sung within a liturgy that also included the congregational singing of suitable chorales. It was therefore, perhaps, only a question of time before chorales were included within the passion as well as around it. A further factor was the continuing development of specific passion chorales within Lutheranism. In the sixteenth century there were chorales such as *Christus, der uns selig macht* (a German version of the thirteenth-century Latin hymn *Patris sapientia, veritas divina,* that early Lutheran hymnals took over from the German hymnals of the Bohemian Brethren), and the classic passion hymn *O Mensch bewein dein Sünde gross,* by Sebald Heyden, dating from 1525. During the seventeenth century there was an intensification in the writing of passion chorales, largely in reaction to the devastation and suffering of the Thirty Years' War. Such chorales include

Johann Heermann's *Herzliebster Jesu* (1630), Paul Stock-
mann's *Jesu Leiden, Pein und Tod* (1633), and especially Paul
Gerhardt's *O Haupt voll Blut und Wunden* (1656), a translation of the fifth section, *Salve, caput cruentatum,* of Arnulf von
Löwen's thirteenth-century poem on the wounds of the crucified Christ.

These passion chorales led to the development of a specific
subgenre of passion music: the chorale passion. Sometimes one
chorale was employed throughout the setting of the passion,
such as Georg Böhm's St. Luke Passion (1711), which used all
fourteen stanzas of Johann Olearius's *O Jesu Gottes Lamm*
(1671).[42] Georg Philipp Telemann's Danzig St. Matthew Passion (1754), however, includes a sequence of thirty-four stanzas
from various passion chorales.[43]

The development of the oratorio passion after Selle is somewhat imperfectly known, since many of the scores are no
longer extant; only their libretti or some documentary references survive.[44] As late as the early eighteenth century the developing oratorio passion had still not displaced the earlier
responsorial passion: both existed side by side in Lutheran
worship.

The Passions of Johann Sebastian Bach

Bach's passions[45] were written for performance in the liturgy of the two principal churches in Leipzig, but they were
not intended to replace the Walter responsorial passions, which
continued to be sung—the St. Matthew Passion for Palm Sunday, and the St. John Passion for Good Friday.[46] Bach's passions, following the pattern established by his predecessor,
Johann Kuhnau, were composed for Good Friday vespers and
were thus intended to complement the liturgical passions of
Walter. But Bach's passions included *secco* recitatives, *da capo*
arias, choruses, and chorales, adding a meditative dimension in
contrast to Walter's austere versions of the unaltered biblical
narrative.

Good Friday vespers in Leipzig had a simple liturgical
structure:

1. Hymn: *Da Jesus an den Kreuze stund*
2. Passion, part I
3. Sermon
4. Passion, part II
5. Motet: *Ecce quomodo moritur* (Gallus/Handl)[47]
6. Verse and Collect
7. Benediction
8. Hymn: *Nun danket alle Gott*

Bach was actively involved in composing and performing various passion settings for practically the whole of his time in Leipzig. The following list records only those passions composed by Bach, or that included music composed by him, and performed during his time in Leipzig:

1724   John Passion (BWV 245), first version
1725   John Passion, second version
1726   Kaiser's St. Mark Passion, including movements composed by Bach, first performed in Weimar in 1713 or earlier; additional chorales included for this Leipzig performance[48]
1727   Matthew Passion (BWV 244), earlier version
1729   Matthew Passion, earlier version (?)
1730   Anonymous Luke Passion (BWV 246), including at least one movement by Bach
1731   Mark Passion (BWV 247)[49]
1732? John Passion, third version
1736   Matthew Passion, later version
1739   [Revision of John Passion begun]
1742? Matthew Passion, later version
1745? Anonymous Luke Passion, later version[50]
1748? *Pasticcio*, incorporating the music of Handel and Keiser[51]
1749   John Passion, fourth version

The Non-Liturgical Passion Oratorios

Bach's St. John and St. Matthew Passions, the former more dramatic and the latter more reflective, are by general consent the most sublime examples of passion music. They mark the culmination of the oratorio passion written for performance within the Lutheran liturgy. But the development of the non-liturgical passion oratorio had already begun before Bach composed his first passion, a phenomenon that would eventually lead to the demise of the liturgical oratorio passion.

In 1676 the Hamburg city council decided that performances of passions could be given in the five principal city churches[52] during Lent, establishing a practice that continued for almost half a century. However, most of the passions that were heard during this period were pastiches of music written by several composers: of the 46 printed libretti of passions performed between 1676 and 1721, only 18 were the work of one composer.[53] When Georg Philipp Telemann became the musical director of the five principal churches in Hamburg, it was established that he should compose a new passion each year, based on all four Gospels in sequence. Thus between 1722 and 1762 Telemann composed no less than 46 settings, of which only 20 are extant.[54] Similarly, Telemann's successor, Carl Philipp Emmanuel Bach, composed 20 passions, based on all four Gospels in sequence, between 1769 and 1788.[55] Essentially oratorio passions for liturgical use, they too adhered closely to the biblical narratives.

But there was another tradition of Hamburg passion performances. In 1712 an influential passion libretto was written by one of the leading literati in Hamburg, Barthold Heinrich Brockes (*Der für die Sünde der Welt gemarterte und sterbende Jesus aus den vierten Evangelisten*). It proved to be extremely popular as devotional literature, undergoing more than thirty different editions between 1712 and 1722. The libretto is a poetic paraphrase of the biblical narrative of the passion from all four Gospels, to which are added poetic stanzas that introduce various allegorical figures, such as the daughter of Zion[56] and the faithful soul, but it makes limited use of chorales. The first composer to set the libretto was Reinhold Keiser, and the first performance in 1712 was given in Brockes' home, to an audience of more than 500.[57] It was performed again the following year, and over the next five years three other leading composers set the libretto to music: Telemann in 1716 (revised 1722), Handel in either 1715 or 1716, and Mattheson in 1718.[58] In 1719 Mattheson probably performed all four of these settings in Hamburg cathedral and the St. Marie-Magdelene church.[59] The passion oratorio was admitted into the churches, but as an independent musical work and not as part of the liturgy.

Until 1761 the Hamburg Drillhaus (the militia drill hall) served also as the primary concert hall for secular concerts and was the venue for performances of oratorios, including, from time to time, passion oratorios. Thus the passion oratorio established an identity outside the ambit of the liturgy and became part of the repertoire of the secular oratorio concert.

Telemann's extremely popular passion oratorio, *Das selige Erwägen des Leiden und Sterbens Jesu Christ,* was first performed in the Drillhaus in 1728; in later years it was performed in churches in the Hamburg area.[60] Apart from this passion oratorio, however, the year 1728 marked a decline in performances of passion oratorios in the Hamburg churches, a phenomenon Smither links to Mattheson's resignation that year as director of music at the cathedral.[61] But there were other factors, such as the growing influence of Pietism, that militated against performances of passion oratorios in churches. Two incidents can be cited. In 1732 Christian Gerber, a Pietist, published his *Historie der Kirchen-Ceremonien in Sachsen* (Dresden and Leipzig, 1732) and included the following report:

> The passion story, which had frequently been sung in simple plain chant [i.e., the Walter-type responsorial passion], humbly and reverently, began to be sung with many kinds of instruments in the most elaborate fashion, occasionally mixing in a little setting of a passion chorale which the whole congregation joined in singing, and then the mass of instruments fell to again. When in a large town this passion music was done for the first time, with twelve violins, many oboes, bassoons, and other instruments, many people were astonished and did not know what to make of it. In the pew of a noble family in church, many ministers and

noble ladies were present, who sang the first passion chorale out
of their books with great devotion. But when this theatrical music
began, all these people were thrown into the greatest bewilder-
ment, looked at each other, and said: "What will come of this?"
An old widow of the nobility said: "God save us, my children! It's
just as if one were at an opera comedy." But everyone was genu-
inely displeased by it and voiced complaints against it.[62]

In *Der Musikalische Patriot* (Hamburg, issued in parts from
1728), Mattheson records the following:

On Maunday Thursday, 1731, in the Drillhaus [at a performance
of a passion oratorio], at the words of Christ "I thirst," an officer
called out loudly, "Me too!" In the Katharinekirche, on the Third
Sunday after Easter, Pastor Wolff preached and expounded the
question whether it is right to so prostitute the Passion.[63]

Pietists objected to theatricality in church music, especially
the music that expressed the heart of the Christian gospel.
They therefore advocated a simplification of worship, which included the discontinuance of elaborate liturgical forms and
their associated music, and the promotion of a simple congregational hymnody.[64] As the century progressed the Rational-
ists adopted a similar position, but their concern was to elimi-
nate archaic elements from worship in favor of "enlightened"
simplicity.[65] Even in Hamburg, an enlightened city with regard
to opera compared with elsewhere in Germany, Telemann had
successive problems with regard to performances of passion
oratorios. For example, in 1748 a female opera singer was pre-
vented from singing in a performance of a passion oratorio in
the Michaeliskirche.[66]
 By the end of the eighteenth century the liturgical passion
had mostly disappeared from the Lutheran liturgy. Passion
oratorios and cantatas could be heard at afternoon vespers on
certain Sundays in Lent and during Holy Week,[67] but more
and more they were limited to nonecclesiastical buildings, and
performed by choral societies, such as the Berlin Singakad-
emie (founded in 1791), rather than by church choirs.

The Anglican Tradition

The general European Calvinist Reformation of the sixteenth century eschewed all forms of church music, save for the congregational metrical psalm. Although in later centuries the scope of church music expanded in the Reformed churches, there were no settings of the passion.[68]

In England the singing of the passion continued for a time in the middle of the sixteenth century.[69] In the 1549 Prayer Book the St. Matthew Passion was given as the gospel for Palm Sunday, the St. John Passion the gospel for Good Friday, and the St. Luke Passion was divided to become the gospels for Wednesday and Thursday of Holy Week. The lesson rubric in the service of matins specifically dealt with the continued practice of singing the biblical lections: "And (to the end that the people may the better hear) in such places where they do sing, there shall the lessons be sung in a plain tune after the manner of distinct reading: and likewise the epistle and gospel."[70] Almost certainly, therefore, vernacular passions were sung to Sarum passion tones during the Edwardian years, 1549–1553. But the continued use of plainsong with the vernacular was criticized by leading reformers, like John Hooper, bishop of Gloucester,[71] and soon after the accession of Mary, Prayer Book services were prohibited. During the Marian years the Latin passions returned, sung according to the Latin usage of the Sarum rite.[72] It is possible that after the accession of Elizabeth I in 1558, and the reissuing of the Prayer Book in 1559, vernacular passions were sung to the Sarum passion tones during Holy Week, but if so, the practice was short-lived, since the general Calvinist ethos of Elizabethan Anglicanism, and the particular rise of Puritanism, militated against the continuance of liturgical chant in the English church. Thus passion music was effectively eliminated from the music of the Anglican church for approaching three hundred years, until after the impact of the nineteenth-century Oxford Movement had been felt.

There was, however, an exception during the eighteenth century. The second part of Handel's *Messiah,* first performed in the New Music Hall, Dublin, on April 13, 1742, is effectively passion music. As Winton Dean has perceptively stated: "The greatness of *Messiah*—Handel's only sacred oratorio in the true sense and therefore untypical—derives on one level from its unique fusion of the traditions of Italian opera, English anthem, and German passion, and on the other from the coincidence of Handel's personal faith and creative genius to express, more fully than in any other work of art, the deepest aspirations of the Anglican spirit."[73] It was nevertheless created as an extra-liturgical oratorio; its early performances were in theatres and opera houses,[74] and when it was eventually performed in chapels and churches it was as a sacred concert. At a later date movements were incorporated into the worship of the English church, but they functioned liturgically within the Anglican anthem tradition rather than as passion music per se.

PASSION MUSIC IN THE NINETEENTH AND TWENTIETH CENTURIES

In addition to the ubiquitous *Der Tod Jesu* by Graun, the first half of the nineteenth century[75] saw two other musical expositions of the passion composed, published, and widely performed: Ludwig van Beethoven's *Christus am Oelberge* [Christ on the Mount of Olives], written in 1803, revised in 1804, and published in Leipzig in 1811; and Ludwig Spohr's *Des Heilands letzte Stunden,*[76] composed in 1834 and first performed in 1835 at a church concert on Good Friday in Kassel. Both were the subject of some controversy: Beethoven's oratorio was criticized for being too dramatic and Spohr's as not dramatic enough.

In England, Holy Week passion music in the Anglican church post-dates both the Oxford Movement, which led to a reassessment of liturgical worship in the Church of England, and the Bach revival that brought an awareness of the Bach passions. The first English performance of the St. Matthew Passion took place in the Hanover Square Rooms in 1854, but the Bach passions did not reach a wide public until they had been published in the enormously popular Novello Octavo series of vocal scores: the St. Matthew Passion in 1871 and the St. John Passion in 1872. That year (1872) John Stainer became the organist of St. Paul's Cathedral, London, and undertook long-overdue reforms of its music. At the age of thirteen (1854), Stainer had sung in the first English performance of Bach's St. Matthew Passion, and had played *continuo* (harmonium) in other performances of Bach's passions. As part of the reforms at St. Paul's Cathedral, he naturally introduced regular performances of the St. Matthew Passion, abridging the work for a first-time-ever performance within the liturgical context of the Prayer Book Commination Service—for which Stainer composed a four-part *a cappella* setting of Psalm 51 based on a chant—on April 8, 1873, the Tuesday in Holy Week. Thereafter the annual performance of the abridged Bach St. Matthew Passion in a service of worship during Holy Week became a popular tradition at the cathedral, and continued long after Stainer left St. Paul's (1888). By then his abridged version of the St. Matthew Passion had been published as a Novello Octavo vocal score, and it is reported that at the service in 1882 around a quarter of the congregation followed the music from Stainer's edition.[77]

It was probably this experience of the liturgical use of Bach's passion music that gave Stainer the impetus to create an English genre of passiontide music, that is, a modest musical setting of a libretto comprising biblical and poetic texts for soloists, choir, and congregation, as exemplified in his *Crucifixion* (1887). Apart from one or two hymn tunes and one chorus, the music is somewhat mundane and cliché-ridden, though its popularity gave rise to other similar, quasi-liturgical works, such as J. H. Maunder's *Olivet to Calvary* (1904) and Arthur Somervell's *The Passion of Christ* (1914).

Twentieth-century Germany is characterized by the composition of liturgical passions that follow earlier models, such as Kurt Thomas's St. Matthew Passion (1926) and Hugo Distler's *Choral-Passion* (1932),[78] both *a cappella* works. Such liturgical composition, often *a cappella,* continued into the second half of the twentieth century.[79]

English passion music of this century has tended to follow in the tradition of *The Crucifixion,* but generally with greater musical integrity than is exemplified in Stainer's model.[80] A sequence of similar compositions, by such composers as Dickenson and Sowerby, has appeared in the United States,[81] though Lutheran composers have tended to be more strictly liturgical in their passions.[82] Passions by Randall Thompson and Daniel Pinkham are essentially concert works for full orchestra, chorus, and soloists.[83]

Many African-American spirituals are in a sense passion music, in that they express the sufferings of slavery in the light of the sufferings of Christ. In Germany this connection led Paul Ernst Ruppel to compose *Crucifixion: Passionsbetrachtung nach Spirituals* (1960), a work for speaker, cantor, choir, trombone, and doublebass that is based on African-American spirituals. A similar connection was made between the martyrdom of the civil-rights leader and the martyrdom of Christ in Nicholas Flagello's *The Passion of Martin Luther King Jr.* (1968), first performed in Washington, D.C., in 1974.

Two concert passions have made an extraordinary impact on the second half of the twentieth century: Penderecki's St. Luke Passion and Pärt's St. John Passion, both employing a Latin libretto and both written by Eastern Europeans—Penderecki, whose background is Catholic, from Poland, and Pärt, whose background is Eastern Orthodox, from Estonia. Krzysztof Penderecki's *Passio et mors Domini nostri Iesu Christi secundum Lucam* was commissioned by West German Radio to celebrate the 700th anniversary of Münster cathedral and was first performed on March 30, 1966. Although inspired by the passions of Bach, it is a strikingly twentieth-century work, employing serial technique and microtonality. It is a reflection on human suffering in a post-Hiroshima and post-Auschwitz age.[84] Arvo Pärt's *Passio Domini nostri Jesu Christi secundum Joannem: per soli, coro misto, strumenti e organo,* written in 1982, published in 1985, is very different, though again very much a twentieth-century composition. This sparse, austere, but incredibly powerful setting of the passion is a minimalist work, constructed from an incredible combination of short thematic fragments. It conveys a chant-like serenity that has struck a responsive chord in many people across the world. Although it is usually performed as a concert work, it really is liturgical music.

CONCLUSION: THE CHALLENGE TODAY

In a passage on scripture in the assembly at worship, Gordon W. Lathrop speaks eloquently about "surrounding the scripture reading with singing."[85] The sung response of the congregation is an essential part of Christian liturgical tradition. Record of the singing of psalms and hymns in response to the passion narratives from the earliest times witnesses to this tradition, as does the specific genre of the chorale passion of later Lutheranism. What Lathrop does not discuss is the singing of scripture itself, a practice that is as old and fundamental as responsive "singing around the texts."[86] The singing of the word of scripture in the liturgy has a long continuity from the earliest times in both eastern and western traditions, and is rooted in Hebrew liturgical tradition. It was also carried over into Protestantism by Luther's insistence on the sung word in worship. Musical settings of the passion can therefore be considered as a most developed form of the sung word. What Lathrop writes later about concert masses applies equally to concert performances of passion music: "From the Christian point of view, a composed mass in a concert hall, however powerful it may be, is nothing but a few shards left from the meeting—like candles left burning in an empty church—without the people, without the rest of the song the people sing and without the interactions of word and bath and meal."[87] Many settings of the passion were written for liturgical use and yet they tend to be heard today only in a concert setting. Part of the problem is that, since the reforms of Vatican II, the sung response, and only the sung response of the congregation, has been the focus of music in the liturgy. What has been neglected is the sung word of scripture to which the liturgical assembly responds in appropriate song. There is the need therefore to rescue some of the most sublime musical expositions of the passion of Christ from the concert hall and return them to where they were originally intended to be heard—in the liturgical assembly of the faithful during Holy Week.

EXCURSUS ON ANTI-SEMITIC TENDENCIES IN PASSION MUSIC

There are two primary problem areas with regard to passion music that can involve an incipient anti-Semitism, one internal, when such music is heard within the community of faith, and the other external, when performances occur in a secular concert hall.

The internal problem with passion music occurs when it is performed with an excess of zeal that is colored by the anti-Semitic mores of the particular Zeitgeist. For example, late medieval society was marred by an intensive anti-Semitism. Thus, in the later thirteenth century, Durandus, in *Rationale divinorum officiorum,* directed that the words of Christ should be sung with a certain sweetness, but that the words of "the impious Jews" should be sung in loud and strident tones.[88] Later polyphonic passions exhibit the significant tendency for the *turba* to characterize the Jews in a similar way, with the tacit implication that they were to blame for the death of Christ.[89] In the course of time, by the seventeenth and eighteenth centuries, such overt anti-Semitic traits were muted, if not altogether excluded. For example, Andreas Marti argues that in Heinrich Schütz's setting of the words of the Jews, "Sein Blut komme über uns und unsere Kinder" ("His blood be upon us and our children"; Matt. 27:25), in his Matthew Passion of 1669 (SWV 479), the composer intended to suggest that this reference to being covered, as it were, by the blood of Christ is more salvific than judgmental.[90] Similarly, any thought that the Jews, or anyone else, are to be blamed for the death of Jesus is significantly undercut by the chorales in Bach's St. John Passion, which insist that each worshiper bears the guilt of the crucifixion.[91] One example is the third chorale (BWV 245:11): "'Tis I whom sins encumber, | My misdeeds far out-number | the sands upon the shore; | These sins it was that brought thee | thy misery, and wrought thee | Of martyrdom the awful store."[92] Again, Johann David Heinichen's *Passion-soratorium*—which is exactly contemporary with Bach's St. John Passion in that both received their first performances on the same day, April 7, 1724, Bach's in Leipzig and Heinichen's in Dresden—begins with the aria: "It is not the bonds that ensnare thee, | nor the fetters, that torment thee! | What tortures and oppresses thee, | O my Saviour, is I!"[93] But congregations have not always heard this fundamental herme-neutic and have been conditioned more by inherited preju-dice than enlightened theology, and in consequence, often by default rather than design, have fostered an anti-Semitic stance. Thus the tendency in recent history, when passion music, both historic and contemporary, is performed within the community of faith, is for the associated preaching and teaching to stress the need to hear the biblical narrative with theological ears: to understand that the drama of the cross declares the culpability of all humanity, that guilt is uni-versal, not particular, and salvation is particular in its univer-sality.

Then there is the persistent external problem of passion music performed in a concert hall rather than in the sanctuary of a church. Here there is no theological framework, no litur-gical context, and certainly no preaching, which in an ecclesi-astical setting interpret and expound its contemporary signifi-cance. This became a particular problem in the medieval period with the development of extra-liturgical passion plays, of which the *Oberammergauer Passionsspiel* is the most well-known later manifestation. Freed from theological and litur-gical restraint, interpolations and additional glosses of a decid-edly anti-Semitic character were introduced into the biblical narrative. Passion music in a secular setting remains a contemporary problem because such music is frequently considered to be a subset of these extra-liturgical passion plays, whereas, as this essay has attempted to demonstrate, it has a somewhat different history. The suspicion persists that musical settings of the passion have a not-too-hidden anti-Semitic agenda and therefore they should only be performed in severely edited versions, if at all. It is a real issue that has to be dealt with, although it is not a new problem. When Mendelssohn directed the first modern concert performances of Bach's St. Matthew Passion in 1829, many movements were omitted. Significantly, the chorales were retained, but many of the arias were deleted, together with other omissions. Michael Marissen has suggested that a primary reason for this action, apart from the necessity of reducing a very long work, was Mendelssohn's Jewish sensibilities, since the cuts include all references to Jews that could be construed as anti-Semitic.[94]

It is customary today for the two passions of Bach to be performed in their entirety, because such marvelous music deserves to be heard. But when they, and other passions, are performed in a secular concert hall, it is imperative for the promoters of these concerts to deal with the perceptions and misperceptions of anti-Semitism in carefully-written programme notes. They should also, where possible, arrange for pre-concert discussions by ecumenical religious leaders and informed musicologists, a practice that has become fairly common in recent years. The modern context of a concert hall is so different from the original conditions within which this music was first heard that it is necessary to review with members of the audience the nature of the different contexts, then and now, in order for them to be able to understand this music in a contemporary environment.

New works composed in the last decade or so, designed to be heard in a nonreligious concert hall, reveal a tendency to move away from the passion narratives to a more episodic approach to the passion. The crucifixion is seen as a universal tragedy affecting humanity as a whole, as in Richard Robbins's minimalistic and almost entirely instrumental *Via crucis* (1994), or James Macmillan's *Seven Last Words from the*

Cross (1993), which includes echoes of Bach chorales. Oskar Gottlieb Blarr's large-scale *Jesus-Passion* (1985), for soloists, adult and children's choirs, and orchestra, is clearly written from the perspective of the second half of the twentieth century. The biblical narrative from three of the Gospels is interspersed with additional texts that include an Aramaic hymn from the Talmud, medieval and modern Hebrew poetry, and excerpts from Alfred Kittner's *Requiem* (1943) in which the Düsseldorf poet recalls his experiences in a concentration camp. In the secular arena of a concert hall in a pluralistic society, the suffering of Jesus needs to be seen in connection with the recent suffering of humanity as a whole, as well as with the particularity of the suffering of Jews in this century. In both contexts—internal liturgical passion music within the community of faith and external concert-hall performances in a multi-faith society—it needs to be remembered that Jesus suffered as a Jew.

NOTES

1. *Egeria: Diary of a Pilgrimage,* trans. and ed. George E. Gingras (New York, 1970), p. 112. For the context of Holy Week observances in Jerusalem in the fourth century, see Thomas J. Talley, *The Origins of the Liturgical Year* (New York, 1986), pp. 42–47.

2. On the psalms associated with the passion in Holy Week in the Tridentine Mass, see William L. Holladay, *The Psalms through Three Thousand Years* (Minneapolis, 1993), p. 221.

3. The basic literature includes: Otto Kade, *Die ältere Passionskomposition bis zum Jahre 1631* (Gütersloh, 1893; reprint, Hildesheim, 1971); H. M. Adams, "Passion Music before 1724," *Music and Letters* 7 (1926): 258–64; Kurt von Fischer, "Zur Geschichte der Passions-komposition des 16. Jahrhundert in Italien," *Archiv für Musikwissenschaft* 11 (1954): 189–205; Basil Smallman, *The Background of Passion Music: J. S. Bach and His Predecessors,* 2d rev. ed. (New York, 1970); José-Vincente Gonzales, "Die Tradition des liturgischen Passionsvortrags in Spanien" (Ph.D. dissertation, University of Munich, 1974); Carl Schalk, "Passion," *Key Words in Church Music: Definition Essays on Concepts, Practices, and Movements of Thought in*

Church Music (St. Louis, 1978), pp. 300–304; Kurt von Fischer and Werner Braun, "Passion," *The New Grove Dictionary of Music and Musicians* (London and New York, 1980; hereafter cited as *NGD*), 14:276–86; Kurt von Fischer, "The Theologia Crucis and the Early Liturgical Passion," *Israel Studies in Musicology* 3 (1983): 38–43; Kurt von Fischer, "Die Passionsmusik von den Anfängen bis zum Ende des 16. Jahrhunderts und deren liturgie- und frömmigkeitsgeschichtliche Voraussetzungen," *Musik und Bildung* 19 (1987): 6–10.

4. Non-Roman rites employed different forms of the passion narratives. For example, in Gallican, Ambrosian, and southern Italian liturgies the narratives were abbreviated, and the Mozarabic rite prescribed an abridgement of a history of the passion, a conflation from all four Gospels.

5. The passion tone formulae are different from the regular gospel tones. Examples of passion tone formulae from eighteen manuscripts dating from between the thirteenth and sixteenth centuries are given in Bruno Stäblein, "Die einstimmige lateinische Passion," *Die Musik in Geschichte und Gegenwart* (Kassel, 1949–1986; hereafter cited as *MGG*), 10:887–98, esp. 891–94. For the more exotic Spanish passion tones, see Theodor Göllner, "Unknown Spanish Passion Tones in Sixteenth-Century Hispanic Sources," *Journal of the American Musicological Society* 28 (1975): 46–71. The principal passion tones, and their later Lutheran forms, are conveniently summarized in Otto Brodde, "Evangelische Choralkunde," *Leiturgia: Handbuch des evangelischen Gottesdienst,* ed. Karl Ferdinand Müller and Walter Blankenburg, vol. 4, *Die Musik des evangelischen Gottesdienst* (Kassel, 1961), pp. 534–39.

6. Significative letters can be seen on the leaf of an eleventh-century setting of the St. Matthew Passion reproduced in *NGD* 14:276, and on a leaf from a tenth-century St. Matthew Passion in *MGG* 10:887; see Smallman, *Background of Passion Music,* pp. 123–24, and David Hiley, *Western Plainchant: A Handbook* (Oxford, 1993), p. 56.

7. Basic literature on the rise of the passion play within the general context of medieval drama includes: Karl Young, *The Drama of the Medieval Church* (Oxford, 1933); Richard B. Donovan, *The Liturgical Drama in Medieval Spain* (Toronto, 1958); Richard H. Hoppin, *Medieval Music* (New York, 1978), pp. 172–86; John Stevens, *Words and Music in the Middle Ages: Song, Narrative, Dance and Drama, 1050–1350* (Cambridge, 1983), pp. 308–71; Susan K. Rankin, "Liturgical Drama," *The New Oxford History of Music,* vol. 2, *The Early*

Middle Ages, ed. Richard Crocker and David Hiley (Oxford, 1990), pp. 310–56.

8. Details of the Holy Week observances are conveniently summarized in John Harper, *The Forms and Orders of Western Liturgy from the Tenth to the Eighteenth Century* (Oxford, 1991), pp. 139–49, and Hiley, *Western Plainchant,* pp. 32–39.

9. *Hymns, Psalms, Spiritual Canticles* (Belmont, Mass., 1974), Nos. 520–522, 529, gives the passion narrative in English with the traditional chant. Although *Worship: A Hymnal and Service Book for Roman Catholics,* 3rd ed. (Chicago, 1986), Nos. 807–809, and 814, only gives the narratives laid out for dramatic reading, the publisher, G.I.A., also issues a separate edition of the English texts set to the traditional passion tones. There are signs of a return to a sung passion in American Catholic churches during Holy Week.

10. In addition to already-cited literature, see: Günther Schmidt, "Grundsätzliche Bemerkungen zur Geschichte der Passionskomposition," *Archiv für Musikwissenschaft* 17 (1960): 100–25; Hans Joachim Moser, *Die mehrstimmige Vertonung des Evangeliums* (Leipzig, 1931; reprint, Hildesheim, 1968); Kurt von Fischer, "Die mehrstimmige und katholische Passion," *MGG* 10:898–911; Theodor Göllner, *Die mehrstimmigen liturgischen Lesungen* (Tutzing, 1969), esp. 2:129–92.

11. In older literature it is designated "choral passion," "dramatic passion," "quasi-dramatic," or "plainsong passion."

12. In older literature frequently referred to as "motet" passion.

13. In older literature the treatise is referred to as the "Maihinger Fragment"; it is now known as the "Füssener Traktat."

14. The original Latin, with a German translation, is given in Göllner, *Die mehrstimmigen liturgischen Lesungen,* 2:131–34.

15. See Patricia Robertson, "A Critical Survey of the Motet Passion" (Ph.D. dissertation, London University, 1957); Arnold Schmitz, "Zur motettischen Passion des 16. Jahrhunderts," *Archiv für Musikwissenschaft* 16 (1959): 232–45; Smallman, *Background of Passion Music,* pp. 131–36.

16. See Kade, *Die ältere Passionskomposition,* pp. 52–62.

17. The *Sepolcro* was more common than the passion oratorio; see Howard E. Smither, *A History of the Oratorio* (Chapel Hill, 1977–1987), 1:366–80.

18. Basic literature, in addition to titles listed in note 3 above, includes: Carl von Winterfeld, *Der evangelische Kirchengesang und sein Verhältniss zur Kunst des Tonsatzes,* vol. 3 (Leipzig, 1847; re-

print, Hildesheim, 1966); Rudolf Gerber, "Die deutsche Passion von Luther bis Bach," *Luther-Jahrbuch* 13 (1931): 131–52; Konrad Ameln and Christhard Mahrenholz, eds., *Handbuch der deutschen evangelischen Kirchenmusik* (Göttingen, 1930–1980); Walter Blankenburg, "Die Protestantischen Passion," *MGG* 10:911–33; Werner Braun, *Die mitteldeutsche Choralpassion im 18. Jahrhundert* (Berlin, 1960); Friedrich Blume et al., *Protestant Church Music: A History* (New York, 1974); Philipp Spitta, "The Passion Music of Johann Sebastian Bach and Heinrich Schütz," trans. and ed. Kenneth E. Miller, *The Choral Journal* 16, no. 2 (October 1975): 5–9, and no. 3 (November 1975): 10–13; Audrey Ekdahl Davidson, *The Quasi-Dramatic St. John Passions from Scandinavia and Their Medieval Background* (Kalamazoo, 1981); Elke Axemacher, *"Aus Liebe will mein Heiland Sterben": Untersuchungen zum Wandel des Passionsverständnisses im frühen 18. Jahrhundert* (Stuttgart, 1984).

19. See, for example, Alister E. McGrath, *Luther's Theology of the Cross: Martin Luther's Theological Breakthrough* (Oxford, 1985).

20. *Luther's Works: American Edition,* ed. Jaroslav Pelikan and Helmut T. Lehman (St. Louis and Philadelphia, 1955–1986; hereafter cited as *LW*), 42:11.

21. *LW* 53:24.

22. Kurt von Fischer (*NGD* 14:281) suggests that the phrase "Vier-Passionen-Singen" refers to the *summa Passionis,* that is, a harmonized (Latin) narrative from all four Gospels. On the other hand, since Luther was concerned to greatly simplify the observance of Holy Week, it is more likely to be a reference to the Roman practice of chanting the passion narrative from all four Gospels on different days of Holy Week. This would seem borne out by the fact, mentioned in the text that follows, that Bugenhagen, Luther's colleague and confessor, brought out a conflated narrative of the crucifixion the same year the *Deutsche Messe* was issued.

23. *LW* 53:90.

24. See Walter Blankenburg, "Historia," *MGG* 6:465–89; Blume, *Protestant Church Music,* pp. 177–85; Smither, *History of the Oratorio,* 2:3–37.

25. There is an interesting witness to the continuation of the practice of chanting the passion in Wittenberg. In the sermon preached at Luther's burial, February 22, 1546, after recounting the Reformer's last hour, Bugenhagen made the comment, "Thereby he [Luther] also *sang* [gesungen] his 'consummatum est' and commended his spirit into his heavenly Father's hands"; Johann

Bugenhagen, *A Christian Sermon [Preached] over the Body at the Funeral of the Venerable Dr. Martin Luther,* trans. Kurt. K. Hendel (Atlanta, 1996), p. 43 [emphasis added].

26. See *LW* 53:73–78, 84–89.

27. See Carl Gerhardt, *Die Torgauer Walter-Handschriften: Eine Studie zur Quellenkunde der Musikgeschichte der deutschen Reformationszeit* (Kassel, 1949). Basic literature on Walter's passions includes: Konrad Ameln and Carl Gerhardt, "Johann Walter und die ältesten deutschen Passionhistorien," *Monatsschrift für Gottesdienst und kirchliche Kunst* 44 (1939): 105–19; Ludwig Finscher, "Ein wenig beachtete Quelle zu Johann Walters Passions-Turbae," *Die Musikforschung* 11 (1958): 189–95; Blume, *Protestant Church Music,* pp. 178–80; Walter Blankenburg, *Johann Walter: Leben und Werk,* ed. Friedhelm Brusniak (Tutzing, 1991), pp. 304–9.

28. See Kade, *Die ältere Passionskomposition,* p. 164; Werner Braun, ed., *Johann Walter sämtliche Werke,* vol. 4, *Deutsche Passionen nach Matthäus und Johannes . . .* (Kassel, 1973), p. xvi.

29. Folios 276v–277r of the Gotha manuscript choirbook are reproduced in facsimile in Smither, *History of the Oratorio,* 2:6–7.

30. The addition of a fourth part was not necessarily added by Walter, since in the "Füssener Traktat" there is a note, entered at a later period, indicating that the *turba* could be sung in four parts; see Göllner, *Die mehrstimmigen liturgischen Lesungen,* 2:136, n. 9.

31. In Torgau, where the Walter passions probably originated, the St. John Passion was no longer customarily sung on Good Friday. The Torgau visitation records of spring 1580 note the following: "For sundry years the German passion has been sung on Good Friday, with polyphonic choral responses. This is now unjustly neglected"; cited in Braun, *Johann Walter sämtliche Werke,* 4:xv, n. 4.

32. The Dresden court diary indicates that "the passion, from the Gospel of John, newly-composed by Kapellmeister Heinrich Schütz, was sung" following the epistle reading of Isaiah 53 and before the sermon, at the Good Friday morning service in 1665; see Eberhard Schmidt, *Der Gottesdienst am Kurfürstlichen Hofe zu Dresden: Ein Beitrag zur liturgischen Traditionsgeschichte von Johann Walter zu Heinrich Schütz* (Berlin, 1966), p. 207.

33. The Dresden court diary records that at the morning worship of Good Friday 1668 "the passion from the Gospel of Mark, composed by Joseph Peranda" was sung; see E. Schmidt, *Der Gottesdienst am Kurfürstlichen Hofe.*

34. Peranda was actually a Catholic but was serving the Lutheran court chapel in Dresden.

35. Latin continued to be used in Lutheran worship, since Luther made it clear that the *Deutsche Messe* did not abrogate the earlier *Formula missae,* and that Latin should continue in use where it was understood, that is, in cities with universities or towns with Latin schools; see *LW* 53:62–63.

36. For example, the Longueval passion appears in the same four Torgau-Walter manuscripts with the two Walter passions (see Gerhardt, *Die Torgauer Walter-Handschriften,* pp. 60–61), and was printed numerous times.

37. Cited in *MGG* 8:1190; see also Blume, *Protestant Church Music,* pp. 180–81, where the date is misprinted as "1528."

38. Joachim à Burck's passion was widely sung throughout Thuringia at the end of the sixteenth century; see *NGD* 11:439 (entry on Johann Machold).

39. A book fair advertisement announced that the passion would be published in Nuremberg in 1594; no printed copy is extant but manuscript copies survive.

40. See John B. Haberlen, "A Critical Survey of the North German Oratorio Passion to 1700" (D.M.A. dissertation, Georgia State University, Atlanta, 1974); Stanley Anthony Malinowski, "The Baroque Oratorio Passion" (Ph.D. dissertation, Cornell University, Ithaca, 1978); Blume, *Protestant Church Music,* pp. 220–22; Smither, *History of the Oratorio,* 2:37–41. As with other types of passion, there are problems of definition with regard to the "oratorio" passion. Some would draw a distinction between the early and later types, the earlier being the "concerted" or "oratorical" passion, and the later the "oratorio" passion. Others would divide the later type into two distinct groups: the "oratorio passion," that is, a liturgical passion in a concerted style, and the "passion oratorio," that is, an extra-liturgical concerted passion. But, as Werner Braun observes, "classification of the 18th-century passion is made difficult by a multitude of hybrid forms"; *NGD* 14:284.

41. On the role of the orchestra in passion music, see Smallman, *Background of Passion Music,* pp. 103–15.

42. Only the libretto has survived; see W. Junghans, "Johann Sebastian Bach als Schüler der Particularschule zu St. Michaelis in Lüneburg," *Programm des Johanneums zu Lüneburg* (Lüneburg, 1870), p. 40.

43. Manfred Fechner, "Nachwort," *Georg Philipp Telemann: Matthäus-Passion 1754* [facsimile of the original manuscript], ed. Eitelfriedrich Thom (Michaelstein, 1986), unpaginated.

44. For example, some of the later seventeenth-century Hamburg passion libretti probably had music composed by Christoph Bernhard, Dietrich Becker, and Joachim Gerstenburg, whose St. Matthew Passion was reportedly written "*a 26,*" that is, with twenty-six choral, vocal, and instrumental parts; none of the music has survived.

45. Basic literature in English on the Bach passions includes: Charles S. Terry, *J. S. Bach: The Passions* (London, 1928; reprint, Westport, Conn., 1971); Smallman, *Background of Passion Music,* passim; Paul Steinitz, *Bach's Passions* (London, 1979); Robin A. Leaver, *J. S. Bach As Preacher: His Passions and Music in Worship* (St. Louis, 1982), passim; Jaroslav Pelikan, *Bach Among the Theologians* (Philadelphia, 1986); Paul S. Minear, *Death Set to Music: Masterworks by Bach, Brahms, Penderecki, Bernstein* (Atlanta, 1987).

46. Gottfried Vopelius, *Neu Leipziger Gesangbuch* (Leipzig, 1682), pp. 179 et seq. and 227 et seq., respectively; see Jürgen Grimm, *Das Neu Leipziger Gesangbuch des Gottfried Vopelius (Leipzig 1682): Untersuchungen zur Klärung seiner geschichtlichen Stellung* (Berlin, 1969), p. 59.

47. In Vopelius's *Neu Leipziger Gesangbuch,* Handl's motet *Ecce quomodo moritur justus* immediately follows the two Walter passions; see previous note. The continued use of the responsory *Ecce quomodo moritur* in Lutheran liturgies of Holy Week was no doubt influenced by Luther's modified version of it, included in his collection of funeral pieces, *Christliches Geseng, Lateinisch und Deutsch, zum Begräbnis* (Wittenberg, 1542), reprinted in Valentin Bapst's *Geystlicher Lieder* (Leipzig, 1545), and Lukas Lossius's *Psalmodia* (Nuremberg, 1553); see Markus Jenny, "Sieben Biblische Begräbnisgesänge: Ein unbekanntes und uneditiertes Werk Martin Luthers," *Lutheriana: Zum 500. Geburtstag Martin Luthers von den Mitarbeitern der Weimarer Ausgabe,* ed. Gerhard Hammer and Karl-Heinz zur Mühlen [= *Archiv zur Weimarer Ausgabe der Werke Martin Luthers* 5] (Cologne, 1984), pp. 455–74, esp. pp. 458–59, 466.

48. See Andreas Glöckner, "Bach and the Passion Music of His Contemporaries," *The Musical Times* 116 (1975): 613–16; see also Andreas Glöckner, "Johann Sebastian Bachs Aufführungen zeitgenössischer Passionsmusiken," *Bach-Jahrbuch* 63 (1977): 75–119.

49. Only the libretto and some of the music are known.

50. BWV 246a; see Yoshitaki Kobayashi, "Zu einem neu entdeck-

ten Autograph Bachs. Choral: Aus der Tiefen," *Bach-Jahrbuch* 57 (1971): 5–12; see also Glöckner, "Bachs Aufführungen," pp. 91–99, 108.

51. See Glöckner, "Bachs Aufführungen," p. 91.

52. St. Petri, St. Nikolai, St. Michaelis, St. Katharinen, and St. Jacobi, but not the cathedral, which maintained an independence from the other churches in the city.

53. See Norbert Bolin, "In rechter Ordnung lerne Jesu: C. Ph. E. Bach's 'Spinnhaus-Passion' (H 776) Hamburg 1768," *Augsburger Jahrbuch für Musikwissenschaft* 5 (1988): 67.

54. See Hans Hörner, *Georg Philipp Telemanns Passionsmusiken: Ein Beitrag zur Geschichte der Passionsmusik in Hamburg* (Leipzig, 1933).

55. See Bolin, "In rechter Ordnung," p. 67, n. 12; see also Stephen L. Clark, "C. P. E. Bach and the Tradition of Passion Music in Hamburg," *Early Music* 16 (1988): 533–41.

56. Bach's librettist, Christian Friedrich Henrici (Picander), parallels this image in the opening chorus of the St. Matthew Passion (BWV 245:1).

57. Smither, *History of the Oratorio,* 2:111.

58. Other composers who also set the Brockes passion libretto include: Johann Friedrich Fasch (1723), Gottfried Heinrich Stötzel (1725), Paul Steiniger, Johann Balthasar, Christian Frieslich, and Jacob Schubach (c. 1750). J. S. Bach's librettist incorporated several texts from the Brockes passion into the St. John Passion (BWV 245:7, 19, 20, 24, 32, 34, and partly also in 35 and 39).

59. Heinz Becker, "Die frühe Hamburgische Tagespresse als musikgeschichtliche Quelle," *Beiträge zur Hamburgischen Musik-Geschichte,* ed. Heinrich Husmann (Hamburg, 1956), p. 36.

60. Richard Petzoldt, *Georg Philipp Telemann,* trans. Horace Fitzpatrick (London, 1974), pp. 170–71; see also Smither, *History of the Oratorio,* 3:347–48.

61. Smither, *History of the Oratorio,* 2:120.

62. Hans T. David and Arthur Mendel, *The Bach Reader: A Life of Johann Sebastian Bach in Letters and Documents,* 2d. rev. ed. (New York, 1966), p. 229. Older Bach literature links this anecdote with one of the passions of Bach, but there is no direct evidence; see ibid., p. 442.

63. Cited in Bolin, "In rechter Ordnung," p. 68, n. 13.

64. It was Pietist pressure that led to the suppression of the responsorial passion, with chorales and instrumental interludes, at Ros-

kilde cathedral, Denmark, in 1736, and its replacement by a sermon;
Davidson, *Quasi-Dramatic St. John Passions from Scandinavia,* p. 3.

65. See Paul Graff, *Geschichte der Auflösung der alten gottesdien-
stlichen Formen in der evangelischen Kirche Deutschlands* (Göttingen,
1937-1939).

66. Hörner, *Telemanns Passionsmusiken,* pp. 49-50. Thirty years
earlier Mattheson had regularly used opera singers for his soloists in
performances of oratorios in Hamburg cathedral. At first the female singers were not allowed to be seen during the performances,
but this prohibition was soon lifted; see Smither, *History of the Oratorio,* 2:117.

67. In the early 1770s Johann Georg Sulzer defined "oratorio" as:
"A spiritual, but completely lyric and short drama, which is performed with music, for use in divine service on high days." In 1802
Heinrich Christoph Koch gives a similar definition, and then adds
that oratorios "often, however, as with our modern church music in
general, depart too much from the noble simplicity that should distinguish our music for divine service and incline too much towards
the style of operatic music"; both cited in Smither, *History of the
Oratorio,* 3:337 and 339, respectively.

68. See Walter Blankenburg, "Church Music in Reformed Europe," in Blume, *Protestant Church Music,* pp. 509-90.

69. The Latin passions were familiar to the populace. Among a
number of English passion carols there is one that specifically cites
the Latin passion narratives. It is found in a sixteenth-century manuscript (Balliol College, Oxford, MS. 354), and was printed in *Christmas carolles newely Inprynted* (London, c. 1550). Stanza 3 concludes:
"Pylate said vnto the Jews, "What say ye?" | Than they cryed with
on[e] voys, Crucyfige! [Crucyfige!]"; see Richard Leighton Green, ed.
The Early English Carols, 2d. rev. ed. (Oxford, 1977), No. 163.

70. Cited in F. E. Brightman, *The English Rite* (London, 1921),
1:136. The same rubric was repeated in the 1552 Prayer Book.

71. See Hooper's letter to Heinrich Bullinger, dated December
27, 1549: "In the churches [in London] they always chant the hours
and other hymns relating to the Lord's Supper, but in our own language. And that popery may not be lost, the mass-priests, although
they are compelled to discontinue the use of the Latin language, yet
most carefully observe the same tone and manner of chanting to
which they were heretofore accustomed in the papacy"; *Original Letters Relative to the English Reformation,* ed. H. Robinson, Parker Society 53 (Cambridge, 1847), 1:72.

72. Among the English exiles in Frankfurt in 1554–1555, it was reported that "in Cathedral churches [in England] they utter their lessons in plain-song"; *A Brieff discours off the troubles begonne in Franckford in Germany Anno Domini 1554* [1575] (London, 1846), pp. xxix.

73. *NGD* 8:112.

74. *NGD* 8:118.

75. See Melvin A. Wells, "Settings of the Passion Story in the Nineteenth Century" (D. M. A. dissertation, Southwestern Baptist Theological Seminary, Louisville, 1990); Martin Geck, *Deutsche Oratorien 1800 bis 1840* (Wilhelmshaven, 1971).

76. In England and America, after its publication by Novello of London, it was known as *Calvary.*

77. See Peter Charlton, *John Stainer and the Musical Life of Victorian Britain* (London, 1984), p. 72.

78. Distler's *Choral-Passion,* for five-voice mixed choir and soloists, employs a libretto based on all four Gospels and was inspired by the passion music of Heinrich Schütz; see Larry Palmer, *Hugo Distler and His Church Music* (St. Louis, 1967), pp. 121–26.

79. Examples include: Ernst Pepping's St. Matthew Passion (1950); Hans Friedrich Micheelsen's St. Matthew (1948), St. Mark (1952), and St. John Passions (1962); Lothar Graap's St. Mark Passion, with five organ meditations (1974); and Anton Heiler's *Passionsmusik* for children's choir and organ (1974).

80. Among the more important examples are: Charles Wood's St. Mark Passion (1921); Sydney H. Nicholson's *The Saviour of the World* (1924); C. Armstrong Gibbs's *Behold the Man* (1955); Kenneth Leighton's *Crucifixus pro nobis* (1961); Alan Ridout's St. John Passion (1964); and Francis B. Westbrook's *Calvary: A Cantata for Passiontide* (1965).

81. Clarence Dickenson, *The Redeemer* (1935, revised 1953); Leo Sowerby's *Forsaken of Man: a Lenten or Good Friday Cantata* (1940).

82. Examples include the St. Mark Passions of Jan Bender (a Dutch-born German citizen on the faculty of Wittenberg University, Ohio, at the time) and Ronald A. Nelson (both 1962), Richard Hillert's St. John Passion (1974), and Richard Wienhorst's *The Seven Words of Christ from the Cross* (1956).

83. Randall Thompson's St. Luke Passion (1965) for soloists, chorus, and full orchestra was written to celebrate the 150th anniversary of the Boston Handel and Haydn Society. Daniel Pinkham's St. Mark Passion (1966) is similarly a full-scale concert work, written for solo-

ists and chorus, with brass, timpani, percussion, double bass, harp, and organ accompaniment.

84. See Minear, *Death Set to Music,* pp. 95–108.

85. Gordon W. Lathrop, *Holy Things: A Liturgical Theology* (Minneapolis, 1993), pp. 18–19; see also p. 124.

86. Ibid., p. 18.

87. Ibid., pp. 112–13.

88. Durandus, *Rationale divinorum officiorum,* ed. John Beletho (Naples, 1859), 506 (Bk. VI, chap. lxviii, 68): "Verba vero impiissimorum Iudaeorum clamose et cum asperitate vocis. . . . "

89. Even Luther, who made harsh references to Jews later in his life, opens his 1519 sermon on the passion of Christ by stating that "singing and ranting" anger against the Jews is not a valid meditation on the sufferings of Christ; see *LW* 42:7.

90. The argument is based on a comparison of the passage in question with Schütz's setting of "Das Blut Jesu Christ . . . machet uns rein von allen Sünden" ("The blood of Jesus Christ . . . cleanses us from all sin"; 1 John 1:7) in the *Kleine geistliche Concerten* of 1636 (SWV 298); see Andreas Marti, "Heil oder Gericht? Das Blut Jesu in zwei Werken von Heinrich Schütz," *Ars et musica in liturgia: Essays Presented to Casper Honders,* ed. Frans Brouwer and Robin A. Leaver (Metuchen, 1994), pp. 145–49. See also Lothar Steiger, " 'Wir haben keinen König denn den Kaiser.' Pilatus und die Juden in der Passionsgeschichte nach dem Johannesevangelium mit Bezug auf Heinrich Schütz und Johann Sebastian Bach: Oder die Frage nach dem Antijudaismus," *Musik und Kirche* 64 (1994): 264–71.

91. The significance of the chorales is not always taken into account in discussions of the treatment of the Jews in the St. John Passion; see Dagmar Hoffmann-Axthelm, "Bach und die 'Perfidia Iudaica': Zur Symmetrie der Juden-Turbae in der Johannes-Passion," *Basler Jahrbuch für historische Musikpraxis* 13 (1989): 31–54, and Michael Marissen, *Lutheranism, Anti-Judaism, and Bach's St. John Passion* (New York, 1998).

92. Translated by Daniel Reuning; used with permission.

93. Translated by Lionel Salter in the accompanying booklet to the CD recording by the Musica Antiqua Köln: Deutsche Grammaphon Archiv 447092-2.

94. See Michael Marissen, "Religious Aims in Mendelssohn's 1829 Berlin-Singakademie Performances of Bach's St. Matthew Passion," *The Musical Quarterly* 77 (1993): 718–26.

PART 4

A Symbolic Modern Dilemma

Should Christians
Celebrate the Passover?

Frank C. Senn

Since the 1960s some Christians have been participating in a form of the Jewish Passover seder as part of their Holy Week observances. It is unclear when this custom began. I have seen copies of Christianized Seders ("Seder" is used here for a script, corresponding to the Jewish Haggadah), duplicated by mimeograph, from the late 1960s and early 1970s. In these scripts or "orders" (*seder* means "order"), it is clear that the seder is designed to be a celebration of the Lord's Supper. In one script, Christ's "words of institution" are inserted at the breaking of the bread at the beginning of the meal and at the third (eucharistic) cup.[1] Another does not attempt explicitly to make the Jewish Passover meal a setting for the Lord's Supper, but it terminates psalms with the *Gloria Patri*[2] and adds the Trinitarian invocation[3] to the concluding Aaronic benediction.

Toward the end of the 1970s it was apparent that the practice of conducting Passover seders in Christian settings was becoming popular. At the same time, there was greater sensitivity to the fact that this is a *Jewish* observance, not a Gentile one. Both the United Methodist Commission on Worship and the Liturgy Training Publications of the Roman Catholic Archdiocese of Chicago published Passover Seders which respected the integrity of the Jewish rite and refrained from inserting Christianizing formulas.[4] In the same vein, Augsburg Publishing House published a Passover Seder by Barbara Balzac Thompson, a Jewish convert to Christianity, which admitted that "Christians are particularly interested in this

ritual meal because it was during a Passover celebration that
Jesus instituted Holy Communion"; nevertheless, she warned,

> Christians will want to avoid any tendency to syncretism, that is,
> mixing the Seder and the Lord's Supper so that the Seder appears
> to be a Christian observance. It is a Jewish ritual used to observe
> the Passover. The Lord's Supper is a Christian sacrament which
> was instituted by our Lord following a specific Passover obser-
> vance.[5]

In spite of the author's warning, this edition of the Passover
Seder was published to help Christians understand and *observe* the Jewish Passover. Why would Christians want to observe a Jewish rite?

As recently as 1994, a Passover Seder was published which
is a compromise between Christianizing the seder and simply
celebrating a Jewish rite. It claims to be "An Authentic Passover Seder," but includes two additions for Christians: the first
is an interpretation of the Easter egg in connection with the
Baytzah (eating the roasted egg); the second is "A Christian
Conclusion to the Seder," called "Agape," which refers to Jesus'
institution of the Lord's Supper in the context of a Passover
seder, but harmonizes the differing synoptic and Johannine
accounts[6] of the institution around the theme of the New
Covenant that "we love one another" (John 13:31). It has the
participants eat the *afikoman* (the loaf that is hidden and then
found again) during the reading of 1 Corinthians 13:1–13 (St.
Paul's great paean to love), and drink the fifth cup (the cup
for Elijah, which was never drunk at the Jewish seder) during
the reading of 1 John 4:7–21.[7]

What shall we say about these Seders for Christian use?
First, it must be admitted that they are sincere. All of the edi-
tions mentioned above have sought to increase Christian un-
derstanding of and respect for the Jewish tradition. The United
Methodist publication was prepared with Jewish consultants.
The Liturgy Training Publication Seder was actually edited by
Rabbi Leon Klenicki. Barbara Balzac Thompson drew upon
her experience of growing up in a Conservative Jewish home.
Joseph Stallinger dedicated his edition to members of Temple

Emanu-El. These Seders are designed to help Christians understand Jewish tradition.

Secondly, some of the Seders for Christian use have continued to stress the Passover context of the institution of the Lord's Supper. Even though it seems that early efforts to celebrate the Lord's Supper or eucharist[8] in the context of a Passover seder have waned, introductory material and, in Stallinger's case, an actual Haggadah in connection with the "Agape" make reference to the institution of the Lord's Supper. It seems that pastors who lead members of their congregation in a seder (or who invite a rabbi to do so) intend this experience to serve as a background for celebrating Holy Communion (and perhaps serve as a way of loosening up lugubrious western Christian liturgical celebrations).

Thirdly, commentators speak of recovering the biblical concept of memorial (*zikkaron, anamnesis*).[9] These commentators recognize the difficulty modern western people have with entering into an historical event so as to become contemporary with the event. How can we say, "In every generation let each man or woman consider it as if he or she personally came forth from Egypt. . . . It was not only our ancestors whom the Holy One redeemed. God saved us along with them"?[10] Our principal way of connecting with history has been through dramatic reenactment. One notices, for example, the popularity in America of living museums, such as Colonial Williamsburg, Greenfield Village, Sturbridge Village, or Plimouth Plantation, in which historical life is reenacted in original settings with period implements and costumes. These replications are high on entertainment value but still serve as ways of connecting people with their heritage. Unfortunately, they combat historical amnesia by promoting nostalgia rather than critical assessment.[11] Christian Passover seders are also high on retrieving historical remembrance through participatory reenactment. The same thing cannot be said about Jewish observances of the Passover seder, for reasons that will be indicated below.

In spite of the compilers' noble aims, questions must be raised about the value of the Christian use of the Jewish seder—precisely in connection with these aims. First, we must question the advisability of Christians observing non-Christian rites and festivals. What Jews think of Christians trying to replicate the holiest Jewish observance is best left to Jewish judgment. Some Jews obviously approve of such undertakings since they have advised and consulted with Christians in preparing materials. Others are critical of the practice because it blurs the particularities of the Jewish and Christian faiths. A look at the evolution of the Passover seder in Judaism will help to sharpen this question, as will a look at the Quartodeciman practice in Asia Minor. Our principal concern about the Christian celebration of Passover seders is whether misleading information is being presented about both Jewish and early Christian practice.

Secondly, we must question whether the Passover context provides the best way to understand the early Christian eucharist.[12] The discrepancy between the synoptic and Johannine versions of the institution of the Lord's Supper cannot be lightly passed over. And the witness of early Christian understandings of the eucharist, particularly as the eschatological feast, must be considered.

Thirdly, we must inquire into the western difficulty with the biblical and patristic understanding of memorial and question whether dramatic reenactment is the best form of commemoration.

The Evolution of the Passover Seder

We need not analyze deeply the long and complicated history of *pesach.* For our purposes it is necessary to remember that the festival has evolved through centuries of development and continues to do so today. The origins of the Passover festival are to be found in both nomadic and agricultural rites (*pesach,* the spring offering of the lamb from the nomad's flock, and *matsot,* the cutting of the grain and eating of unleavened bread) which antedate the time of Israel in Egypt.[13] After Israel's settlement in Palestine, the combined festival was historicized and became a commemoration of the Exodus from Egypt (Exod. 23:14–16). It did not become a national festival, however, until the time of King Josiah's reform, only a few decades before the destruction of the First Temple in Jerusalem and well after the dissolution of the northern kingdom (2 Kings 23:21–22; see also 2 Chronicles 35). This national celebration of liberation was short-lived because of the Babylonian exile and the resulting Diaspora. When the exiles returned to Palestine, they celebrated the festival again under Ezra (Ezra 6:19–22).

Passover reached its high point in national observance during the last century of the Second Temple, when Jews suffered under Roman oppression and messianic hope burned brightly. There was great expectation that a Mosaic deliverer or Elijah himself would come at Passover time to lead Israel in a new exodus from Graeco-Roman cultural and political domination. The ritual of Passover became luxurious, especially the elaborate ceremonies for the sacrifice of the Passover lambs in the Temple. The *Hallel* psalms were chanted by the Levites while the paschal lambs were slaughtered. The meat was then brought into people's homes and was roasted and eaten as *Hallel* was sung and the nucleus of a Haggadah was recited.[14] Because these lambs could not be sacrificed outside of the Temple cult, tens of thousands of pilgrims went up to Jerusalem every year to celebrate Passover. Josephus gives the extraordinary figure of 2,500,000 gathered in Jerusalem for the Passover (*Jewish War* VI. 9. 3), on the basis of a count taken by Cestius in the 60s C.E. On some occasions Jesus of Nazareth was among these pilgrims. Luke reports that every year Joseph and Mary of Nazareth went up to Jerusalem to celebrate the Passover. This Gospel relates the incident of one particular year when the boy Jesus was twelve years old (Luke 2:41 ff.). The ministry of Jesus in the Gospel of John is organized around three annual pilgrimages to Jerusalem at Passover time. The synoptic Gospels, in contrast, present only one long journey from Galilee to Jerusalem. In the week of his death, according to Mark 14:12 ff. (and parallels in Matthew and Luke), Jesus formed a *chavurah* with his disciples to eat the Passover meal.

It is obvious that the celebration of Passover changed after

the destruction of the Second Temple by the Romans in 70 C.E.
The ritual sacrifice of the lambs was no longer possible. The
course of roasted meat on a bone and a roasted egg became
reminders of the Passover sacrifice. The domestic celebration
became more important and the "script" for the domestic celebration became more formalized with the cessation of the
Temple ritual. The Haggadah was elaborately furnished with
texts of symbolic meaning and homiletic interpretations.[15] The
details of this ritual continued to develop, but essentially, the
basic content and framework of the Haggadah was established
by the time of the Mishnah (200 C.E.), tractate Pesachim.[16] The
Passover seder did not reach the form in which it is typically
celebrated today until the Middle Ages, and even then there
were variations according to geographic provenance. It is still
being shaped anew by modern Jews who adapt its contents and
message to such twentieth-century events as the Holocaust,
the birth of the state of Israel, and the impact of feminism as
a liberationist movement. It is precisely this continual evolution of the Passover seder brought about by the adaptation of
tradition to contemporary events and concerns that keeps it
from being merely a dramatic reenactment of a past event. The
Jew who celebrates the Passover seder does not think that he
or she is participating in a dramatic reenactment of the original Passover and Exodus, even though the seder is laden with
symbolic evocations of those events, in the same way that the
Christian who celebrates the seder may think that he or she
is participating in a dramatic reenactment of the context in
which the Lord's Supper was instituted by Jesus.

The point of this brief historical overview of the Jewish
celebration is to show that the Passover seder, as practiced by
Jews today, is not the Passover celebration that might have
been observed by Jesus and his disciples. It would be instruc-
tive for Christians to experience it, perhaps as guests in Jewish
homes and synagogues, but only to understand Judaism as a
living tradition. Whatever they observe there can only hint at
an understanding of what Jesus did "on the night in which he
was betrayed," if indeed he even celebrated a Passover seder

at all. This last disclaimer is occasioned by differences in chronology in the gospel traditions. But before we turn to that problem, we should note the attitude of early Christians toward the Jewish Passover as exemplified by the Christians of Asia Minor in the second century.

The Witness of the Quartodecimans

There were Christians in antiquity who were rigorous about observing the paschal celebration of Jesus on the 14th of Nisan: hence they have been called the "Quartodecimans" or fourteenthers. They inhabited primarily the region of Asia Minor. These Christians were not like the "Judaizers" St. Paul wrote against in his Letter to the Galatians. In fact, their concern was to celebrate the Passover of Christ as the fulfillment of the Passover of the Jews. The Quartodecimans apparently kept the night in vigil which lasted until cockcrow, at which point, according to the *Epistula Apostolorum,* it ended with "my agape and my commemoration" (a reference undoubtedly to the eucharist). In other words, while the Jews were feasting, these Christians observed a fast (the origins of the Easter Vigil). When the Jewish feast was ended at midnight (or slightly after), the Christians celebrated their feast—the eucharist.[17]

The practice of the Quartodecimans precipitated a controversy in the second century concerning the date of the annual Christian Pasch or Easter. The principal disputants, according to Eusebius's *Ecclesiastical History* V.23–25, were Bishops Polycarp of Smyrna and Polycrates of Ephesus, representing the church in Asia Minor, and Popes Anicetus and Victor I, representing the church of Rome. Even though the Roman Sunday observance of Easter finally won out at the Council of Nicea in 325, by which Easter was to be celebrated on the first Sunday after the first full moon of spring,[18] the Quartodecimans made an important contribution to the date of Easter in the Eastern Orthodox Church. In the eastern church, even the Sunday observance of Easter would not take place until *after* the Jewish Passover (usually a whole seven-day period), which accounts for the discrepancy to this day between the dates of the western and eastern celebrations of Easter.

There was also a difference in emphasis between the Quartodeciman Pascha and Easter as it later evolved in other Christian communities. The Roman and other churches celebrated the resurrection of Christ on the first day of the week (as, indeed, each Sunday or "Lord's Day" was observed as a day of resurrection). This meant that they eventually followed the synoptic chronology and separated the death of Christ (Good Friday) from the resurrection of Christ (Easter Day), marking both independently but emphasizing Christ's resurrection. The Quartodeciman celebration emphasized Christ's redemptive death. In his *Peri Pascha* ("Concerning the Passover," c. 165), Melito of Sardis even interpreted the Greek verb *paschein* as "to suffer."[19] He assumes in this paschal homily that the entire work of redemption occurred during the night of 14–15 Nisan; not only the crucifixion and glorification of Christ, but also the incarnation.[20] This homily views the Christian Pasch as a celebration of everything that was done for our salvation. The Quartodecimans arrived at this conclusion by following the Johannine rather than the synoptic tradition, with its emphasis on the incarnation of the divine Logos and its anti-gnostic sacramentalism.

Was the Last Supper a Passover Seder?

The Johannine passion chronology raises the question whether the Last Supper of Jesus was a Passover meal. If the Last Supper was a Passover meal, as the synoptic Gospels maintain, then everything that followed—the arrest, the hearing before the Sanhedrin, the trial before Pontius Pilate, the flogging and execution of Jesus—all had to have occurred on the first full day of the Passover festival itself. Joachim Jeremias was willing to argue that all this could have taken place during the festival without compromising Jewish custom, because his concern was to establish the Last Supper as a Passover seder.[21] Mark 14:12 is specific that Jesus dispatched his disciples to make arrangements for a Passover seder "on the first day of Unleavened Bread, when the Passover lamb is sacrificed" (a chronology followed in Matthew 26:17 ff. and Luke 22:7 ff.). Yet it strains the imagination to think of all this bothersome activity going on during a day that was so tightly-packed with responsibilities for the Temple staff.

The Gospel of John, however, is also quite clear that the Last Supper took place "before the festival of the Passover" (John 13:1). It also places the death of Jesus on the Day of Preparation, at the time when the lambs were being slaughtered in the Temple. Commentators have long assumed that the synoptic chronology is correct, and that the Gospel of John altered the time sequence to accommodate the symbolism of Jesus, "the Lamb of God who takes away the sins of the world" (John 1:29), being put to death at the same time as the paschal lambs were being slaughtered in the Temple. But theological concerns alone would not be sufficient to affect chronology. Furthermore, the synoptic Gospels had their own theological agendas. In fact, Luke may have emphasized the Passover seder as the setting of the Last Supper in order to indicate that the Lord's Supper fulfills and supersedes the Passover. This Gospel has Jesus state that he would not eat the Passover until it is fulfilled in the kingdom of God, and then he proceeds to celebrate it by taking the first cup and breaking the bread (Luke 22:14 ff.).

There have been numerous attempts to reconcile the discrepancies between the two gospel traditions by appealing to special calendars that Jesus might have been following (such as the solar calendar used by the Essenes in which the 15th of Nisan always fell on a Tuesday evening/Wednesday).[22] But these various attempts at reconciliation of the conflicting gospel chronologies have not won widespread critical acceptance because of weak supporting evidence.

There is no doubt that Passover themes were, in fact, included in the Last Supper according to John.[23] Yet the inclusion of such themes settles neither the chronology issue nor the question of whether the Last Supper was a Passover seder. Raymond Brown suggests the more likely scenario that Jesus and his disciples celebrated a meal together in Jerusalem before the beginning of the Passover, which, because of the proximity of the great feast, had paschal overtones. John does not relate the institution of the Lord's Supper in this context. It is possible that the synoptic tradition jumped to the conclusion that it was a Passover meal, whereas John independently retained the more correct chronological information.[24] The net result of this discrepancy, however, is that we cannot claim with absolute certainty that the Last Supper was a Passover seder.

In any event, the meal elements which Jesus focused on for sacramental purposes were not the elements unique to the Passover, such as the roasted lamb and bitter herbs. Rather, he added his words of interpretation to the broken bread at the start of the meal and the cup of blessing over which the thanksgiving would have been said at the end of the meal.[25] These are the elements which would have been common to any meal. Recognizing this fact, the Christian tradition as a whole never even made an effort to use only unleavened bread. In fact, when the western church began to use unleavened wafers in Holy Communion in the ninth century, it was intended to facilitate the reverent handling of the consecrated elements. This was a development that led the Greeks to accuse the Latins of acting "mosaically" and of "eating at the tables of the Jews."[26]

It remains to be pointed out that, for whatever reasons (perhaps an imperial ban on evening meetings of associations in the second century, necessitating early Sunday morning gatherings for the eucharist, or perhaps the custom of ending all-night Saturday vigils with the eucharist at dawn on Sunday, or perhaps some combination of both), Christians continued celebrating the eucharist using only the elements of bread and wine and apart from the context of an actual meal. In fact, already in the earliest account of the Lord's Supper (1 Cor. 11), St. Paul moves in the direction of distinguishing the Lord's Supper from the church's supper ("your own meal"). Thus, the standard Christian eucharistic celebration which emerged during the second century did not use the food most characteristic of the Passover seder; nor was it practiced in the context of an actual meal, as the Passover seder would have required.

Eucharist and Eschatology

The reason why the context of the Passover meal was not essential to the Lord's Supper is that the sacramental meal was the means of celebrating the presence of the crucified and risen Christ among his faithless disciples, not just a way of recalling the blissful days of being with Jesus during his earthly ministry. The resurrection was an eschatological event, not something that could happen in history. The presence of the risen and glorified Christ among his failed disciples, by his very presence bestowing the gift of forgiveness and reconciliation, made the eucharistic meal the "Lord's Supper" (*kyriakon deipnon,* first used in 1 Corinthians 11:20). The celebration of this meal on the first day of the week, observed as the day of resurrection, made that day the "Lord's Day" (*kyriake hemera,* first used in Revelation [Apocalypse] 1:10). The Lord's Supper on the Lord's Day was more a "foretaste of the feast to come" (the marriage supper of the Lamb in Revelation 19:6–7) than a backward-looking historical commemoration of the Last Supper of Jesus and his disciples.[27]

The whole mission and message of Jesus had been charged with eschatological urgency. He proclaimed the kingdom of God and performed signs of healing and exorcism indicative of the presence of God's reign in his ministry and expressive of God's will for the wholeness of the creation (which is also why some of these healings were scandalously performed on the Sabbath). Jesus looked forward to feasting in the kingdom of God, and his eating with outcasts and sinners was a realization of the kingdom-feast in which "many shall come from east and west and will eat with Abraham and Isaac and Jacob in the kingdom of heaven," while those who thought they should have been included would find themselves excluded (Matt. 8:11 ff.; Luke 13:29 ff.). The very fact that the meal celebrated by Jesus with his disciples in the upper room "on the night in which he was betrayed" is called the "Last Supper" in the Christian tradition is a recognition that there had been many "suppers" during Jesus' ministry which served as anticipations of the banquet of the kingdom of God.

This "Last Supper" anticipated Jesus' death, which the synoptic Gospels viewed as a sacrifice sealing the new covenant. To the Markan words of institution Matthew added, "for the forgiveness of sins" (Matt. 26:28), which was associated with the acquittal of the last judgment. The earliest literary account of the institution, by Paul, interpreted the meal as a "proclamation of the Lord's death until he comes" (1 Cor. 11:26). The remembrance of Christ in the eucharistic meal prompted an urgent plea for Christ's coming again (*maranatha,* "Our Lord, come," 1 Cor. 16:22; *Didache* 10:6). The crucified Jesus is also the risen Christ and the ascended Lord who will come again as universal Judge and Ruler. Just as Matthew emphasizes the eschatological judgment of acquittal (the forgiveness of sin) as the condition and gift of communion, so Paul warned the Corinthians to eat and drink "worthily" because of the presence of the One who comes again as Judge. He charged that their divisive behavior at the Lord's Supper had already brought negative judgment upon them ("That is why many of you are weak and ill, and some have died," 1 Cor. 11:30).

In sum, the eucharistic meal in the early church was not just a historical commemoration of what took place "on the night in which he was betrayed" (although it was historically anchored to the sacramental institution of that night); rather, it was the celebration of the presence of the risen One with his wayward disciples, conveying by his very presence in the shared meal the gift of eschatological forgiveness and reconciliation.[28]

Effective and Affective Memorial

In view of the foregoing, how do we account for the desire of some Christians to celebrate the Jewish Passover as a ritual means of putting them in closer touch with the historical Jesus? Clearly the Passover seder now observed by Jewish communities is not identical with the Passover meal of Jesus' time. In particular, the sacrificial cult of the Jerusalem Temple, which was so crucial to the gospel interpretations of Jesus' death as the paschal lamb, no longer exists. We cannot even say with certainty that the eucharistic rite Jesus commanded his disciples to observe was instituted in the context of an actual Passover seder. Even the witness of the Quartodecimans, who observed Passover eve with a fast and a vigil, did not commemorate the Last Supper as a Passover feast, but celebrated Jesus' passover from death to life as a fulfillment of the Passover hopes and expectations. St. Paul too proclaimed Christ's Passover as the inauguration of a new way of life. "For Christ, our paschal lamb, has been sacrificed. Let us, therefore, celebrate the festival, not with the old leaven, the leaven of malice and evil, but with the unleavened bread of sincerity and truth" (1 Cor. 5:7–8). Indeed, I would argue that Paul, the former Pharisee and student of Gamaliel, was doing what the Jews have always done: he was "updating" the meaning of the Passover festival to address new circumstances. We might note as well that references to the Last Supper are found only in institution narratives included in later eucharistic prayers, but that some early eucharistic prayers (e.g., *Didache* 9–10, and the East Syrian Anaphora of Addai and Mari) lack an institution narrative altogether. Even the Anaphora of Hippolytus, so influential on current Christian eucharistic rites, lacks a reference to the formula, "on the night in which he was betrayed"; instead it refers to the one who was "handed over to a death he freely accepted." But the thrust is totally eschatological: Jesus freely accepted this death "in order to destroy death, to break the bonds of the evil one, to crush hell underfoot, to give light to the righteous, to establish his covenant, and to show forth the resurrection," in anticipation and celebration of which he took the bread and cup, giving thanks, and giving these gifts to his disciples as communion in his body and blood.[29]

Those who claim that celebrating the Passover seder helps modern western Christians (perhaps modern western Jews as well) better apprehend the biblical understanding of "memorial" have put their fingers on the heart of the issue. The western mind has difficulty understanding *anamnesis* as reactualization. In the classical Graeco-Roman worldview the "really real" is the symbolic; in the western worldview it is the empirical. The classical view of symbol lingered on well into the Middle Ages, but occasioned eucharistic controversies in the ninth through the eleventh centuries as it clashed with the more indigenous view of "symbol" and "reality," creating irreconcilable misunderstandings. By the twelfth century people had begun to acquire "a fresh sense of the immediacies of concrete experience, a new attachment to physical actualities," which led to the rise of the natural sciences.[30] This new attention to the sensual also played an important role in heightening eucharistic realism during the Middle Ages, prompting devotions centered around exposing the host rather than eating it.

It is not surprising that in this cultural context, memorial became *memesis,* imitation or reenactment, or *recordatio,* recollection achieved through affective means. One thinks of the ways in which biblical events were presented to the faithful during the Middle Ages: in allegorical commentaries on the mass (beginning already with Theodore of Mopsuestia in fourth-century Syria, but reaching a high point during the Carolingian Renaissance, especially in the *Expositio Missae* of Amalarius of Metz), which in turn prompted a ceremonial that aimed at making the mass a reenactment of the passion of Christ. Biblical events were also portrayed in the pictures in stained-glass windows, in paintings on the walls of church buildings, in statuary carved in stone, in chancel dramas and mystery plays. In a culture which reenacted in ritual drama the Palm Sunday triumphal procession (e.g., at Salisbury) and the Maundy Thursday footwashing (e.g., at Milan), which found a role for little liturgical music dramas (e.g., *Quem pastores* at Christmas, *Victimae paschali laudes* at Easter), and which produced passion plays enlisting the participation of whole populations of villages (a tradition that continues in America in "living Nativity scenes" and drive-through "Passion dioramas"), it is not surprising that a fondness would develop for Passover seders in an attempt to come historically close to the Last Supper and to the historical Jesus.

It is also not surprising that Christian observance of Passover seders began in the Reformed tradition (although they have also been observed in Roman Catholic and Lutheran parishes). The chief characteristic of Zwinglian/Reformed/ Puritan spirituality has been a historical criticism which attempts to peel away the layers of tradition in order to get at and therefore be able to experience the original event. The celebration of the Lord's Supper thus became a reenactment of the Last Supper, so as to be put in mind of Christ's sacrifice for our redemption. The accoutrements and practices of later liturgical history—altars, candles, gold or silver vessels, vestments, kneeling for reception of Holy Communion—were abolished in favor of tables, wooden or pewter vessels, street clothing for ministers (in this case academic gowns), and sitting "about" or "at" the communion table for the distribution.[31] The whole thrust of the Reformed/Puritan celebration of the Lord's Supper was to make it as close to what Jesus did in the upper room as the Reformers' knowledge allowed. This tradition of "historical realism" has flourished in America, where it contributed profoundly to the biblicism of the "American religion"—i.e., the quest to discover and do what is in the Bible without the intervening hermeneutical traditions of Jewish sages, church fathers, ecumenical councils, creeds, summas, liturgies, confessions, and so on.[32]

The whole western Christian tradition since the Middle Ages has operated with an affective rather than an effective understanding of memorial: that is, with a sense that making the participant one with the saving event requires a dramatic reenactment of the original event which elicits a subjective response from the participant (who experiences the event anew in the celebration), rather than relying on the creative power of the word and rite to make the celebration one with the saving event. Odo Casel, the celebrated monk of Maria Laach Abbey in Germany earlier in this century, tried to recover the effective understanding of memorial found in the Bible and the church fathers by means of the concept of cultic reactualization (*Gegenwärtigung*). He wrote: "The mystery of worship makes present among us the saving act of Christ in word and rite."[33] The saving act is re-presented (not represented in the sense of portrayal) by performing the rite. So, by taking bread and wine, giving thanks over them in remembrance of Christ's redemptive acts, and eating and drinking the bread and wine as communion in the body and blood of Christ, the redemptive acts of Christ are present with their salutary benefits in the contemporary celebration. This sense of effective memorial requires ritual enactment, but not cult drama. The community of faith does not do what Christ did in the upper room by way of replicating that event; rather it does what Christ commanded it to do in its own time and place, as spelled out in the "rubrics" of the institution narratives (taking, blessing, breaking, giving).

The reformer Martin Luther also strained after a more effective understanding of memorial, although he emphasized the creative and redemptive power of the word of God more than the performance of the rite (although by no means excluding the necessity of performing the rite as instituted and mandated). But against the dramatic spectacle of the Roman mass interpreted allegorically in the *Expositiones missae*, on the one hand, and the Zwinglian memorial of the Last Supper on the other, both of which in Luther's view cultivated spiritualism ("the inward thoughts of the heart"), Luther said that "This memorial requires a sermon."[34] For Luther "remembrance" (*Gedächtnis*) must be an act of proclamation. The words of scripture, of the sermon, of prayer, as well as the "visible words" of the sacramental rite, elicit the response of faith but do not depend on that response for their efficacy. John Calvin, like Luther, also had a lively sense of the presence of God in the preaching of the word and believed that one receives Christ through the obedient ritual use of the signs of bread and wine.[35]

Luther and Calvin, in their theologies of the word of God, come close to the understanding of "the word" (*davar*) in the Hebrew Bible. Words cause things to happen—the word of God above all. God's word is God's action. "By the word of the Lord were the heavens made . . . for God spoke and it came to pass" (Ps. 33:6, 9). God's word goes forth from his mouth and does not return to God empty; "but it shall accomplish that which I purpose, and prosper in the thing for which I sent it" (Isa. 55:11).[36]

Thus, the satisfaction modern western (especially American) Christians have experienced in celebrations of the Passover seder is located in the wider cultural predilection for affective religion. The western approach to cultic memorial, also profoundly influenced by the subjectivism of the Enlightenment, is rooted in this cultural context. For this reason I see no likelihood of a widespread return to and embracing of the kind of effective memorial found in the Bible and patristic liturgy, in the faith and practice of the Reformation (particularly in Luther and Calvin), or in the "mystery theology" of Odo Casel. But at least in this one case we may say that if we are truly interested in a shared experience with Jewish brothers and sisters of the observance of the Pasch, co-opting the seder as a Christian celebration of what Jesus may have done is not the way. We should instead give renewed attention to the Christian Pasch (the Easter Vigil) with its Proclamation (the *Exultet*) and long series of readings from the Hebrew Bible, so as to arrive at a common experience of our life with the God of Israel who is also the Abba of our Lord Jesus Christ.

Pesach and Pascha: A Shared Experience

What needs to be shared between Jews and Christians, to bind us together in the biblical faith, is our common experience of the mighty acts of God. The original night of the Passover in Egypt was a night of pure terror which required absolute obedience and trust on the part of the people of Israel. As the angel of death passed over their homes, claiming every first-born human and animal in Egypt, the Israelites had to obey the instructions of Moses to perform the apotropaic act of painting the blood of the lamb on the doorposts of their dwellings; and they had to trust that by this act their first-born would be spared. In the same way Jesus had to obey the Father's will by submitting even to death on the cross, and then

entrust himself in death to his heavenly Father. The biblical
narratives read at the Easter Vigil contain elements of destruction: the destruction of chaos by God's creative word/act; the
destruction of the sinful world by the waters of the flood and
the salvation of Noah and his family and all those animals in
the ark; God's instruction to Abraham to sacrifice his only
son Isaac; the Israelites crossing the Red Sea and the drowning
of Pharaoh's soldiers and horses; Jonah crying from the belly
of the great fish; and Shadrach, Meschach, and Abednego
thrown into the fiery furnace for refusing to worship King
Nebuchadnezzar's golden image. A quaint rabbinic gloss on
the Exodus story of the crossing of the sea pictures God re-
buking the angels in heaven for not weeping over the destruction of the beautiful Egyptians who are God's children too.
The point is that terror and destruction are real and cannot
be easily explained away. We are left in the hands of the living
and true God who can destroy and save.

The Passover of the Jews has been celebrated many times
during nights of terror. It has not only been a festival of liberation but a festival of fear.[37] Jews in medieval Europe were
rounded up and killed because of the "blood libel" which
charged that they killed Christian children to get blood for
making *matsah*. Also during the Middle Ages the secret Jews
of Spain and Portugal (the Marranos) celebrated the Passover
according to what they could learn about it from the Latin
Bible (and therefore as it was practiced during the time of the
kings and prophets of ancient Israel) because they could not
get Jewish books. There were secret Passover seders in the Jewish ghettoes of Eastern Europe during times of persecution
and the Nazi Holocaust. The aspect of Passover as a festival of
fear is not learned by non-Jews, including Christians, without
going into Jewish communities as guests to hear the stories of
faith since the time of the Jewish-Christian schism at the end
of the first century C.E.

Christians share with Jews the terrors of "the Paschal Feast
in which the true Lamb is slain, by whose blood the doorposts
of the faithful are made holy." Jews and Christians share the

dangers of "this night." For "this indeed is the night" in which the children of Israel are delivered from Egypt and "led dryshod, through the Red Sea." "This is the night in which, breaking the chains of death, Christ arises from hell in triumph."[38]

We recall the calendrical juxtaposition of Passover and Easter. In some years these two festivals occur on the same calendar date or in close proximity to each other. Dialogue between Jewish and Christian faith communities might follow the separate celebrations of *Pesach* and *Pascha*. The common human experiences of fear and faith can be explored and shared in these discussions.

Such dialogue will be aided if the Christian Pasch does not minimize the terrors and dangers of this night, or other terrors and dangers we face in daily life and in historical existence, by explaining away all that is terrible and dangerous. The celebration of the Easter Vigil has its physical dangers. It begins around a bonfire which gives light and warmth, but which also poses a threat should it get out of control. The congregation processes into a church building that has been plunged into darkness as dark as the darkness of a grave or a tomb (even the "exit" lights are turned off). That may be "spooky" enough; but the numerous hand-held candles also constitute a danger that would worry local fire departments and possibly even violate local safety ordinances. The night of vigil comes to an end with candidates for baptism being plunged into the waters of baptism, for which some baptismal pools remind us of drowning as well as birthing. The baptismal rite itself calls for a renunciation of the Evil One as well as a confession of faith in God the Father, Son, and Holy Spirit; and proper pre-baptismal catechesis names instances of methodical evil, wanton destruction, and innocent suffering in the world. Often such suffering is the consequence of pure opposition to God's rule and will. But such evil and sin is not to be explained away; it is to be faced squarely and renounced firmly as preliminary to the confession of faith in the triune God.

The point is that the true Christian Passover is the Easter Vigil, and it expresses both Christian continuity and

discontinuity with the Jewish Passover. Until congregations
have learned to observe and celebrate well their own paschal
feast, they have no business trying to celebrate someone else's.
And even those congregations which do celebrate the Christian Passover well need to reconsider the practice of celebrating the Jewish one, for reasons offered in this essay. On the
other hand, a proper celebration of the Christian Passover
gives Christians food for sharing in interfaith dialogue, which
could lead to affirming our common experience of life under
the gracious rule of a faithful and loving God.

NOTES

1. This practice prompted my earlier article, "The Lord's Supper, Not the Passover Seder," *Worship* 60 (1986): 362–68.
2. It has been a standard Christian practice to terminate both
Old Testament psalms and New Testament canticles with the doxol-
ogy, "Glory to the Father and to the Son and to the Holy Spirit; as
it was in the beginning, is now, and will be forever. Amen."
3. "In the Name of the Father and of the Son and of the Holy
Spirit."
4. See "A Passover Meal (seder) with Commentary," *From
Ashes to Fire: Services of Worship for the Seasons of Lent and Easter,*
Supplemental Worship Resources 8 (Nashville, 1979), pp. 214–30; *The
Passover Celebration: A Haggadah for the Seder,* ed. Rabbi Leon
Klenicki, introduction by Gabe Huck (The Anti-Defamation
League of B'nai B'rith and The Liturgy Training Publications of the
Archdiocese of Chicago, 1980). The United Methodist Church has
been especially sensitive to anti-Semitic expressions in the liturgical
tradition by rewriting the infamous Reproaches in the Good Friday
Liturgy. The Archdiocese of Chicago, under the leadership of Joseph
Cardinal Bernardin, has made a special effort to develop fraternal
relationships with the Jewish community of metropolitan Chicago.
5. Barbara Balzac Thompson, *Passover Seder: Ritual and Menu
for an Observance by Christians* (Minneapolis, 1984), p. 3.
6. "Synoptic" Gospels refer to the Gospels according to St.
Matthew, St. Mark, and St. Luke, which critical studies have shown
to "look toward" one another, probably with Mark being a "source"

used by Matthew and Luke. "Johannine" refers to the Gospel according to St. John, which critical studies regard as an independent tradition from the synoptic Gospels not relying on the synoptic sources.

7. See Joseph M. Stallinger, *Celebrating an Authentic Passover Seder: A Haggadah for Home and Church* (San Jose, 1994).

8. See Frank C. Senn, "Eucharistic Liturgy, Names for the," in *The New Dictionary of Sacramental Worship*, ed. Peter Fink (Collegeville, 1990), pp. 448–51.

9. See especially the introductions in the Liturgy Training Publication Seder and in Stallinger, *Celebrating an Authentic Passover Seder.*

10. *The Birnbaum Haggadah,* ed. Philip Birnbaum (New York, 1969), p. 94.

11. See Michael Kammen, *Mystic Chords of Memory: The Transformation of Tradition in American Culture* (New York, 1991), pp. 531 ff.

12. The names "Eucharist," "Lord's Supper," and "Holy Communion" are used interchangeably in Christian literature and among Christian denominations.

13. See Thierry Maertens, *A Feast in Honor of Yahweh* (Notre Dame, 1965), pp. 100 ff.

14. See Hayyim Schauss, *Guide to Jewish Holy Days: History and Observance* (New York, 1938; 1962), especially pp. 48 ff.

15. See A. Z. Idelsohn, *Jewish Liturgy and Its Development* (New York, 1932; 1960; 1967), pp. 176 ff.

16. See *The Mishnah,* trans. with introduction by Herbert Danby (Oxford, 1933), pp. 136 ff.; or *The Mishnah: A New Translation,* ed. Jacob Neusner (New Haven, 1988), pp. 249–57.

17. See Thomas J. Talley, *The Origins of the Liturgical Year* (New York, 1986), pp. 5 ff.

18. See Adolf Adam, *The Liturgical Year* (New York, 1981), p. 59.

19. See A. Hamman, *The Paschal Mystery* (Staten Island, N.Y., 1969), p. 31.

20. Following rabbinic belief that the creation of the world occurred in the spring of the year, at Passover time, the Quartodecimans reasoned that the new creation, which began with the incarnation of the Word, also began in the spring of the year. Hence, the Annunciation to the Virgin Mary was celebrated originally on the same day as Jesus' death, and remains to this day March 25. Talley and others have suggested that this calendrical calculation is the

origin of the date of Christmas, since nine months after March 25 is December 25.

21. See Joachim Jeremias, *The Eucharistic Words of Jesus,* trans. Norman Perrin (New York, 1966).

22. Strongly defended by A. Jaubert, *The Date of the Last Supper* (Staten Island, N.Y., 1965), but unfavorably received by exegetes, including Jeremias, Benoit, and Brown.

23. See P. Benoit, "The Holy Eucharist," *Scripture* 8 (1956): 97–108.

24. Raymond E. Brown, *The Anchor Bible: The Gospel according to John XIII–XXI* (Garden City, N.J., 1970), p. 556.

25. The unique sequence of cup-bread-cup in the longer narrative in Luke is dealt with in a convincing way in Arthur Vööbus, *The Prelude to the Lukan Passion Narrative* (Stockholm, 1968).

26. See Jaroslav Pelikan, *The Christian Tradition,* vol. 2, *The Spirit of Eastern Christendom (600–1700)* (Chicago, 1974), pp. 176–79.

27. See Geoffrey Wainwright, *Eucharist and Eschatology* (Oxford and New York, 1981), who explicates the meanings of the eucharist as the antepast of heaven, the parousia of Christ, and the realization of the church as the firstfruits of the new creation.

28. See Norman Perrin, *Recovering the Teaching of Jesus* (New York, 1967), p. 107.

29. See the texts of these eucharistic prayers, also called "anaphoras" (from the invitatory "Lift up your hearts/minds") in *Prayers of the Eucharist: Early and Reformed,* ed. and trans. with commentaries by R. D. C. Jasper and G. J. Cuming, 3rd ed. (New York, 1987).

30. See Lynn White, Jr., "Natural Science and Naturalistic Art in the Middle Ages," in *Medieval Religion and Technology: Collected Essays* (Berkeley, 1978), pp. 27–33.

31. *The Westminster Directory for the Publique Worship of God* (1644) devised these rubrics for posture as a compromise between Presbyterians who sat "at" the table passing the elements to one another and the Congregationalists who sat "about" the table (i.e., in their pews) and had the elements brought to them by ministers. See *Liturgies of the Western Church,* selected and introduced by Bard Thompson (New York and Scarborough, Ontario, 1961), p. 369; discussion on p. 352.

32. See Harold Bloom, *The American Religion: The Emergence of the Post-Christian Nation* (New York, 1992), p. 81.

33. Odo Casel, *The Mystery of Christian Worship and Other Writings,* ed. Burkhard Neunheuser (Westminster, Md., 1962), p. 142.

34. See Carl F. Wislöff, *The Gift of Communion: Luther's Controversy with Rome on Eucharistic Sacrifice* (Minneapolis, 1964), p. 89.

35. See Brian A. Gerrish, *The Old Protestantism and the New* (Chicago, 1982), especially pp. 111 ff.

36. See Gerhard von Rad, *Old Testament Theology,* vol. 2 (New York, 1965), pp. 81 ff.

37. See Schauss, *Guide to Jewish Holy Days,* pp. 57 ff.

38. From the *Exultet* of the Easter Vigil. See *Lutheran Book of Worship,* Ministers Edition (Minneapolis, 1978), p. 144.

Contributors

PAUL F. BRADSHAW, an Anglican priest, is professor of liturgy at the University of Notre Dame and editor-in-chief of *Studia Liturgica*. Among his recent books are *The Search for the Origins of Christian Worship* (SPCK/Oxford University Press, 1992), *Two Ways of Praying* (SPCK/Abingdon Press, 1995), and *Early Christian Worship: An Introduction to Ideas and Practice* (SPCK, 1996).

MARTIN F. CONNELL teaches in the School of Theology at Saint John's University in Collegeville, Minnesota. He is the author of *A Parish's Introduction to the Liturgical Year* (Loyola Press, 1997) and *The Guide of the Revised Lectionary* (Liturgy Training Publications, 1998).

JOSEPH GUTMANN is professor emeritus of art history, Wayne State University, and an ordained rabbi from Hebrew Union College–Jewish Institute of Religion, Cincinnati. Among his eighteen books are *The Temple of Solomon, No Graven Images, Hebrew Manuscript Painting, The Dura-Europos Synagogue,* and *The Jewish Life Cycle*. He lives in Huntington Woods, Michigan, with his wife of forty-five years, Marilyn.

LAWRENCE A. HOFFMAN is an ordained rabbi and professor of liturgy at the Hebrew Union College–Jewish Institute of Religion, New York. His books include *The Canonization of the Synagogue Service* (University of Notre Dame Press, 1979), *Beyond the Text* (Indiana University Press, 1988) and *Covenant of Blood: Circumcision and Gender in Rabbinic Judaism* (University of Chicago Press, 1995). He is the general editor of *Minhag*

Ami: My People's Prayer Book (Jewish Lights Publications, 1997–), a projected eight-volume series containing the liturgy of the synagogue and a series of modern commentaries.

Maxwell E. Johnson is an ordained pastor in the Evangelical Lutheran Church in America and Associate Professor of Liturgy at the University of Notre Dame. His publications include *The Prayers of Sarapion of Thmuis* (Rome: Pontifical Oriental Institute, 1995) and *Living Water, Sealing Spirit: Readings on Christian Initiation* (The Liturgical Press, 1995).

Robin A. Leaver, an ordained Anglican, is a professor of sacred music at Westminster Choir College of Rider University, Princeton, and visiting professor of liturgy at Drew University, Madison, N.J. He has written widely on liturgy and music and is the editor of the series of monographs, *Studies in Liturgical Musicology,* and coeditor of the series, *Drew University Studies in Liturgy.* His most recent book (coedited with Joyce A. Zimmerman) is *Liturgy and Music: Lifetime Learning* (The Liturgical Press, 1998).

Frank C. Senn is an ordained minister in the Evangelical Lutheran Church in America. He received his doctorate in liturgical studies from the University of Notre Dame and has held academic appointments at the Lutheran School of Theology at Chicago and the University of Chicago Divinity School. Pastor of Immanuel Lutheran Church in Evanston, Illinois, since 1990, and past president of the Liturgical Conference and the North American Academy of Liturgy, his works include *Christian Worship: Catholic and Evangelical* (Fortress Press, 1997) and *A Stewardship of the Mysteries* (Paulist Press, 1998).

Efrat Zarren-Zohar is an ordained rabbi from Hebrew Union College–Jewish Institute of Religion, New York, and has served since 1993 as Director of Adult Education and Outreach at the Central Agency for Jewish Education in Miami. She resides in Hollywood, Florida, with her husband, Dr. Zion Zohar, and son, Matan Yitzhak.

Index

Abrahams, Israel, 80, 120–21, 130n. 54

à Burck, Joachim (Moller), 155

Acts of the Apostles, 98, 102, 105n. 1

Acts of the Martyrs, use of term "Great Sabbath," 29–30

afikoman (see also matsah): in Christianized seder, 184; derivation of term, 113, 126n. 22; interpretations of, 112–13, 127nn. 22, 29; regulations for eating, 111, 118–19

African-American spirituals, 165

Akiba, Rabbi, 76, 85; death of students linked to the *S'firah,* 79–80, 81, 83, 87, 91n. 31

Akiva, Rabbi, 91n. 35

Alexandrian Christianity, 37, 47, 57, 65; origin of forty-day fast seen in, 44–47, 49–50, 53n. 35, 64

Alexandrian Judaism, 57

Alfasi, 130n. 47

Ambrose, 117

amoraim, 120, 127n. 29; regulations on Passover, 113–15, 116, 126n. 9

Amphiloque (bishop of Iconium), 104

anaphoras, 195, 203n. 29

angels, depicted in medieval Haggadahs, 136, 140, 141

Anglican Church (Church of England), 162–64

Anicetus (pope), 189

Annunciation, the, 203n. 20

anti-Semitism: in deaths of Pionius and Polycarp, 31; medieval, 167, 200; tendencies in passion music, 167–70; twentieth-century Christian efforts to combat, 202n. 4

Apostolic Constitutions, 18, 101

Apostolic Traditions (attributed to Hippolytus), 21, 37, 43, 44–45, 51n. 6

Aramaic language, 123

Armenia, early Christian tradition, 23, 40, 42, 43, 62

arts, 2, 7–8, 10; Haggadah illumination traditions, 132–43

Ascension, Feast of the, 97–99, 100–102, 103–5

Ashkenazi, 125n. 5; Haggadah illumination tradition, 132, 133, 136–40, 141–42

Ash Wednesday, 47

Athanasius, 22, 39, 47, 96

atonement, 9–10

Augsburg Publishing House, 183–84

Baal, ritual for, *omer* linked with, 75, 90n. 10

Babli, the, 112, 114, 119–21

Babylonia, ancient, celebration in honor of victory of Marduk, 92n. 54

Babylonian Jews, 15, 187; Passover seder customs, 114–15, 118–19, 121, 129nn. 42, 43, 47

Bach, Carl Philipp Emmanuel, 159
Bach, Johann Sebastian, 157–59,
    163–64, 165, 168–69, 177nn.
    56, 58
Bahr, Gordon J., 126n. 14
Baldovin, John, 38
Balin, Carole, 10
baptism, 8, 42–44, 47–48, 64–67
    on Easter, 42–43, 55, 65, 201;
    Council of Nicea on, 46–47,
    48; preparation for, 36, 37,
    39–41, 45–46, 49–50, 51n. 6,
    52n. 15, 54n. 48
    preparation for not associated
    with Easter, 57, 59, 61, 64, 95
Bar Kochba rebellion, 91n. 31
Bar Yochai, Rabbi Shimon, 85–86
Baumstark, Anton, 44, 56
Beethoven, Ludwig van, 163
Ben Asher, Jacob, 82
benediction(s): in contemporary
    S'firat Ha'omer ritual, 87;
    over bread, 116–17, 118,
    129n. 43
Bernardin, Joseph Cardinal, 202n. 4
Bible, the (see also New Testament;
    Old Testament): 1534 Ger-
    man, 153; medieval illustra-
    tions, 132; scenes from in
    Spanish Haggadahs, 140;
    singing of texts from, 166
    (see also music, church)
bikkurim (first fruits), 74
Binding of Isaac, depiction of, 141
Bird's Head Haggadah, 136–37
birkat hamazon (after-dinner
    Grace), 129n. 47
bitter herbs (maror), 7, 118–19; de-
    piction in Haggadah illumi-
    nations, 132, 139, 140, 142
Blarr, Gottlieb, 170
Block, Abraham, 91n. 31
blood, symbolism of, 128n. 32
Boethusians, 77–78, 91n. 22

Böhm, Georg, 157
bonfires, as Lag Ba'omer custom,
    84–86
books: medieval illustrations, 132–
    43; role in Jewish and Chris-
    tian traditions, 134–35
bows and arrows, playing with, as
    Lag Ba'omer custom, 84–85
Bradshaw, Paul F., 1–12, 43, 44, 55
Braun, Werner, 175n. 40
bread, 7, 115–17 (see also matsah)
    as element of the eucharist, 192
    second offering of S'firat
    Ha'omer in form of, 74, 77
    as symbol of salvation, 115–17,
    123; in the Passover seder,
    10, 109–25
Brockes, Barthold Heinrich, 159–
    60, 177n. 58
Brown, Raymond, 191–92
Bugenhagen, Johannes, 153, 173nn.
    22, 25
Byrd, William, 151
Byzantine Christian tradition, 37,
    42, 53n. 35

Cairo Genizah, 132
Calvin, John, 198–99
Calvinism, 162
candles, use during Easter vigil, 201
Canonical Epistle (Peter of Alexan-
    dria), 44–45
Canons of Hippolytus, 44–45, 96
Casel, Odo, 197–98, 199
catechumens, 8, 39, 44, 48, 52n. 15,
    105n. 10; pre-paschal prepa-
    ration, 36, 37, 40, 45–46,
    48–50
Chag Hakatzir (Feast of Reaping),
    73
chag hamatzot (Passover), 110
Chag Hashavuot (Feast of Weeks),
    73–74
Chama bar Chanina, Rabbi, 26

chanting of the passion narratives, in liturgy: Catholic, 147–48, 150, 173n. 22; Protestant, 153, 173n. 25, 178n. 71

charoset, 128n. 32, 141

Chasidic Jews, 85

Chavasse, Antoine, 22–23, 28, 40, 41, 52n. 15, 63

children, 3, 84–85

chorales, inclusion in passions, 156–57, 168–70, 180n. 91

choral passion. *See* polyphonic passions, responsorial

Choral-Passion (Distler), 164, 179n. 78

Christianity (*see also individual denominations and topics*): shared experiences with Judaism, 199–202

Christians, as illustrators of Haggadahs, 133

Christmas, 149, 204n. 12

Chromatius of Aquileia (bishop). 101

chronology: as approach to the Great Sabbath in Christian tradition, 29–32; as approach to periods of time related to Lent, 60–62

Chrysostom, John, 23, 48, 67, 101

Church of England (Anglican Church), 162–64

cleansing from impurity, in Jewish tradition, 25–26, 27, 34n. 25, 41, 55, 60, 61, 63, 66

climate, importance for *S'firat Ha'omer,* 72–76

commemoration, post-Constantian liturgy focused on, 36–37

Common Prayer, Book of (Anglican), 162, 164, 178n. 70

concert performances of Catholic masses, 166 of passion music, 159–60, 161, 162–63, 165–66; anti-Semitic tendencies in, 167, 168–70

Congregationalists, 204n. 31

Connell, Martin, 10, 94–106

Conservative Judaism, *S'firat Ha'omer* ritual, 88–89

Coquin, R.-G., 44, 46, 56

1 Corinthians: **5:7–8,** 66, 127n. 31, 195; **16:8,** 105n. 1; **11** on the Last Supper, 115–16, 127n. 31, 128n. 32, 192, 193, 194; **13:1–13** read during Christianized seder, 184

corpse-uncleanliness, in Jewish tradition, 25–26, 27

counting period, *S'firat Ha'omer* as a, 73–75, 76–78, 81; contemporary ritual, 87–89; Lag Ba'omer as thirty-third day of, 82–87

covenant, 28–29

craft guilds, medieval, closed to Jews, 133

crops, in biblical Israel, significance of *omer* for, 72–75

cross, the, Lutheran theology of, 151

crowd. *See turba*

crucifixion. *See* Passion of Christ

cultic reactualization (*Gegenwärtigung*), 197–99

Cup of Elijah, 125n. 5, 184

Cyril of Alexandria, 96

Cyril of Jerusalem (bishop), 38, 40, 67

Dalmais, I. H., 27

Dalman, Gustav, 87

Darmstadt Passover Haggadah, 137–38, 139

Daube, David, 126n. 22

Days of the Counting of the Omer. *See S'firat Ha'omer*

dead, the (*see also* mourning): con-

dead, the, (*continued*)
  nected with harvest time, 80,
  91n. 35
Dean, Winton, 163
deliverance (*see also* salvation):
  matsah as symbol of, 109–10,
  123–25; paschal lamb as symbol of, 115; petition related
  to in the Lord's Prayer, 117
Derenburg, Joseph, 87
desacrilization, rite of, 74
Deuteronomy **16:9–10**, 71, 73–74,
  90n. 19
Deutsche Messe (Luther), 152, 153,
  173n. 22, 175n. 35
Diaspora, following the Babylonian exile, 187
Dickenson, Clarence, 165, 179n. 81
Didascalia Apostolorum, 38
Distler, Hugo, 164, 179n. 78
Diversarum hereseon liber (Filastrius), 101–2
Dix, Gregory, 37, 38
Dominica (in) mediana, 22, 39
dramatic passion. *See* polyphonic
  passions, responsorial
dramatic reenactment, as means
  for connecting with history,
  185, 197–98
Dura-Europos synagogue, 135–36
Durandus, 167

Easter, 66–68, 95–96, 103, 149
  baptism (*see* baptism, on Easter)
  date for, 22–23, 24, 27, 189–90,
  201; Nicene decision on, 46
  preparation for, 36–38 (*see also*
  Lent)
  symbolic shaping of time and
  meaning, 1–11
Eastern Christianity, 37, 42, 47,
  53n. 35; date of Easter for,
  189–90; Good Friday passion
  narratives, 146–47, 171n. 4

Easter vigil, 4–5; as the Christian
  Passover, 199–200, 201–2
Ecclesiastical History (Socrates),
  21, 38–40, 41, 42, 47
ecology, context of *S'firat Ha'omer,*
  72–76
Edward VI (king, England), 162
Egeria (Etheria): accounts of Lent,
  21–22, 47–48, 103, 146; accounts of Pentecost, 97–99,
  100, 101, 105n. 10
eggs, symbolism of, 142
Egypt, 57, 96–97, 132, 199–200 (*see
  also* Alexandrian Christian-
  ity); deliverance from (*see*
  Exodus, the)
Elbogen, Ismar, 35n. 41
Eleazar, Rabbi, 75–76
Elijah, coming of, 19, 125, 184, 187
Elizabeth I (queen, England), 162
Elvira, Council of, 101
English language, use of: in Anglican liturgy, 178n. 71; in passion narrative for Holy
  Week masses, 148, 172n. 9; in
  twentieth-century passion
  music, 165, 179nn. 80, 81
Epiphany, 42–43, 60, 64–65, 149
Episcopalians, 54n. 47
Epistula Apostolorum, 189
Erna Michael Haggadah, 138
eschatology, in Christianity, 36, 38,
  95, 117, 193–94
eschatology, in Judaism: messianism, 11, 85, 187; significance
  in medieval Haggadah illustrations, 136, 141–42
eucharist, 192, 203n. 12 (*see also*
  Last Supper)
celebration of, 195, 203n. 31 (*see
  also* mass[es]); as culmination of baptism, 60, 66–67;
  early Christian, 186; meanings of, 204n. 27; parallel

between seder and for
  Hoffman, 65–67
Eusebius, 31, 189
evangelist, voice of in sung passions, 147–49
Exodus, Book of, 24, 58, 73–74
  12, 95, 110
  12:1–20, 28, 41; as feature of
    Shabbat Hachodesh, 17, 24–
    25, 27, 28, 41
  illustrations from in Spanish
    Haggadahs, 140
Exodus, the, 88–89, 200; Haggadah
  illustrations depicting, 136,
  140; *matsah* as historical
  recollection of, 112, 115, 122;
  the seder as commemora-
  tion of, 186–88
Expositiones missae, 196, 198
Ezekiel **36:23–36,** 28–29, 41

fasting, in Christian tradition, 101–
  2, 189
  not permitted during fifty-day
    Pentecost season, 94–95, 96,
    98, 100, 101
  pre-paschal, 21–23, 27–29, 36, 37–
    38, 47, 49–50, 54n. 48 (*see
    also* Lent); forty-day custom,
    44–49, 58; three-week cus-
    tom, 22–23, 28–29, 36, 39–40,
    55–58, 61–62
fasting, in Jewish tradition, 9, 23,
  114
Feast of Reaping (*Chag Hakatzir*),
  73
Feast of Weeks (*Chag Hashavuot*),
  73–74 (*see also* Shavuot)
Filastrius of Brescia (bishop), 101–2
Finkelstein, Louis, 78
Fischer, Kurt von, 173n. 22
fish, symbolism of, 142
Flagello, Nicholas, 165
folk character and humor, in me-

dieval Haggadah illustra-
  tions, 139
folk traditions, medieval, for *S'firat
  Ha'omer,* 71–72
Formulae missae (Luther), 152,
  175n. 35
forty, references to (*see also* fasting; Lent): significance, 22,
  58–59, 64
"Four Questions," in the
  Haggadah, 121
four sons, Haggadah illustrations
  of, 137, 144n. 7
Fox, Robin Lane, 30–31
fresco painting, Greco-Roman, 135
Frishman, Elyse, 89
*Füssener Traktat (Maihinger Frag-
  ment; Passionale*), 149–50,
  154, 172n. 13, 174n. 30

Galatians, Letter to the, 189
Garden of Eden, symbolism of
  bread in, 116–17
Gaster, Theodor, 80, 85, 87
Gedächtnis (remembrance), for
  Luther, 198
Gegenwärtigung (cultic reactualiza-
  tion), 197–99
Genesis, Book of, illustrations
  from in Spanish Haggadahs,
  140
Gennadius of Marseilles, 99
Geonim, 75–82, 91n. 31, 113–14,
  129n. 47 (*see also* Rabbis,
  the)
Georgian Lectionary, 40, 62
Gerber, Christian, 160–61
Gerhardt, Paul, 157
Germany: Haggadah illumination
  tradition, 132, 133, 136–39;
  passion music, 151–63, 164–
  65, 179nn. 78, 79
Gerstenburg, Joachim, 176n. 44
ghettos, of Eastern Europe, 200

Ginsberg, H. Louis, 73, 90n. 20
Gloria Patri, 183, 202n. 2
Gold Haggadah, 139–40
Goldschmidt, Daniel, 119, 130n. 53
Good Friday, 5, 28, 47, 96, 190; in
	the Eastern church, 46, 146–
	47; Protestant observance of,
	152–53, 157, 162; Reproaches,
	202n. 4; vespers, 157–58
Gospels (*see also* John, Gospel of)
	link between the Passover *mat-*
	sah and *pesach*, 116
	synoptic, 187, 190, 202n. 6 (*see*
	also Luke; Mark; Matthew);
	accounts of the Lord's
	Supper, 184, 190–91; Last
	Supper seen as a seder, 116,
	127n. 31, 185, 190–91
Gotha manuscript choirbook, 153,
	174n. 29
Great Sabbath: in Christian tradi-
	tion, 8–9, 18, 29–32, 60; in
	Jewish tradition (*Shabbat*
	Hagadol), 6, 8–9, 17–20, 23,
	29–32
Great Week, 36–37, 46, 56
Greco-Roman world, 187; festive
	meals, 113, 130n. 52; lost illus-
	trated Jewish manuscripts
	unlikely, 134–36
Greenberg, Rabbi Irving, 89
Gregory Nazianzus, 43
Gregory of Nyassa, 101
Gregory XIII (pope), 148
Grimme, Hubert, 92n. 54
Guidetti, Giovanni, 148
Gutmann, Joseph, 10, 132–45

Haftarah, 15–17, 19–20, 23
Haggadah(s), 2, 5, 18, 112, 125n. 5,
	187 (*see also ha lachma*
	anya; seder); illuminated
	manuscripts, 10, 132–43;
	twentieth-century Christian-
	ized forms, 5, 183–86

Hai Gaon, 81–82, 110
haircuts: prohibition against during
	S'firat Ha'omer, 78, 82, 92n.
	40; received by boys during
	hillula festival, 85–86
ha lachma anya ("Behold the
	bread of affliction"), 111,
	130n. 54, 141, 142; interpreta-
	tions of, 119–22, 124, 130n. 52
Hallel, 18, 187
hamotsi (benediction over bread),
	116–17
Handel, George Frederick, 160,
	162–63
Handl, Jacob (Gallus), 151, 158,
	176n. 47
Hareuveni, Nogah, 73, 74–75
Harvest, feast of. See Shavuot
harvest season, 80 (*see also S'firat*
	Ha'omer)
Havdalah ceremony, 142
Hayarchi, Abraham, 83, 86
Hebdomada (in) mediana, 22, 39
Heilands letzte Stunden, Des (*Cal-*
	vary) (Spohr), 163, 179n. 76
Heinichen, Johann David, 168
Henrici, Christian Friedrich (Pican-
	der), 177nn. 56, 58
"Hillel sandwich" (*korekh*), 111,
	118–19, 123, 129n. 47
hillula, 85–86
Hippolytus of Rome, 21, 37, 43, 44–
	45, 51n. 6, 63, 95, 195
Historia Ecclesiastica (Socrates),
	21, 38–40, 41, 42, 47
historicism, 104, 197; Dix's theory
	of, 37, 38
Historie der Kirchen-Ceremonien in
	Sachsen (Gerber), 160–61
Hoffman, Lawrence A., 1–12, 15–
	35, 41–42, 55–68, 109–31
Holocaust, the, 200; influence on
	the Passover seder, 188
Holy Communion. See eucharist;
	Last Supper

Holy Saturday, pre-paschal fast on, 47

Holy Spirit, sending of, 95, 97–98, 100, 103 (*see also* Pentecost)

Holy Thursday, 48, 56, 96

Holy Week, 4, 36–38, 152–53 (*see also* music, church, for Holy Week); Protestant observance of, 152–53, 154, 162, 173n. 22; twentieth-century Christian participation in form of seder as part of, 183–86

Homilies on Leviticus (Origen), 44–45

Hooper, John (bishop of Gloucester), 162, 178n. 71

Hosea, Book of, 16, 28, 75

human development, parallel with seen in the *S'firat Ha'omer,* 89

Huna, Rav, 119–21

illustrations: Haggadah, 10, 132–43; medieval Christian books, 132–34, 144n. 7

incarnation, 190, 203n. 20

Irenaeus of Lyons, 31, 95

Israel: as Land under Roman sphere of influence, 81; as state, influence on the Passover seder, 188

Italy, medieval
Christianity, 97, 99–100, 104
Judaism: Haggadah illuminations, 132, 140–41, 142; *Shabbat Hagadol,* 17

Jellinek, A., 18

Jeremias, Joachim, 190

Jerome, St., 22, 39, 102, 117

Jerusalem, in early Christianity, 97–99 (*see also* Egeria); Lenten period, 38, 47–48, 55, 65, 103

Jerusalem, significance in Judaism,

125 (*see also* Temple, the); depicted in the Bird's Head Haggadah, 136–37; pilgrimages to, 73–74, 187

Jesus, 10, 104, 187, 199–200 (*see also* Ascension; Passion of Christ; resurrection); baptism of, 42, 56, 61, 64–65; forty days fast in the wilderness, 37, 45, 49–50, 56–57, 59, 61, 64, 67; incarnation, 190, 203n. 20; as the Passover, 60, 64; Pionius and Polycarp seen as imitating death of, 31–32; voice of in monophonic passions, 147–48

Joel ben Simeon, 138–39

John, Gospel of, 104, 187, 202n. 6
account of the Lord's Supper, 184, 190–93
date of the crucifixion, 128n. 31, 190
passion narrative (**18–19**) (*see also* St. John Passion); role in Holy Week liturgy, 146–47
readings from during last three weeks of Lent, 39–40, 52n. 15, 53n. 35
references to the Great Sabbath, 8–9, 18, 20, 29–30, 31–32, 60

Johnson, Maxwell, 8, 36–54, 55–68

John the Baptist, 64–65

Josephus, 91n. 27, 113, 122, 134, 187

Joshua, Rabbi (Rabbi Simon), 75, 124

Jounel, P., 27

Jubilees, calendar of, 91n. 22

Judah, Rabbi, 76

Judah, Rav, 113–14

Judaism (*see also individual topics*): shared experiences with Christianity, 199–202; singing of words of scripture in liturgical tradition, 166;

Judaism (*continued*)
  unique customs depicted in
    illustrated Haggadah manu-
    scripts, 141–43
Judenstern (Sabbath lamp), 142
Justin Martyr, 19, 27

Kabbalists, on the *S'firah,* 88
Kaddish, 117
Kairuwan Jewry, 130n. 47
Keisler, Reinhold, 159
Kiddush, 121–22
Kittner, Alfred, 170
Klein, Isaac, 88–89
Klenicki, Rabbi Leon, 184
Koch, Heinrich Christoph, 178n. 67
korekh ("Hillel sandwich"), 111,
    118–19, 123, 129n. 47
Kuhnau, Johann, 156, 157

Lag Ba'omer, 71–72, 82–87, 92nn.
    41, 51, 54; determination of
    date for, 83–84
Lages, Mario Ferreira, 28, 40, 55,
    63, 65
lamb, paschal (*pesach*)
  consumption at the seder, 111,
    113–14, 118–19, 122–23, 129n.
    47; *matsah* as replacement
    for, 110, 114–16, 117–18,
    122–23
  sacrifice in the Temple, 186–87,
    195
  taking and slaughtering, 121,
    187–88; relationship to the
    Great Sabbath, 18, 24, 29
lamb, paschal, Jesus as, 95–96, 128n.
    31
Last (Lord's) Supper, 115–16, 123,
    128n. 32, 184, 190–94, 203n.
    12 (*see also* eucharist); cele-
    bration of as affective or ef-
    fective memorial, 197–99,
    204n. 31; seen in the synop-

tic Gospels as a seder, 116,
    127n. 31, 185, 190–91; twenti-
    eth-century Christian cele-
    bration of seder seen as cele-
    bration of, 183–85, 188
Lathrop, Gordon W., 166
Latin language, use of: in Lutheran
    worship, 154–55, 175n. 35; in
    passion music, 165–66,
    178nn. 69, 71
Lazarus Saturday, 37, 42, 46, 47
Leach, Edmund, 7
leaven of sin, cleaning one's self
    from, 55, 61, 63
Leaver, Robin, 10, 146–80
Lechner, Leonhard, 155, 175n. 39
lectionaries, Christian, 23, 40, 53n.
    35, 153; Georgian and Arme-
    nian, 23, 28, 40, 62; on read-
    ings for last three weeks of
    Lent, 39–40, 41, 52n. 15
lectionaries, Jewish, 5, 8, 15–20,
    28, 41
Lemuria (Roman festival), 80
Lent, 4, 8, 152, 154, 159–60
  length of time for, 21–23, 27–29,
    36, 46–47; forty-day custom,
    22, 36–38, 39, 44–50, 56–62,
    63–64, 67; three-week cus-
    tom, 22–23, 28–29, 36, 38–44,
    50, 55–58, 63–68
  "micarême," Lag Ba'omer com-
    pared to, 87
  origins, 21–23, 27–29, 36–50;
    Hoffman-Johnson dialogue
    on, 55–68; Jewish, 15, 20,
    41–42
Leo I (the Great) (pope), 43, 48,
    52n. 15
Levi, Rabbi, 26, 111
Levine, Sandy (Kinneret Shiryon),
    89
Levi-Strauss, Claude, 7
Leviticus **23:10–21,** 71, 74, 76–77, 81

Lightfoot, J. B., 30
liminal events, number forty applied to, 58–59
literalism, in use of language, 59
Longueval, Antoine de, 150–51, 155, 175n. 36
Lord's Prayer, symbolism of bread in, 117
Lord's Supper. *See* Last Supper
Löwen, Arnulf von, 157
Luke, Gospel of, 16, 187; Lord's Prayer, 117; passion narrative (**22–23**), 146–47, 191, 204n. 25 (*see also* St. Luke Passion)
Luria, Isaac, 92n. 51
Luther, Martin, 151–54, 166, 173n. 25, 180n. 89, 198–99
Lutherans, 54n. 47, 197; passion music, 151–63, 165, 166, 179n. 82

Macmillan, James, 169–70
Maihinger Fragment. See Füssener Traktat
Maimonides, Moses, 88, 123
Malachi **3:4–24,** 17, 19–20, 23
manna, Lag Ba'omer seen as celebration of, 92n. 54
Marissen, Michael, 169
Mark, Gospel of, 46; *Mar Saba Clementine Fragment,* 46, 53n. 35; passion narrative (**14–15**), 19, 127n. 31, 128n. 32, 146–47, 190–91, 194 (*see also* St. Mark Passion)
maror. See bitter herbs
marriage, prohibition of: during harvest season in ancient Rome, 80–81; during *S'firat Ha'omer,* 78–81, 83
Mar Saba Clementine Fragment, 46, 53n. 35
Marti, Andreas, 167
Martimort, A. G., 27

martyrdom: feasts as baptismal occasions, 43; of Pionius and Polycarp, 9, 29–32
Mary I (queen, England), 162
mass(es), Catholic, 149, 196, 198 (*see also* eucharist); concert performances, 166; Holy Week, 147–52
matsah (*see also* afikoman): depiction in Haggadah illuminations, 132, 140, 141, 142; Hillel's custom for eating, 111, 118–19, 123, 129n. 47; Passover regulations on, 110–11, 117–19, 125n. 7, 126n. 9, 129n. 42; as replacement for *pesach,* 110, 114–16, 117–18, 122–23; as symbol of salvation, 10, 109–25
Mattheson, Johann, 160–61, 178n. 66
Matthew, Gospel of: Lord's Prayer, 117; passion narrative (**26–27**), 19, 146–47, 191, 194 (*see also* St. Matthew Passion)
Maximus of Turin, 99–100
May Day ceremony, Lag Ba'omer as a, 85
meals: festive Greco-Roman, 113, 130n. 52; shared by Christ with others, 193–94 (*see also* Last Supper)
meat, symbolism of, 142 (*see also* lamb, paschal)
Melito of Sardis, 190
Melloh, John, 4
memorial: biblical concept of (*anamnesis; zikkaron*), 185, 196; effective and affective, 194–99; as *memesis* or *recordatio,* 196
Mendelssohn, Felix, 169
Messiah (Handel), 162–63
messianism, in Judaism, 11, 85, 141–42, 187

"micarême," Lag Ba'omer compared to, 87
Middle Ages, 80, 196
    Christianity during, 2, 20, 104, 148
    first discussions of the Great Sabbath, 17–18, 19
    Judaism during, 6, 8–9, 71–72, 85; anti-Semitism, 167, 200; Haggadah illumination traditions, 132–43
Mid-Pentecost, Feast of, 103–4
midrash, 28–29, 59, 79, 116–17
Mihaly, Eugene, 116–17, 126n. 10
Mishnah, 17, 120, 124, 188; interpretation of *afikoman,* 127nn. 22, 29; Passover regulations, 112, 113–14, 121–22, 126n. 9; on *Shabbat Parah* and *Shabbat Hachodesh,* 24–26, 28, 35n. 41
Missale Romanum, Tridentine, 52n. 15
monasticism, medieval, 96, 132, 148
monophonic passions, 147–48
Morgenstern, Julian, 92n. 54
Moses, 58; Haggadah illustrations depicting, 135–36
motets, 155–56; through-composed passions, 149, 150–51, 172n. 12
motsi (benediction over bread), 116–17, 118, 129n. 43
mourning: Lenten practices relaxed on "micarême," 87; *S'firat Ha'omer* associated with, 78–84, 87
music, church, 10, 162
    for Holy Week, 146–70; anti-Semitic tendencies in, 167–70; nineteenth- and twentieth-century, 163–67, 169–70; pre-nineteenth-century, 151–63
Muslims, 86, 132
Musurillo, Herbert, 31

mystics: Christian, 148; Jewish, 85, 88, 92n. 51, 120

narrative (storytelling), as ritual, 3–8
Natronai Gaon, 79, 81
New Testament (*see also* Gospels; *individual books by name*): Luther's German text, use in responsorial passions, 153; readings from as part of Christianized seder, 184; on revelry as part of the seder, 113; translation from Greek into Latin, 102
"Next year in Jerusalem," 125
Nicea, Council of, 38, 49, 55, 101, 189; origin of forty-day fast before Easter, 44, 46, 48, 56, 64
North Africa, early Christianity in, 43, 55–56, 63, 67
Numbers, Book of, 74; **19:1–22,** 17, 24, 25, 28, 41

Obrecht, Jacob, 150–51, 155
Octave of Easter, 103
Offer, Joseph, 16
Old Testament, 91n. 27 (*see also* individual books by name*); accounts of interval between Passover and Shavuot, 71; bread as symbol of salvation in, 116–17; medieval illustrations, 132, 140; Pentateuchal readings for Sabbath and holy days, 15–17, 26–27
omer. See S'firat Ha'omer
oratorio passion, 155–57, 172n. 17, 175n. 40, 176n. 44, 178n. 67; non-liturgical, 151, 156, 158–61
oratorios, definitions, 178n. 67
Ordines Romani, 147
Origen, 44–45, 65, 95

Orthodox Judaism, *S'firat Ha'omer* ritual, 88–89
Oxford Movement, 162, 163

Palestinian Jews, 15, 55, 57, 61; Passover seder customs, 114–15, 118–19, 121, 129nn. 42, 43, 47
Palestinian Talmud, 26, 127n. 22
Palm Sunday, 37, 46, 47, 96, 142, 148, 196; Protestant observance of, 152–53, 157, 162
Papa, Rav, 129n. 43
Pärt, Arvo, 165
Pascha, 27 (*see also* Easter; Passover); preparation for, 36, 55, 57–58 (*see also* fasting; Lent)
Passionale. See Füssener Traktat
Passion of Christ, 49, 151
  crucifixion, 149, 168; date of, 128n. 31, 190, 191
  music for liturgy of, 146–70; anti-Semitic tendencies in, 167–70; nineteenth- and twentieth-century, 163–67, 169–70; pre-nineteenth-century, 147–63
  non-liturgical music, 151, 156, 158–61, 165–66, 179n. 83
passion oratorio. *See* oratorio passion
passion plays, 148, 168–69, 196
passion tone formulae (music), 147–48, 171n. 5
Passover, 27–29, 34n. 25, 66–68, 199–201 (*see also* Haggadah; seder)
  Easter vigil as the true Christian, 199–200, 201–2
  illustrated in medieval Haggadahs, 136
  linking with Shavuot, 74–78
  preparation for, 5–6, 8–9, 20; relevance for early Christians, 27–28, 41–42, 59–60

as sacred time, 1–11, 24–25, 27, 190, 201 (*see also S'firat Ha'omer*)
  Shabbat Hagadol as Sabbath preceding, 17, 29, 31
Paul, St., 64–65, 189, 195 (*see also* Corinthians; Romans)
Penderecki, Krzysztof, 165
penitence, 9–10, 17, 48
Pentecost, in Christian tradition, 10, 101
  as fifty-day period in early Christianity (*quinquagesima*), 94–99, 102, 105n. 10; Feast of Mid-Pentecost, 103–4; transition to single day, 97–100, 105
  as a single day, 102–3, 103; fourth- and fifth-century transition to, 97–100, 105; as Jewish feast of Shavuot in the New Testament, 94, 105n. 1
Pentecost, in Jewish tradition. *See* Shavuot
Peranda, Marco Gioseppe, 154, 174n. 33, 175n. 34
Peri Pascha (Melito), 190
pesach. See lamb, paschal (*pesach*)
Peter Chrysologus (bishop of Ravenna), 104
Peter of Alexandria, 44–45
Pharisees, 71, 77–78
Philo, 91n. 27
Phinebas, Rabbi, 76
Pierce, Joanne, 2, 4
Pietism, 160–61, 177n. 64
pilgrimages, in Christian tradition, 99
pilgrimages, in Jewish tradition, 86; to Jerusalem, 73–74, 187; to tomb of Shimon Bar Yochai, 85–86, 92n. 51
Pinkham, Daniel, 165, 179n. 83
Pionius, 9, 20, 29–32, 60

piyyutim, recitation of, 125, 141
plainsong passions, 148, 162, 179n. 72 (*see also* polyphonic passions, responsorial)
Polycarp (bishop of Smyrna), 9, 20, 29–32, 60, 189
Polycrates (bishop of Ephesus), 189
polyphonic passions, 149–51, 155–56, 167; responsorial, 148–50, 153–54, 157, 162, 172n. 11, 177n. 64, 179n. 72; through-composed, 149, 150–51, 154–55, 172n. 12
polytheism, 74–75, 90n. 10
poor, the, *ha lachma anya* seen as invitation to, 119–22, 130n. 52
prayer(s), 2, 73
Presbyterians, 204n. 31
printing press, effect on illustrated Haggadah manuscripts, 142–43
prophet-derived Sabbath names, 16–17, 19–20
Protestantism, 54n. 47, 166, 202n. 4; celebration of the Lord's Supper, 197–99, 204n. 31; Christianized Passover seders, 183–86, 197; passion music, 151–65, 166, 179n. 82; Reformation, 152, 162, 199
p'rusah, customs for eating, 118, 129n. 43
Psalters, medieval illustrations, 132, 140
Purim, celebration of, 30

Quadragesima (*Tessarakoste*), 44, 47, 50
Quartodecimans, 186, 189–90, 195, 203n. 20
quasi-dramatic passion, 149–50, 172n. 11 (*see also* polyphonic passions, responsorial)
quinquagesima. See Pentecost, in Christian tradition

Rabbis, the, 19, 75–78, 113–14, 122 (*see also* Geonim)
Rashi (Shlomo Yitzhaqi), 26, 82
redemption, 142 (*see also* salvation); wine as symbol for, 128n. 32
Reformation, Protestant, 152, 162, 199
Reformed churches, 162, 197
Reform Judaism, practice of counting the *omer* abandoned by, 88
Regan, Patrick, 48
remembrance (*see also* memorial): for Luther (*Gedächtnis*), 198; as post-Constantian liturgy focus, 36–37
resurrection of Christ, 18, 193–94; focus on during fifty-day Pentecost season, 95, 97–98, 104
revelry, afterdinner, *afikoman* interpreted as, 112–14, 127n. 22
Rhau, Georg, 154–55
rishonim, 129n. 42
Roman Catholic Church: Christianized Passover seders, 183, 184, 197; passion music, 147–51; Stations of the Cross, 54n. 47, 151
Romans **6**, reinterpretation of baptism, 43, 49, 64–65
Rome, ancient, 80–81, 85, 92n. 40 (*see also* Greco-Roman world); as center of primitive Christianity, 22, 47, 55–56, 63, 67
Rosh Hashanah, and the "Sabbath of 'Return,' " 16–17
Ruppel, Paul Ernst, 165

sabbath (*shabbat*), 15–17, 19–20 biblical meaning, 77; in Leviticus **23:10–12,** 76–77, 90nn. 19, 20

"Sabbath of 'Return,' " 16–17
Sabbath of the (red) heifer
(*Shabbat Parah*), 17, 20,
24–29
Sabbath of "This Month" (*Shabbat
Hachodesh*), 17, 20, 24–29
Sadducees, 77–78
salvation, in Christianity, 109, 116–
17; symbols for, 115–16,
127n. 29
salvation, in Judaism, 109, 116–17
(*see also* deliverance);
matsah as symbol of, 10, 109–
25, 126n. 10
Samaritans, 77
Samuel the prophet (third cen-
tury), 85–86, 112, 114–15
Sarajevo Haggadah, 140
Schocken Haggadah, 140–41
"Scholars Festival," 84–87 (*see also*
Lag Ba'omer)
Schütz, Heinrich, 154, 167, 174n. 32,
179n. 78, 180n. 90
Second Council of Braga (572
C.E.), 41, 62
seder, 6, 186–89 (*see also* Haggadah)
bread as symbol of salvation in,
10, 109–25
Christian adoption of as a
Christian event, 10, 183–86,
196–97; alternative to, 199–
202
context of not essential to the
Lord's Supper, 193–94
depiction of in illuminated
Haggadahs, 132–33, 137–38,
141–42
the Last Supper as in the synoptic Gospels, 116, 127n. 31,
185, 190–91
parallel between eucharist and
for Hoffman, 65–67
twentieth-century celebration
of, 188–89, 194–95
Sefardic (Sephardic) Jews, 80, 82–

85, 110, 141; Haggadah illumination tradition, 132, 133,
135, 139–40, 141
Sefer Hachinukh (anon.), 88
Sefer Mateh Moshe, 18
Selle, Thomas, 155, 157
Senn, Frank, 10, 183–205
Sephardic Jews. *See* Sefardic Jews
Septuagint: illustrated scrolls, possibility of, 134; on meaning
of *shabbat* in Leviticus **23,**
77
Seven Last Words, devotion of, 54n.
47
Severus of Antioch, 104
S'firat Ha'omer (*omer; S'firah*), 9–
10, 71–89; in biblical pe-
riod, 72–75; contemporary
practices, 87–89; date for beginning of, 90n. 19; Lag
Ba'omer customs, 82–87;
from post-biblical through
geonic period, 75–78; prohibitions for period, 78–82
Shabbat Hachodesh (Sabbath of
"This Month"), 17, 20, 24–29
Shabbat Hagadol (Great Sabbath),
6, 8–9, 17–20, 23, 29–32
shabbat kodesh, 19–20
shabbatot, use to refer to "weeks,"
90n. 19
Shabbat Parah (Sabbath of the
[red] heifer), 17, 20, 24–29
Shavuot (Feast of Weeks), 73–74,
78, 91n. 27 (*see also* counting period); New Testament
"Pentecost" as designation
for, 94, 105n. 1; *S'firat
Ha'omer* as link between
Passover and, 9–10, 71–89
Sherira Gaon, 110, 129n. 47
Shibboleh Haleket, 18, 110
sh'lemah, customs for eating, 118,
129n. 43
Silberman, Lou, 54, 92n. 40

Siricius (pope), 39, 43
Socrates (fifth-century historian),
    21, 38–40, 41, 42, 47, 55–56,
    59, 62, 63–64
Sowerby, Leo, 165, 179n. 81
Spain, early Christianity in, 41, 43,
    62, 65, 101
Spain, Jews in: customs, 80, 82, 83–
    84, 141; Haggadah illumina-
    tion tradition, 132, 133, 135,
    139–40, 141
spirituals, African-American, 165
Spohr, Ludwig, 163, 179n. 76
St. John Passion, 148, 152, 162
    music, 151, 153–54, 155, 157, 165,
    174nn. 31, 32; of J. S. Bach,
    158–59, 164, 168, 177n. 58,
    180n. 91
St. Luke Passion, 148, 162; music,
    154, 157, 165
St. Mark Passion, 148; music, 154,
    156, 158, 174n. 33
St. Matthew Passion, 148, 152, 162
    music, 153–54, 155, 157, 164,
    176n. 44; anti-Semitism seen
    in, 167–68; of J. S. Bach, 158–
    59, 163–64, 177n. 56
St. Paul's Cathedral (London), 164
Stainer, John, 164–65
Stallinger, Joseph, 184–85
Stations of the Cross, 54n. 47, 151
Stein, Sigmund, 130n. 52
Stevenson, Kenneth, 4
storytelling (narrative), as ritual,
    3–8
Sulzer, Johann Georg, 178n. 67
Sunday(s) (see also Easter; Palm
    Sunday): celebration of the
    Lord's Supper on, 193–94;
    fifty-day Pentecost modeled
    on, 99–100
sunset, working after, prohibited
    during S'firat Ha'omer, 78,
    81–82

symbolism, 2, 7–10, 59, 196
    for salvation: for Christianity,
    115–16, 127n. 31; matsah as
    in the seder, 10, 109–25,
    126n. 10
synagogue: recitation of Haggadah
    in depicted in Spanish
    Haggadahs, 141; ritual, the
    omer transformed into, 87–89
synoptic gospels (see also Matthew;
    Mark; Luke): accounts of
    Jesus' baptism, 64–65
Syria, early Christian tradition, 37,
    42, 65, 104

Taft, Robert, S.J., 38
Talley, Thomas, 8, 37–38, 98–99,
    203n. 20; on Lenten tradi-
    tions, 21–22, 40, 41–46, 50,
    53n. 35, 56–57, 63
Talmud(s), 17, 19, 26, 87–88, 127n.
    22, 170; the pesach linked
    with the Passover matsah,
    114–15, 116
tannaitic Judaism, 120–21, 124;
    Passover regulations, 111,
    113–15, 126n. 9
Tarfon, Rabbi, 128n. 32
Targum, 135
Telemann, Georg Philipp, 157, 159,
    160, 161
Temple, the, 187
    destruction of, 122, 187; effect
    on celebration of Passover,
    187–88; effect on ritual of
    bringing the omer, 71, 87
    pilgrimage to during S'firat
    Ha'omer, 71, 73–74, 75
    sacrifice of the paschal lamb,
    186–87, 195
Ten Commandments, Revelation
    of, 88–89; Shavuot seen as
    date of, 78, 91n. 27
Tertullian, 31, 36, 43, 63, 95

Tessarakoste (*Quadragesima*), 44, 47, 50

Thirty Years' War, passion chorales written as reaction to, 156–57

"This is my body" (*see also* Last Supper): Paul's use of bread as salvational symbol, 115–16

Thompson, Barbara Balzac, 183–84

Thompson, Randall, 165, 179n. 83

Tigay, Jeffrey H., 90n. 19

time

    chronology: as approach to the Great Sabbath in Christian tradition, 29–32; as approach to periods of time related to Lent, 60–62

    sacred, 1–11 (*see also individual sacred days and periods by name*)

tones, musical, for voices singing the Passion, 147–48, 153–54, 162, 171n. 5

Torah, 91n. 27 (*see also* Old Testament); Pentateuchal readings for Sabbath and holy days, 15–17, 26–27; scrolls, procession with to gravesites of Bar Yochai and Samuel the prophet, 85–86

Torgau-Walter manuscripts, of Lutheran responsorial passions, 150, 153–54, 174nn. 30, 31, 175n. 36

Tosafot, 17–18

Tosefta, 26, 28, 120; on Passover, 112–13, 115, 122, 127n. 29

triduum, 6, 96

Trinitarian invocation, included in Christianized seder, 183, 202n. 3

Tur (law code), 82, 110

turba (crowd), voice of: in monophonic passions, 148; in polyphonic passions, 149, 153–54, 167, 174n. 30

Turin, churches of, fifth-century, 97, 99–100

Turner, Victor, 7

typology: as approach to the Great Sabbath in Christian tradition, 29–32; as approach to relationship between Passover and Lent, 61–62, 63–68; as approach to use of term "forty," 59–60, 64

United Methodist Church, 183, 184, 202n. 4

unitive mode of liturgical celebration, 4

Van de Paverd, Frans, 48

Vatican II (Second Vatican Council), 148, 166–67

vespers, during Lent, 152, 157–58, 161

Victor I (pope), 27, 189

Wainwright, Geoffrey, 204n. 27

Walter, Johann, 150, 153–54, 157, 174nn. 30, 31, 175n. 36, 176n. 47

Washington Haggadah, 138–39

wine, 7; as element of the eucharist, 192; regulations on drinking of at seder, 112–13, 128n. 32; symbolism of, 128n. 32

Ya'ari, Avraham, 85

Yerushalmi, the, 112–13, 120; on the Passover seder, 112, 114–15, 119, 126n. 13, 128n. 32

Yochanan ben Nuri, Rabbi, 91n. 35, 112

Yom Kippur, 9, 16–17, 123

Yuval, Israel, 2, 9, 20, 23, 29, 60

Zarren-Zohar, Efrat, 10, 71–93
Zeitlin, Solomon, 8–9, 18–20, 23,
    126n. 10
zekher, rabbinic use of as symbolic,
    128n. 32
Zerachiah Halevi, Rabbi, 83

Zion, daughter of, image of in pas-
    sion librettos, 159, 177n. 56
zoocephalic figures, in medieval
    Haggadah illuminations, 137
Zunz, Leopold, 18
Zwinglian spirituality, 197, 198